BIODIVERSITY

THE UK ACTION PLAN

Presented to Parliament by the Secretaries of State for the Environment and for Foreign and Commonwealth Affairs, the Chancellor of the Exchequer, the President of the Board of Trade, the Secretaries of State for Transport , Defence, National Heritage and Employment, the Chancellor of the Duchy of Lancaster, the Secretaries of State for Scotland, Northern Ireland, Education and Health, the Minister for Agriculture, Fisheries and Food, the Secretary of State for Wales and the Minister for Overseas Development by Command of Her Majesty.
January 1994.

Cm 2428   LONDON: HMSO   £18.50 net

FOREWORD

In June 1992 the Prime Minister and over 150 other heads of state or governments signed the Convention on Biological Diversity at Rio de Janeiro. They did so to express a shared belief that action must be taken to halt the worldwide loss of animal and plant species and genetic resources. They recognised that each country has the primary responsibility to save and enhance biodiversity within its jurisdiction. At the same time they agreed to draw up national plans and programmes and to share resources to help implement them.

This document represents the first United Kingdom biodiversity action plan. It has been drawn up to a tight timetable, as the Prime Minister promised shortly after Rio, to demonstrate our commitment to the Convention. We accept that we have a contribution to make to the richness of the world's wildlife. The Darwin Initiative, the Aid Programme, the development of biodiversity action plans for our Dependent Territories and the fine work of our Institutions will help towards this aim. We also accept that we should further develop our strategies and programmes to ensure the conservation and, where possible, the enhancement of biodiversity within the UK. As the plan shows the Government and others in the UK are already strongly committed to the objectives of the convention, and are putting them into practice.

The plan which follows commits the Government, but just as we were not able to draw up the document without a wide and vigorous contribution from people and organisations who care about our natural heritage, so we shall not be able to deliver the plan without their active participation. The Government can take a lead and establish a framework but whether, in the end, we and our children enjoy a country which is richer or poorer in species and habitats depends on all of us.

We welcome debate and comments on the plan from home and abroad. We regard it as a first attempt to draw together a demanding programme of activity and commitment. To accelerate progress, and to sustain the open process by which this document has been prepared, the Government has agreed to set up a Biodiversity Action Plan Steering Group with membership drawn from central and local government, agencies, collections, academic bodies and non-governmental organisations. Its task will be to oversee the development of a range of targets for biodiversity so that they can be adopted in 1995 the European Nature Conservation Year. The Steering Group will also help to monitor the implementation of the actions contained in this plan. We look forward to continuing co-operation in this process.

JOHN GUMMER	IAN LANG	JOHN REDWOOD	SIR PATRICK MAYHEW	BARONESS CHALKER OF WALLASEY
Secretary of State for the Environment	Sectretary of State for Scotland	Secretary of State for Wales	Secretary of State for Northern Ireland	Minister for Overseas Development

CONTENTS

OUTLINE OF THE ACTION PLAN

SECTION 1

This section describes the United Kingdom's biological resource, and its importance in relation to Europe and the rest of the world. Chapter 1 explains the commitments made at the United Nations Conference on Environment and Development (the "Earth Summit"). It defines what is meant by biodiversity, why it is important and the objectives of the action plan. Chapter 2 examines the growth of our scientific knowledge, our scientific tradition and collections, and the role of scientific research in conserving our biodiversity. It sets out our commitment to continue this tradition by underpinning policy and programmes with sound science. Chapter 3 looks at UK biodiversity from a historical and geographical perspective. It describes the range and variation of species and habitats, and the genetic variation within species to be found in the UK, and why UK biodiversity is special and significant.

SECTION 2

This section describes the UK's strategy and programmes, and examines threats, problems, and opportunities. Chapter 4 looks at conservation within habitats (in-situ) and how the nature conservation agencies implement government strategy through the designation of protected areas and, increasingly, through measures to restore biodiversity in the wider countryside. Chapter 5 examines conservation outside natural habitats (ex-situ) and the techniques which are employed for conserving plants, animals and micro-organisms through collections, storage and propagation (among others). Chapter 6 is concerned with the sustainable use of those natural resources which contribute to biodiversity and how they may be conserved and enhanced for future generations. Chapter 7 explains the role of environmental awareness and education, and the contribution that can be made by all sectors of our society. Chapter 8 describes the support the UK gives to biodiversity overseas and our special responsibility for Antarctica, the Crown Dependencies and the Dependent Territories. Chapter 9 explains the importance of information and data and the need to establish a national biota database.

SECTION 3

The final section, chapter 10, draws the components of the action plan together, and provides a forward work programme. It describes the mechanisms for implementation, reporting and review, and proposes a new Biodiversity Action Plan Steering Group which will have responsibility for overseeing the development of targets for biodiversity, and the techniques and programmes necessary to achieve them. The outcome will be reported in 1995 which has been designated by the Council of Europe as the European Nature Conservation Year.

NOTES

This three stage approach is generally in line with the UN Environment Programme guidelines, of national assessment of country study/national strategy/action plan. Because of the UK's tradition and science base developed over 200 years, we have decided to include the country study, the strategy and the action plan in one document.

The adjective 'British' is used throughout the action plan to mean 'of the United Kingdom'.

The definition of biodiversity provided by Article 2 of the Biodiversity Convention is:

> 'The variability among living organisms from all sources including, inter alia, terrestrial, marine and other aquatic ecosystems and the ecological complexes of which they are part; this includes diversity within species, between species and of ecosystems.'

This plan addresses biodiversity in this sense with primary reference to the UK, but with a chapter on UK responsibilities overseas. It does not consider the issue of biotechnology which is also dealt with in the Biodiversity Convention, as this is covered in the parallel document *Sustainable Development: The UK Strategy*.

SECTION 1

CHAPTER 1

SETTING THE SCENE

1.1 Charles Darwin wrote in *The Origin of Species*:

> 'Why, if man can by patience select variations most useful to himself, should nature fail in selecting variations useful, under changing conditions of life, to her living products? What limit can be put to this power, acting during long ages and rigidly scrutinising the whole constitution, structure, and habits of each creature — favouring the good and rejecting the bad? I can see no limit to this power, in slowly and beautifully adapting each form to the most complex relations of life.'

If this was true when Charles Darwin presented his paper to the Linnean Society in 1858, it is equally true today. Biodiversity ('or variability within nature') is life around us. It is a wonder and a delight, but it is also a concern and a responsibility. The natural diversity within species and between species and ecosystems forms the basis for natural selection. It is salutary to remember that in effect life is not created on earth today; all living cells are descended, in an unbroken line, from some remote ancestor in the distant geological past. We are a part of nature, the biosphere being an intricate tapestry of interwoven life forms which help to constitute the marine, freshwater and terrestrial landscapes of the world and which give the richness to our natural heritage in the United Kingdom.

1.2 And yet this natural inheritance is increasingly under threat. Human activities are changing and destroying habitats, natural ecosystems and landscapes on an increasing scale. This has led to a demonstrable rise in the level of concern amongst scientists and the wider public who recognise that biodiversity must be treated more seriously as a global

The Earth Summit was the largest environmental gathering of world leaders.

resource to be protected and conserved according to principles of ecological, economic and social sustainability. Protecting and enhancing biodiversity were therefore among the critical issues addressed at the Earth Summit.

THE EARTH SUMMIT

1.3 In June 1992 around 150 Heads of State or Governments attended the United Nations Conference on Environment and Development (the 'Earth Summit') at Rio de Janeiro. This was the largest ever gathering of world leaders and signalled that environmental concerns had assumed a very high priority on the world's political agenda.

1.4 The Convention on Biological Diversity was an important component of the Earth Summit and was signed at Rio by over 150 countries including the United Kingdom (and by the European Community). Article 6A of the Convention

THE EIGHT-POINT PLAN

The Prime Minister wrote to leaders of all European Community and G7 countries proposing the following eight-point plan:

- to ratify the Climate Change Convention and publish national plans to implement it;
- to publish plans for action on biodiversity, and to establish the basis for ratification of the Convention;
- to publish national plans for the implementation of the forestry principles;
- to publish national plans for the implementation of the Rio Declaration and Agenda 21;
- to give financial support to developing countries for the implementation of Agenda 21 through Official Development Assistance (ODA) and for the replenishment of the Global Environment Facility (GEF);
- to take the lead at the 1992 UN General Assembly in the establishment of the Sustainable Development Commission;
- to put our weight behind establishing an international review process for the forestry principles;
- to take the lead in the restructuring of the GEF so that it can in time be established as the permanent financial mechanism for the Climate Change and Biodiversity Conventions.

requires each Contracting Party to 'develop national strategies, plans or programmes for the conservation and sustainable use of biological diversity, or adapt for this purpose existing strategies, plans or programmes which shall reflect, inter alia, the measures set out in this Convention relevant to the Contracting Party concerned'. Shortly after the Rio meeting the Prime Minister announced an 8-point plan for follow-up action to the Earth Summit which included publishing an Action Plan for biodiversity.

1.5 The Earth Summit contained a number of other major agreements as well as the Biodiversity Convention. One major output was the Rio Declaration, a Statement of Principles which addressed the need to balance the protection of our environment with the need for sustainable development. Agenda 21, an action plan for the next century, aims at the integration of environmental concerns across a broad range of activities. These include industry, agriculture, energy, transport, recreation and tourism, land use and fisheries. The UK is issuing simultaneously with this Plan, a national sustainable development strategy, which explains our implementation programme. We will report our progress to the new Commission on Sustainable Development.

1.6 The UK signed the Convention on Climate Change which commits all ratifying countries to prepare national programmes to contain greenhouse gas emissions, and to return emissions of carbon dioxide and other greenhouse gases to 1990 levels by the year 2000. A Statement of Principles for the sustainable management of forests was also agreed at Rio. The UK is issuing programmes for these initiatives in parallel with this Action Plan.

1.7 The UK intends to ratify the Biodiversity Convention given satisfactory progress towards securing safeguards regarding our concerns on the financial provisions of the Convention. The Prime Minister announced in Rio that the UK would offer additional help to developing countries for the conservation and sustainable use of their biological resources through the Darwin Initiative.

1.8 These UK plans and strategies represent a serious response to the commitments made in Rio. They are also inter-connected. For example the Sustainable Development Strategy contains chapters on wildlife and habitats and biotechnology. The need to integrate environmental concerns into Government policy and decision-making is well recognised. Within each Department responsibility for environmental aspects of policy lies with a designated 'Green Minister'. A Ministerial Committee on the Environment has been set up to

consider questions of environmental policy. The Fifth Environmental Action Programme produced by the European Commission is designed to set the strategic framework for the Community's environmental policy until the year 2000.

1.9 Although the protection and enhancement of biodiversity is extremely important in its own right, it should be seen as inseparable from the initiatives arising from the Earth Summit. Those preparing this Action Plan have worked closely with colleagues who have responsibility for sustainable development, climate change, sustainable forestry and the Darwin Initiative.

WHAT IS BIODIVERSITY?

1.10 Biodiversity is the variety of life forms we see around us. It encompasses the whole range of mammals, birds, reptiles, amphibians, fish, insects and other invertebrates, plants, fungi, and micro-organisms such as protists, bacteria and viruses.

1.11 No-one knows for certain the number of Earth's species. Informed opinion suggests a figure of between 5 and 30 million. But the concept of biodiversity goes beyond multiplicity of species. It includes the genetic and morphological variability within a species and the assemblages of plants, animals and micro-organisms which together form their ecosystems and natural habitats. Article 2 of the Biodiversity Convention defines biological diversity to mean:

'The variability among living organisms from all sources including, inter alia, terrestrial, marine and other aquatic ecosystems and the ecological complexes of which they are part; this includes diversity within species, between species and of ecosystems.'

1.12 Three levels of biodiversity are apparent from this definition:
(a) diversity between and within ecosystems and habitats;
(b) diversity of species, and
(c) genetic variation within individual species.

It is important to stress the linkage between species and habitats. Changing a habitat will often affect the diversity of species contained within it, and conversely a change in the number and assemblage of species may affect the nature of the habitat. A crucial test of the "health" of a local environment is reflected in the wildlife community appropriate to the area or habitat. If the rate of change or loss is markedly greater than ordinary evolutionary processes would imply, this could indicate a systematic problem to which we should pay serious attention.

THE IMPORTANCE OF BIODIVERSITY

1.13 The introduction to chapter 15 of Agenda 21 reads as follows:

'Our planet's essential goods and services depend on the variety and variability of genes, species, populations and ecosystems. Biological resources feed and clothe us and provide housing, medicines and spiritual nourishment. The natural ecosystems of forests, savannahs, pastures and rangelands, deserts, tundras, rivers, lakes and seas contain most of the Earth's biodiversity. Farmers' fields and gardens are also of great importance, while gene banks, botanical gardens, zoos and other germplasm repositories make a small but significant contribution. The current decline in biodiversity is largely the result of human activity and represents a serious threat to human development.'

Human development, and the human use of land and natural resources, have always affected other species and their habitats; and have often accelerated the processes of change or loss of biodiversity. No ecosystem in the UK has been unaffected by human activity, whether directly or indirectly; and most of the landscapes that we now regard as traditionally British have been created or heavily modified by man. This century has seen a formidable increase in the pace and scale of human intervention in the natural world and, as a result, an accelerated pace of loss of biodiversity.

1.14 The conservation of biodiversity is not necessarily without cost. We must therefore be clear why biodiversity matters so that a balanced view can be formed. One reason is insurance. Biodiversity should be maintained because future practical needs and values are unpredictable and our understanding of ecosystems is insufficient to be certain of the impact of removing any component. Genetic diversity provides the variability within which a species can adapt to changing conditions. The less diverse environmental systems are, the less likely it is that gene pools and reservoirs, indeed genetic variability of all kinds, will be available to substitute for others that are depleted. Furthermore, if the effective population size falls below a certain level, the species is likely to die out. Diverse environmental systems normally enhance the resilience to cope with ecological stresses and perturbations, such as climate change.

1.15 Many losses are irreversible. There is also considerable uncertainty about the values, including economic values, that future generations may attach to biodiversity. For example few would have predicted that the Pacific Yew, a tree believed to be of little value, is now thought to contain one of the most promising potential cures for different forms of cancer. While it is probable that only a small proportion of the as yet unexploited species are likely to be of practical use to the human race it is prudent to seek to preserve as many as possible since we do not yet know which are the potentially useful species.

The Pacific Yew, a tree once believed to be of little value, now thought to contain one of the most promising potential cures for certain cancers.

1.16 No organism lives in isolation from other living things and each has its own way of life which contributes to the balance of nature. The inter-dependence and successful functioning of all these parts is a key contributory factor to the healthiness of the planet as a whole. If we continue to pollute the atmosphere, contaminate land and water, and degrade our ecosystems by, for example, destroying forests, wetlands and marine environments, then the planet will suffer accordingly. The totality of the problem is addressed by the Sustainable Development Strategy, but the harmonious and healthy functioning of all the organisms which constitute 'life' is the concern of the Biodiversity Convention, and hence of this Plan.

1.17 A simplified marine food chain demonstrates how organisms interact with each other and their surroundings. The mud in our coastal waters contains microscopic animals, meiofauna, which occur at some 45 million per square metre. They are at the bottom

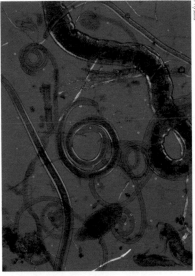

A sample of meiofauna separated from sediment. To date, over 350 species of meiofauna have been identified in the estuarine reaches of the Thames alone.

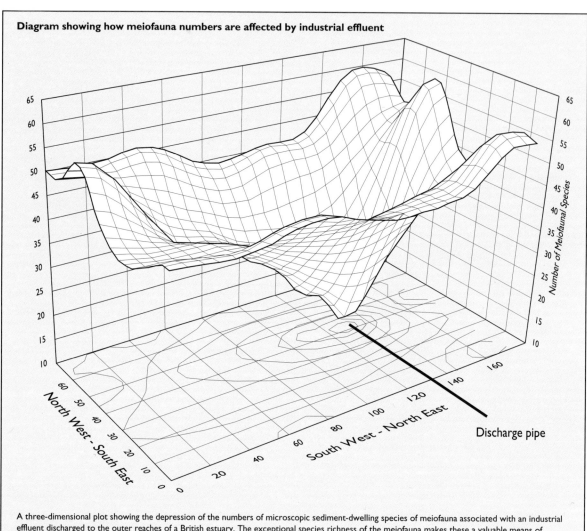

Diagram showing how meiofauna numbers are affected by industrial effluent

North West - South East

South West - North East

Number of Meiofaunal Species

Discharge pipe

A three-dimensional plot showing the depression of the numbers of microscopic sediment-dwelling species of meiofauna associated with an industrial effluent discharged to the outer reaches of a British estuary. The exceptional species richness of the meiofauna makes these a valuable means of detecting and monitoring environmental stress. (Area shown approximately 1.7 x 1.7 km)

of the food chain, and clean mud by feeding on detritus, fungi, bacteria, and micro-algae. They are a source of food for larger invertebrates such as crabs and shellfish, which are eaten in turn by sea mammals, fish, birds and man. The seawater over the mud is rich in diversity and numbers of microscopic plankton, the food source for commercial fish such as cod and herring. A wealth of food chains occur in the marine environment and similar food webs exist throughout the biosphere.

1.18 If a particular species or group of organisms is damaged then other species in the web will be affected. Communities of marine meiofauna are particularly sensitive to pollution from factory and sewage discharge. An outfall in the Humber Estuary, for example, reduced dramatically the number of meiofaunal species from around 60 to only 10. If these apparently insignificant microscopic organisms at the base of the food chain are affected there could be long term effects on other organisms. A balanced assemblage of species and healthy food webs in an ecosystem ensure the satisfactory functioning of all parts of that system.

1.19 The economic argument for biodiversity develops this further. A species has a commodity value if it can be made into a product that can be bought or sold in the market place. This may be food, clothing or medicine. This natural resource is finite insofar that it may be exploited faster than it can reproduce itself, and should be managed. Depletion of these natural resources will affect the global exchange economy.

1.20 Genetic variability in cultivated and domestic species is, and probably always will be, an extremely important social and economic resource. It was genetic variability which enabled early man to develop the crops and livestock which were a pre-requisite of settled agriculture and which now enable breeders to develop new varieties. The continued development and stability of agriculture, especially in the longer term, depend to no small extent on our capacity to continue doing this.

1.21 A value may also be placed on eco-tourism, products derived from wildlands, and ecological processes such as watershed protection. Wetlands, for example, act as natural filters for surface waters, and are now being used deliberately for waste water treatment. Their successful action depends upon the type of soil, the water plants in the wetland and the microbes around their roots.

1.22 Integrity, productivity and diversity of nature are all interlinked and mutually dependent. Functional integrity is the proper functioning of ecosystems leading to the cycling of the elements and the operation of the planetary life support system. Productivity can, of course, be enhanced by reducing diversity in those areas we cultivate intensively, but to maintain the productivity of our cultivars we depend on there being a reservoir of wild relatives, and a pool of genetic material we can go back to in order to reinforce our selection.

1.23 Productivity often depends on diversity and it is important to balance trade-offs between development and conservation. Now that farmers' fields are expanding to squeeze the wild habitats the availability of diversity to support productivity cannot be taken so readily for granted as it used to be. Land use is a mosaic, and the crucial issue is to balance the elements of the mosaic so that the three key attributes – productivity, integrity and diversity – are all sustained.

1.24 There are other, less obvious, values of biodiversity. Ecosystems provide important natural functions. Flood plains and washlands act as natural release valves for rivers in flood; the diversity of vegetation on mud flats and sand dunes reduces coastal erosion, and woods and hedges act as wind breaks. Upland vegetation is particularly good at binding soil and lessening erosion while beds of seaweed reduce wave action. If an ecosystem is altered in a detrimental way these functions may be lost and the habitats which the ecosystem supports destroyed. The benefits of preserving such systems can be measured in terms of avoided damage.

1.25 Biological resources may be renewable, but in human terms may take a substantial time to recover. Of particular interest is an experiment conducted over the past 150 years at the Rothamsted Agricultural Research Station. The experiment relates to fertiliser application to grassland. Grassland plots have received different fertiliser applications for 150 years. Control plots have received nothing. Analyses show that control plots have the highest number of herbaceous species (60), a rich diversity with no particular species dominating. Fertilised plots low in nitrogen have been taken over by leguminous species (which fix their own nitrogen) while high nitrogen plots are dominated by grasses. Plots which received fertilisers initially, but not for the last one hundred years, still reflect their treatments by loss of species diversity, demonstrating that diversity cannot be regained overnight.

1.26 Some species have an intrinsic commercial value which can be costed and are priced accordingly (eg the fishing and forestry industries). However, the price often reflects immediate demand rather than the true value of sustainable cropping, and over-exploitation ensues. There is considerable potential commercial value in products from species which may have medicinal benefits, and the gene pools which are essential for breeding new and better varieties of crops and domestic animals.

1.27 The moral and aesthetic reasons for conserving biodiversity are less tangible but of great importance. Nature conservation has become an issue for UK public policy over the last 100 years for reasons which are essentially non-economic. We conserve species and habitats because they are beautiful or because they otherwise enrich our lives. The culture of a nation is closely allied to its landscapes and wildlife. Poets, painters, writers and composers have been inspired by the nature around them. As Keats wrote in his Ode to a Nightingale:

> 'Thou wast not born for death, immortal Bird!
> No hungry generations tread thee down;
> The voice I hear this passing night was heard
> In ancient days by emperor and clown.'

1.28 The moral argument adds to this perspective the view that we should hand on to the next generation an environment no less rich than the one we ourselves inherited. We believe that a culture which encourages respect for wildlife and landscapes is preferable to one that does not. Human beings exercise a determinative power over other creatures. Whether hundreds of thousands of species survive depends on the decisions of humans. With this dominion comes responsibility, and we reaffirm the UK's commitment set out in *This Common Inheritance* to taking this stewardship very seriously.

1.29 Biodiversity is under threat globally and there are serious issues to address in the UK. Ecosystems are fragile and normally can only adapt at natural rates of change. Their inherent resilience to natural change depends on the ability of components to adapt to new circumstances at the same pace as the rate of change. The diversity of species and their genetic pools enable this to occur. However the rates of changes in the environment brought about by man (eg through pollution and land use changes) far exceed those at which species can adapt. This has two major effects. The rate of loss of species far exceeds the development of new species, and thus the global genetic pool is diminished (and can never be replaced), and the habitats within which the remaining species reside are irredeemably diminished.

1.30 In 1862 Alfred Russell Wallace wrote about his concern for man's actions on nature in the following terms:

> 'and if we continue to devote our chief energies to the utilisation of our knowledge of the laws of nature with the view of still further extending our commerce and our wealth, the evils which necessarily accompany these when too eagerly pursued, may increase to such gigantic dimensions as to be beyond our power to alleviate.'

1.31 The Government signed the Biodiversity Convention at Rio to signify its conviction that urgent action is necessary to slow the loss of the world's biodiversity. If we do not take this action we shall suffer both economic and spiritual loss. Moreover we shall hand on to our successors a planet which is poorer than the one we were privileged to inherit. The cumulative weight of these arguments compel us, at national and at international level, to give high priority to fulfilling our responsibilities towards biodiversity.

THE BIODIVERSITY ACTION PLAN

1.32 The publication of the UK Action Plan is in response to Article 6 of the Biodiversity Convention, to develop national strategies for the conservation of biological diversity and the sustainable use of biological resources. The Action Plan is intended to be dynamic, rather than

Charles Darwin

static. We fully recognise the need to develop and refine it in the near future, as well as to establish an effective monitoring mechanism.

1.33 Although Government is in the lead with the preparation of the Action Plan it is in no sense a matter solely for Government. It requires action by the whole community. The UK has a rich tradition in the study of the natural world, exemplified by such figures as Gilbert White, Joseph Banks and Charles Darwin, and our voluntary sector is very strong and diverse. We have consulted widely across all sectors of society in preparing this Action Plan, having written to over 300 organisations and receiving over 1,000 pages of text from learned societies, universities, research institutes, local authorities, the voluntary sector and individuals. The commitment and concern shown by respondents, and the large consensus of agreement between them over major issues are indicative of the general level of support.

1.34 A two-day seminar organised jointly by JNCC and DOE was held in May 1993 at the Royal Geographical Society, where key issues were discussed and a series of workshops held. These, also, helped to inform chapter editors who were drawn from a variety of backgrounds

OVERALL GOAL

To conserve and enhance biological diversity within the UK and to contribute to the conservation of global biodiversity through all appropriate mechanisms.

UNDERLYING PRINCIPLES

1 Where biological resources are used, such use should be sustainable.
2 Wise use should be ensured for non-renewable resources.
3 The conservation of biodiversity requires the care and involvement of individuals and communities as well as Governmental processes.
4 Conservation of biodiversity should be an integral part of Government programmes, policy and action.
5 Conservation practice and policy should be based upon a sound knowledge base.
6 The precautionary principle (see glossary) should guide decisions.

OBJECTIVES FOR CONSERVING BIODIVERSITY

1 To conserve and where practicable to enhance:
   (a) the overall populations and natural ranges of native species and the quality and range of wildlife habitats and ecosystems;
   (b) internationally important and threatened species, habitats and ecosystems;
   (c) species, habitats and natural and managed ecosystems that are characteristic of local areas;
   (d) the biodiversity of natural and semi-natural habitats where this has been diminished over recent past decades.
2 To increase public awareness of, and involvement in, conserving biodiversity.
3 To contribute to the conservation of biodiversity on a European and global scale.

including Government, agencies, academia and non governmental organisations (NGOs). We would like to place on record our thanks and gratitude to the many people who have contributed to this Action Plan. While we appreciate the perspective of those who are looking only for a list of actions, the Government believes that it is necessary to draw together a conspectus of our biodiversity and resource and the effort already being made to conserve and enhance it as a basis for a forward plan.

1.35 The overall goal and objectives that this process has developed for the Action Plan are defined (see box). As well as addressing UK biodiversity, for which we have direct responsibility, we also seek to contribute to the conservation of global biodiversity. This is reflected in the objectives and underlying principles which form the basis for the proposals contained in the body of this report. The final chapter draws these proposals together, and includes targets and proposals for monitoring and review so that future progress may be measured.

CHAPTER 2

UK SCIENCE BASE

INTRODUCTION

2.1 This Chapter outlines the way in which the biological sciences have helped to develop a closer understanding of the nature and importance of biodiversity. Drawing upon a long tradition of survey and research in natural history, undertaken by both the public and voluntary sectors, the UK is well placed to make a distinctive contribution to the conservation of its own wildlife heritage and to the evolving agenda for sustainable development on a global scale.

2.2 Environmental considerations have assumed an increasing significance in Government. William Waldegrave, the Minister responsible for the Office of Science and Technology, wrote, in 1992, in response to a report on Environmental Research Programmes prepared by the then Advisory Council on Science and Technology (ACOST):

> 'Sound science should underpin all environmental policy. The environment cannot speak for itself and we require a clear understanding of its present and future condition to guide its stewardship. Research to improve our understanding for future action is still one of the best precautionary measures.'

2.3 The following sections describe the growth of our scientific knowledge, our scientific tradition and collections, and the role of scientific research in conserving our biodiversity.

THE GROWTH OF SCIENTIFIC KNOWLEDGE

Taxonomy

2.4 From the time the Swedish botanist, Carl Linnaeus, devised his classificatory system in the eighteenth century, taxonomists have endeavoured to build up inventories of plant and animal life. The system has been used to distinguish one species from another, and for naming them in such a way as to ensure information can be exchanged unambiguously. Only recently, however, has it become possible to assemble a global inventory. Modern analytical techniques were needed, for example, before a detailed taxonomy of Bryophytes could be attempted. Only through the most advanced forms of marine technology is it possible to discover, let alone analyse, the species occupying the most remote and difficult environments of the ocean bed. Even so, the challenge remains immense. Scientists still have little idea how many species of organisms inhabit the earth, even to the nearest order of

magnitude. Each year, large numbers of new species continue to be found.

SPECIES AND THEIR EVOLUTION

2.5 The basic unit of biological diversity is the species. Although defining a species might seem straightforward, both the concept and agreeing a practical working definition have proved contentious among biologists. This is largely due to the variety of ways living organisms have evolved and their different means of reproduction.

2.6 A species can be defined either as those populations of living organisms which can interbreed to produce viable and reproductively successful offspring; or as those populations of living organisms which are genetically similar by virtue of common ancestry. The first definition works for most animals and many plants. The second is useful for those organisms which reproduce asexually by simple division (viruses, bacteria and many micro-organisms), for plants which reproduce vegetatively, or for animals which give birth to young without fertilization of eggs.

2.7 Individuals within a species are more similar to each other than they are to individuals of other species. The attributes of each living organism are determined by their genetic constitution and the conditions experienced during their development: sometimes informally referred to as the effects of **nature** and **nurture** respectively. Within a species there is typically considerable variation in characteristics controlled by genes. While some characteristics under genetic control are easily seen (such as eye colour in humans), others are not obvious (such as variation in the biochemistry or physiology of an organism).

2.8 Because the survival and reproduction of each individual are affected by the genetic constitution, the frequencies of different gene types will change over time. The effects of natural selection in changing populations, and hence species, over time were first proposed by Charles Darwin and Alfred Russell Wallace in a joint paper. These ideas were discussed in depth by Charles Darwin in 'On the Origin of Species' (1859). Here, natural selection acting upon heritable variation, coupled with the survival of only a proportion of each generation, were the factors suggested as being the principal means by which species originate and change.

2.9 Once genetic variation is lost from within a species, for instance because the population has declined to a few closely related individuals, it takes a long time to be regained. What is more, the new range and type of variation will be different from what was present previously. In essence this is due to genetic variation being a product of a combination of circumstances (just like species themselves), which cannot be repeated by nature or human design.

Biological systematics

2.10 The concept of evolution through natural selection, developed by Darwin and his contemporaries in the late nineteenth century, meant taxonomy became more than simply cataloguing and naming. Biological systematics (as taxonomy is also known) sought to describe and explain the role played by evolutionary relationships in bringing about the extraordinary diversity of organisms, both at the present day and at different times in the past. A difference in perhaps a single biological trait might be enough to act as an isolating mechanism, preventing a group of individuals from interbreeding with others. Once segregated, a new species would begin to evolve, becoming ever more different as the suite of different traits was enlarged.

Biogeography

2.11 The related science of biogeography was given shape by Alfred Russell Wallace in the mid-nineteenth century (his definition of 'biogeographical realms' is still used), and further developed as botanists, at the turn of the century, began to map the distribution of individual plant species and the vegetation communities that comprised them. They realised that the patterns that emerged, although complex, were far from random. A succession could often be discerned. Where the clearance of a space provided scope for fresh colonisation, and herbs and shrubs might initially flourish, woodland species might in time come to prevail. The transition to sylvan thicket was rarely smooth. Early ecologists were intrigued about the relative importance of climate, soil-water conditions, and what came to be called the 'biotic' factor (including humans) in determining the distribution of plant and animal life. The terminology of sociology was adopted to describe patterns of plant 'community' and 'society'.

Ecosystems

2.12 The concept of the ecosystem was developed in the inter-war years, to help describe and explain the intricate relationships that were found to exist among the different forms of organic life, and with the environment in which they existed. Through the concept of food chains and webs, zoologists (or rather, animal ecologists) began to explore the significance of trophic relationships between species and the consequences for productivity, expressed in terms of biomass. Charles S. Elton devised an ecological pyramid to help explain how the productivity of plants might be greater than that of herbivores, which in turn were more productive than carnivores. In terms of structure, marine life seemed much less orderly than that on land. Feeding relationships were dominated by size, rather than species. Large 'particles' might consume 'small' particles, irrespective of species. As an individual of a species grew, it might consume individuals of species that had previously preyed upon it.

Island biogeography

2.13 Through empirical observation, the theory of 'island biogeography' was developed, whereby the number of species occupying an island was related to the area of that island. There was an intuitive belief that richness was maintained by the dynamics of local extinction and immigration. The greater the number of cross-links in an ecosystem, the more assured its stability and, therefore, protection from perturbations. The application of non-linear mathematical techniques has, however, severely challenged such notions of structure and permanence. Through a closer recognition of the realities of life, a more realistic approach to environmental management is beginning to emerge. Species diversity is now perceived to consist of two components. Species *richness* reflects the number of species in an ecosystem, and species *evenness* comprises the extent to which assemblages are dominated by relatively few species. In unchanging environments, both will usually increase. The network of inter-relationships will become so complex as to be highly vulnerable to any kind of natural or artificial perturbation. There may, however, be a greater resilience where communities, within the long-established system, have had to cope with a natural and predictably-wide variation in local conditions.

Population biology

2.14 To dwell on species richness is to risk overlooking what is happening within the populations of those species. Whilst comfort might be taken from the fact that 'only' 1% of Britain's invertebrate species may have become extinct this century, that fauna has become markedly depauperate in terms of the size and distribution of species populations. Within population biology, the evolving relationship between species survival and changes in the abundance and range of populations has come to be recognised as both significant and complex. Other things being equal, geographically-restricted species tend to have local populations that are characteristically small, thereby making them doubly vulnerable to extinction. Although densities are likely to decline towards the edge of a range, the varying incidence of birth and death, immigration and emigration, is likely to result in multi-modal patterns of abundance. While such factors will have operated throughout 'ecological' time, evolutionary history might continue to play a part. The fact that a species might be phylogenetically disposed to being rare has an obvious relevance in deciding priorities for investment in the protection of species and their populations.

Through greater access afforded by satellite imagery research has become more credible at the global scale.

2.15 Through the greater access afforded by new technologies and satellite imagery, research has become more credible at the global scale. It is gradually becoming possible to draw on the total experience of research in both the terrestrial and marine environments. It becomes instructive to draw analogies between, say, the very finely-scaled variability in the deep ocean-bottom faunas and those of the tropical rainforest, where they are determined in the relatively-quiet climate by the fall of individual trees. In neither situation do the communities ever reach a state of equilibrium. Instead, there are mosaics of local assemblages in different stages of recovery from the last perturbation. Since species vary in their incidence and rate of response, and further disturbances may occur, chance may play a significant role in the pattern that emerges.

2.16 As knowledge of the environment has increased, so too has a sense of the difficulty of interpreting what has been found. How does biodiversity affect ecological processes? The fact that agricultural monocultures have not already brought about environmental disaster suggests there may, in some circumstances, be a considerable redundancy of species in communities. Through commercial fishing, a large proportion of the top predators is removed from the North Sea ecosystem. Whilst such population losses must have had an impact on the structure of the ecosystems concerned, and the energy flow within them, it is not always clear how this is expressed. Understanding how locally less-diversified populations might affect the functioning of those ecological processes, essential for the maintenance of the ecosystem structure, is still rudimentary, despite the growing success of mathematical modelling.

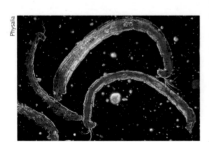

How do changes in the biodiversity of microscopic creatures affect ecological processes?

2.17 Perhaps, the greatest impediment remains one of total ignorance how organisation and structure at one level of spatial or temporal scale and complexity may influence those at both higher and lower levels. What may be a 'drop' of water to a whale is the whole ocean to a phytoplankton cell. Population changes in terrestrial plant systems may occur over months, centuries or even millennia, whereas those in pelagic phytoplankton communities might take place over only a few days to tens of years. The life of the rainforests and abyssal benthos may be utterly different in a physical sense, without a single common species of plant or animal, and yet the significance of that diversity might be dwarfed by the presence of bacteria, which saturate both these two extreme environments and every other place on earth. In a non-linear world, impacts might cascade up and/or down scales of variability, and between the different organisational levels of assemblages and ecosystems.

The precautionary principle

2.18 Where there is so much uncertainty, there is consensus that everything possible should be done to conserve species and their populations up to the point where the cost would become unacceptable to human society. The precautionary principle should prevail. For the policy-maker, the greatest challenge is to define what is an acceptable cost. There is no shortage of dire warnings. From spasms of extinction, as inferred from the fossil record, there is reason to believe it might take some twenty times longer for the biosphere to recover from the current rate of mass extinctions than humankind has existed on the planet. It is 5 million years since the first hominids appeared. Society needs, however, something to fight for, as well as against. Perhaps less emphasis might be placed on the irreversibility of mass extinction, and more on the scope which the conservation of *living* resources offers, in terms of enriching and enlarging the global estate through more sustainable forms of development. Through scientific method, not only might the enormity of the pressures on biodiversity be better defined, but the techniques may be found by which species and their populations can be conserved more effectively, working with, rather than against, the aspirations of Governments, industries and cultures of individual societies.

THE UK TRADITION AND ITS INSTITUTIONS

Founding figures

2.19 It may be claimed that more is known about the natural history of Britain than any other country. This in part reflects the fact that there is only 3% of the global total of recorded terrestrial species, in an area representing about 0.07% of the planet's land area. It also reflects a long tradition of observation and study. Gilbert White's volume of letters, *The Natural History* *and Antiquities of Selborne*, was published at the time of the French Revolution. Arguably the first genuinely ecological text to be written, it sought to record and interpret the intimate observations made by White as curate of this Hampshire parish over a 25-year period. The fourth most-reprinted book in the English language, it acted as both a precursor and model for a widening and deepening of interest in the living world.

2.20 As authors ranged beyond simple lists of species they had found, the growing number of natural-history journals and published Floras and Faunas began to offer ecological insights into the variety and dynamism of wild plant and animal life. The Scottish naturalist, Francis Buchanan White, recounted in 1895 how the chief factor in determining the flora of the banks of the river Tay was the river itself, through its ability to transport material and provide 'suitable habitats for the plants', destroying sooner or later what it had formed, only 'to repeat the construction in some other part of the river'. Such naturalists brought both an astonishingly broad knowledge of the physical and biological sciences to their observations, and they often had a deep knowledge of foreign literature.

2.21 Through the example of the founding figures of British ecology, A.G. Tansley and the animal ecologist, Charles S. Elton, the tradition was established of detailed observational studies, trials, and experimentation in the field. Crucial insights were gained from extensive tours of the Empire and North America, and the more focused studies of university expeditions. Through such insights, major advances were made in discerning how order might evolve within the seemingly-chaotic 'living' world. Collaboration with foresters in the Imperial service, for example, produced biogeographies and a rudimentary understanding of the tropical-forest environments.

The Linnean Society

2.22 Drawing heavily on its status as the capital of the world's greatest industrial and imperial power, nineteenth-century London was unrivalled for the size of its repositories of knowledge and the efficacy with which scholarship was disseminated. The papers and collections of Linnaeus, purchased after his death and brought to London, formed the centrepiece of the Linnean Society of London, founded in 1788 and today the oldest biological society in existence. Darwin's paper on the origin of species was presented in the Society's rooms in 1858.

Collections

2.23 Historians have made much of the Victorians' predilection for gathering data, particularly in statistical form. As the centre of an Empire, there was an abundance of opportunity to

The Naturalists painted by L J Watson. (Left to right) E B Ford, A G Tansley, A S Watt and C Diver on an East Anglian heath in the summer of 1949.

collect and study specimens of plant and animal life from all parts of the world. Collections of facts were published in the form of Blue Books, lectures, or displayed as museum collections. Pressure of space caused the natural-history exhibits of the British Museum to be transferred to new premises in South Kensington in 1880. Whether the incentive was commercial or military, a scientific underpinning was essential. The botanic gardens founded by George III at Kew, on the banks of the river Thames, became from the 1840s the leading centre for the study of material collected on numerous expeditions. From the royal collection of animals in the Tower of London, the young Zoological Society of London began in 1829 to assemble what rapidly became the world-famous Zoological Gardens in Regent's Park.

Nature preservation

2.24 It was from such early centres of scientific

A natural history exhibit at the British Museum

Wicken Fen, Cambridgeshire. Britain's first nature reserve.

excellence that much of the stimulus came for establishing nature 'preserves', nature-study classes in schools, and legislation to protect fisheries, birds, and other forms of wildlife. Much effort was invested in trying to stamp out the international trade in exotic bird plumage. Whilst the extinctions brought about by the hunting and the over-collecting of specimens aroused most censure, Britain's pioneering role as an industrial and urban nation also carried a heavy environmental price, both in terms of pollution and habitat destruction. Britain also led the way in the search for ways of mitigating, if not altogether eliminating, the consequent effects.

2.25 An article in the scientific journal, *Nature* in March 1914, began,

'It is only too true that man is slowly but surely destroying the beautiful wild animals and plants of the world, and is substituting for them queer domesticated races which suit his convenience and his greed, or else is blasting whole territories with the dirt and deadly refuse of his industries, and converting well-watered forest lands into lifeless deserts by the ravages of the axe.'

And the article continued,

'The "country" with its manured fields, its well-trimmed hedges and artificial barriers, its parks planted with foreign trees and shrubs, its roadways stinking of tar and petrol, and its streams converted into chemical drains or else into over-stocked fish-stews, is only rendered less repulsive than the town by the survival here and there of a pond or a copse or a bit of ancient moor-land (happily too swampy for golfers) where nature is still allowed to pursue her own way.'

The article was written by the distinguished zoologist and former Director of the Natural History Department of the British Museum, Sir Edwin Ray Lankaster. It introduced the work of the Society for the Promotion of Nature Reserves (SPNR), which had been founded in 1912 to help preserve areas of importance for their wildlife.

2.26 The Yorkshire naturalist and early ecologist, William B. Crump, recounted in an article, published a year earlier in *Country Life*, the achievement of the National Trust for Places of Historic Interest and Natural Beauty, a voluntary body founded in 1895. Wicken Fen in the Cambridgeshire fenland had been acquired to protect its distinctive and rich plant and insect life. More was required than simply erecting a perimeter fence and advertising the designation of a nature reserve. At Wicken Fen, the agricultural use of the neighbouring land caused the peat soils of the reserve to become even drier. The open-fen vegetation gave way to marsh-thicket and woodland. For Crump, these first insights into practical problems of wildlife management presented a challenge. In his words, a nature reserve was

'no mere refuge for vanishing or persecuted species. It is an outdoor workshop for the study of plants and animals in, and in relation to, their natural habitats; a twentieth century instrument of research as indispensable for biological progress as a laboratory or an experimental station.'

2.27 It fell to the oldest ecological society in the world, the British Ecological Society, founded in 1913, to take the most decisive step in establishing a series of national nature reserves in Britain. At the instigation of such leading ecologists as Tansley and Elton, a nature reserves committee was appointed, in the early part of the second world war, to assist in listing 'places suitable for preservation'. Such far-sightedness ensured that, among the documents before Government ministers in 1945, there was a memorandum from the Society, setting out a policy for nature conservation and nature reserves, to be administered by an ecological research council equipped with laboratories 'for the comprehensive study of ecological and population problems both pure and applied'. Out of the confusing interplay of post-war reconstruction, there emerged, in 1949, the first official body to be established anywhere in the world solely devoted to wildlife protection, namely the Nature Conservancy.

THE SUPPORTING ROLE OF RESEARCH

2.28 Such a scientifically-informed approach to 'stewardship' draws heavily on the rich diversity of groups engaged in basic and strategic research within the universities and research councils. The Natural Environment Research Council (NERC) was appointed as one of the country's five research councils, in 1965, to promote an integrated approach to research, survey and training in the natural environmental sciences. Initially the Nature

Conservancy was one of the component bodies of the Council. Following the transfer of the reserves and advisory functions of the Conservancy to the planning sector of Government in 1973, the research stations and staff remained within the Council, as the larger part of a new Institute of Terrestrial Ecology. NERC, through its continuing support for high quality basic and strategic research, survey and postgraduate training in earth, terrestrial, freshwater, marine and atmospheric sciences in its research institutes and units and in the universities, and its stewardship of a number of important environmental databases and collections, plays a key role in advancing the scientific understanding of biodiversity and sustainable management of the environment. The need for continued taxonomic research as part of these endeavours has been recognised in a recent NERC initiative in Taxonomy designed to promote new training and research in taxonomy in a number of UK universities.

2.29 Individually, and increasingly through collaboration, other UK Research Councils have also played a role. As well as sponsoring, research at the agriculture/environment interface, with the NERC and Economic and Social Research Council, the Agricultural and Food Research Council has launched a major programme with the Medical Research Council in comparative genome analysis, as part of a wide promotion of new techniques for studying systematics and evolution.

2.30 The Government's White Paper 'Realising our Potential: A Strategy for Science, Engineering and Technology' stated the Government's intention to redraw the boundaries between the research councils, creating six councils spanning engineering, the natural and social sciences and providing each council with a clear mission statement. The reformed Councils will come into operation on 1 April 1994.

2.31 Two of the six research councils will be carrying out work of direct importance to the maintenance of biodiversity – the Natural Environment Research Council (NERC) and the Biotechnology and Biological Sciences Research Council (BBSRC). The BBSRC will subsume the work currently undertaken by the Agricultural and Food Research Council (AFRC) and the work in biotechnology and biological sciences currently being undertaken by the Science and Engineering Research Council (SERC).

2.32 The research councils missions will be to promote and support high-quality basic, strategy and applied research and related post-graduate training in their areas of responsibility. For BBSRC this will be biological systems and the aim will be to enhance the management of biological resources and their

utilisation and interactions with the environment. For NERC it will be terrestrial marine and freshwater biology and Earth, atmospheric, hydrological, oceanographic and polar sciences and Earth observation. The councils will be expected to place special emphasis on meeting the needs of users of its research and training output, thereby enhancing the United Kingdom's industrial competitiveness and quality of life.

2.33 Drawing on their nineteenth-century headstart, the Natural History Museum, the Royal Botanic Gardens at Kew and Edinburgh, the Welsh and Scottish National Museums, together with many other city and university museums and botanic gardens, as well as zoological gardens, have

Trainee taxonimists identifying freshwater invertebrates.

continued to develop as essential data bases. Some hundred years after its establishment on a separate site in South Kensington, the British Museum (Natural History) remains one the outstanding museums of the world for its collections, exhibitions and science. Its integration with the adjacent Geological Museum in the late 1980s created in effect a Museum of the Natural World. The reference collections of about 67 million specimens, both biological and geological, and the data associated with them, are an essential resource, both for research and for environmental and commercial management generally. The Royal Botanic Gardens at Kew and Edinburgh have continued to provide an international service in plant identification, naming and classification, based on comprehensive collections and the expertise of their staff. Some 3,000 specimens each year are received at Kew for identification. Of 5.5 million vascular plant and 600,000 fungi specimens, some 400,000 constitute the world's largest collection of type specimens. They act as primary reference points for international nomenclature. London Zoo had remained the best known of over 50 zoological collections in the UK, its captive breeding-programme playing a key role in the conservation of some of the world's most endangered species. The Zoological Society's further integrated venture, the Institute of Zoology, constitutes the largest zoo-based centre for conservation research and comparative medicine.

2.34 In 1970, European Conservation Year, the British Government published a White Paper, *The protection of the environment: the fight against pollution*. It was the first to appear on the subject, and emphasised how more research was required on pollutants themselves, on their effects on human health, and on their general influence on plant and animal communities. The White Paper emphasised how,

> *'because ecological systems are complicated and change continually in response to many factors other than pollution, we need a background of basic and often long-term ecological knowledge before we can accurately interpret all the actions of pollutants.'*

A few months earlier, in February 1970, a standing Royal Commission on Environmental Pollution had been appointed, as a further demonstration of how Britain was active both at the international level and in preparing 'its own environmental defences'.

The holistic approach

2.35 The protection of 'habitat' and control of pollution have been perceived traditionally as discrete problems, even within the same Government Department, industry or conservation body. It was not until the 1980s that a more holistic approach began to emerge, as all parties recognised the intimate relationship of the two types of threat to the environment. A powerful stimulus for bringing these two strands of environmental concern together, and with them their respective bodies of expertise and experience, has been the increasing demands of both European Community and domestic legislation for environmental impact assessments of proposed developments. EIAs link these environmental concerns with other relevant matters, such as conservation of the built heritage, thereby facilitating a fully integrated approach to the range of environmental issues.

1990 White Paper

2.36 This major shift in perception was reflected in the publication of Britain's first comprehensive White Paper on the Environment, in September 1990, with the title, This Common Inheritance. Britain's Environmental Strategy. The 350 commitments and proposals for action sought to address both habitat protection and pollution control at all levels in the public and private sectors. The role of research and monitoring was emphasised as a means of basing policy on 'fact, rather than fantasy'. On both global and regional issues, it was the policy of Government to concentrate on research areas where Britain had particular strengths to contribute.

SUMMARY

2.37 The UK has a long and respected tradition of science-based environmental policy, supported by the knowledge it possesses about its natural history. This has been acquired through the patient industry and scientific endeavour of many people. The knowledge base is a substantial asset, but in looking to the future we must improve the quality of information and its availability. We must seek to ensure that 'sound science' underpins our policy and programmes, and that environmental education, and particularly the ecological sciences, reach an even higher standard of excellence.

CHAPTER 3

UK BIODIVERSITY

INTRODUCTION

3.1 This chapter describes the key determinants of geology, geomorphology, soils, climate and human activities which have helped to shape the UK's habitats and wildlife. The UK's biodiversity is expressed in terms of numbers of species, genetic variation within species, and combinations of species which occur together on land and around our shores. Following a description of the main UK habitats, and a brief account of UK patterns and trends in biodiversity, the chapter explains why UK biodiversity is special and significant in comparison with Europe and the rest of the world.

3.2 The UK's geographical position as a collection of temperate offshore islands on the north-eastern Atlantic edge of Europe, together with its diverse geology, geomorphology, soils, and the results of past human management has resulted in a diversity of habitats each with characteristic assemblages of plants and animals.

3.3 The main UK habitats can be described as woodlands, heathlands, lower grasslands, coastal areas (cliffs, estuaries, saltmarshes, sand dunes and shingle shorelines), marine, freshwater habitats (lakes and ponds, rivers and streams, canals and grazing marsh ditches), peatlands, uplands, farmland and urban areas; a diverse and pleasant land.

Found on wet heaths, and bogs, sundews increase their supply of nitrogen by trapping and digesting insects.

KEY DETERMINANTS INFLUENCING THE DEVELOPMENT OF UK BIODIVERSITY

3.4 The UK has great variety of landscapes and wildlife within a small area. Of the factors which have made our countryside what it is today, and given us our characteristic biodiversity, three aspects are paramount; rocks and their landforms, climate and human influence. Each aspect has historical significance because the processes which have shaped our land are ancient: we can only understand the present by reference to the origins of our landscape and wildlife.

Rocks, landforms and soils

3.5 The earth sciences of geology and geomorphology have themselves a long history of exploring the rocks and landforms of the UK. The nature of underlying rocks and the processes which have moulded them into the patterns of hills and valleys, of rivers and coasts we see today, have a profound influence on the distribution of species and their habitats. Remarkably, most periods of geological history are found in the rocks of the UK. There is more variety in a hundred kilometre journey across the UK than over several thousand kilometres of north-eastern Europe. Repeated episodes of glaciation during the last million years have eroded our mountains into glacial landforms and have deposited much boulder clay and other material north of a line from the Thames to the Bristol Channel.

3.6 Weathering of rocks, of differing hardness and contrasting mineral composition, gives rise to many different soil types. Soil organisms modify the weathered surface layers, and in conjunction with colonising plants, create deeper, more complex soils which in turn allow a succession of larger plants to grow. While alluvial soils in the lowlands have a high potential for agriculture, forestry and wildlife, most upland areas are less productive for human purposes and support plants such as dwarf shrubs, mosses and lichens adapted to the characteristically shallow nutrient-poor soils. On wet heaths and peatlands and in acid pools in bogs where the supply of nitrogen always limits plant growth, the sundews, butterworts and bladderworts increase their supply by trapping and digesting insects.

3.7 Just as plants show preferences for acid or base-rich soils, with differing organic content and contrasting physical structures, so many animals are restricted to soils of a particular type. Snails need calcium for their shells and thrive in chalk and limestone districts; an assemblage of ground beetles is confined to areas with sandy, free-draining soils while others are found only on waterlogged peat.

Climate

3.8 After the last glaciation, about 12,000 years ago, ice had retreated from the lowlands and the climate was cold and wet. The land surface resembled the tundra of northern Scandinavia today, with many lakes and waterlogged soils, with vegetation spreading northwards as the ice melted. A record of pollen and insect remains (mainly beetles) has been preserved in peat deposits which became established in low-lying areas. This reveals a succession of birch, willows and herbs becoming established, with a remarkably rapid colonisation of beetles known to be associated with warmer climates as temperatures rose.

3.9 Over the next 5,000 years the climate became drier and warmer than it is today; the **Boreal Period**. Britain was joined to continental Europe by land bridges, with the Thames flowing into the Rhine as a tributary. Pioneering birch woodland spread northwards, followed by Scots pine, hazel, elm and oak. Later lime, alder and ash arrived and woodlands had a complement of species similar to today, though in differing relative abundances.

3.10 By the end of the Boreal Period the land bridges disappeared as sea level rose. Ireland became separated from Britain before many plants and animals had time to colonise, hence Northern Ireland has fewer species than the remainder of the UK. The isolation of Britain as an island has reduced further invasion of sedentary species, though birds and flying insects have continued to arrive and become established here. The climate then became cooler and wetter until the Sub-Atlantic Period 2,500 years ago, which was similar to our current climate. In the lowlands broadleaved woodlands had a richer mammal fauna than today, with lynx, bear, wolf, and beaver still present (these mammals were later depleted and then exterminated by human activities). Pine forests became confined to Scotland and extensive wetlands occurred in river valleys and other low-lying areas. The distribution patterns of some species continue to expand or contract as a result of climate changes. A recent example is the range expansion of the white admiral butterfly during the 1930s, which is thought to have been largely the result of warmer June temperatures.

Human influence

3.11 Human activities have altered the original distribution patterns and habitat associations of wildlife in the British landscape. Thus although geology, geomorphology, soils and climate have set the limits for biological diversity in the UK, people have now become the prime regulators of the biodiversity we see around us. Much of the land surface is now farmed, forested, lived or worked upon; even our most remote hills and mountain tops are grazed or trampled.

3.12 Forest clearance began in Neolithic times and Neolithic people evidently had considerable impact on biodiverstiy. From Roman times the British landscape became clearly dominated by human activities, with succeeding cultures having greater and greater impact. By the Middle Ages many woodland boundaries were similar to those of today and cultivation and grazing by stock accounted for much of the intervening land. In the late eighteenth century the Enclosure Acts changed patterns of land ownership, and subsistence farming was replaced by the production of crops for sale on the open market, rather than domestic or local consumption. These developments all had a fundamental effect on the diverse character of our landscape and its biodiversity which we value so highly today. Moreover, historical features which reflect these developments, such as ancient monuments, land boundaries and historic buildings, now often play host to a diverse range of species, while archaeological and historical investigation help to illuminate our understanding of biodiversity in the UK. The increasing urban population at the time of the Industrial Revolution made new demands on land for housing, industry and transport. Woodland management and new plantations reflected growing demands for timber,

David Woodfall, Countryside Commission

Shropshire includes fine examples of small fields with dense hedges characteristic of ancient landscapes in this part of Britain.

mostly satisfied by imports from forests in North America and elsewhere. A further consequence of the growth in industry was increasing pollution of air and water, leading to dramatic reduction in ranges of lichens and freshwater species in rivers.

3.13 Throughout the nineteenth century land drainage and more sophisticated farming practices increased agricultural production, but at the expense of the loss of many wetlands and ancient grasslands, together with their characteristic wildlife. This century has seen further loss of countryside to urban and transport developments, and increasing arable and livestock outputs from intensively managed farmland. These changes, while bringing economic benefits, in many cases resulted in losses of our biodiversity. For unimproved lowland grasslands it is estimated over 97% were lost between 1932 and 1984; for lowland heathlands in England over 70% were lost between 1830 and 1980. Restoration of biodiversity is time-consuming and expensive; what is easy to lose quickly is hard to regain, even slowly.

Land classification

3.14 Complex variations of rocks, landforms, climate and human activity across Britain give rise to local patterns of biodiversity. In order to simplify this complexity and provide a framework for extrapolating records of local biodiversity to the national scale, the Institute of Terrestrial Ecology (ITE) has developed a **Land Classification of Great Britain**. In this approach each one kilometre square is assigned to one of 32 Land Classes on the basis of a range of environmental attributes obtained from maps (including climate, geology, altitude, drainage, relief, coastal physiography and man-made features such as roads and buildings). Squares within each Land Class have a similar range of basic environmental characteristics. The ITE Land Classes have been used as a sampling framework in national surveys of biodiversity, in particular the Countryside Survey 1990.

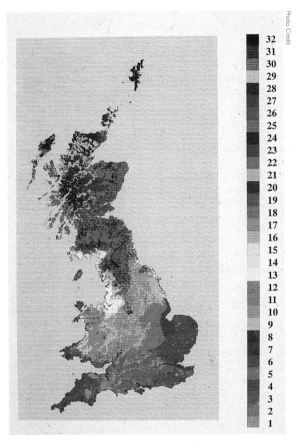

Distribution of the 32 ITE land classes in Great Britain.

FIVE VIEWS OF BIODIVERSITY IN THE UK

3.15 The following five sections consider biodiversity in the UK at five interconnected levels. These range from the local to the global, and from within species to assemblages or communities of species. There are examples and summary statistics to illustrate the major themes, and to give overviews of the nature and scale of the UK's biological richness. We begin by looking at genetic variation within species and its significance for people and wildlife. We then review estimates of the number of species in the UK, before looking at the combinations of species which occur together on our land and around our shores. Next, patterns of biological diversity across the UK demonstrate the great variety we can observe within a relatively small geographical area, and we conclude by viewing our biodiversity in a wider European and world context to evaluate our wider responsibilities.

VARIATION WITHIN SPECIES IN THE UK

3.16 In this section we will look at some examples of the inherited genetic variation known to occur within British

It is essential to avoid areas of importance for wildlife when planning for transport routes or other similar developments.

species. It should be borne in mind that all species vary in many characters, but in most cases this variation remains little known or undocumented. It is easier to observe variation as expressed in obvious structural or colour characteristics. However, many subtle biochemical or physiological features may be even more important for the survival of individuals and the evolution of species.

3.17 The importance of within-species variation for the survival of species is that, through the process of natural selection, it allows populations of a species to change in their genetic constitution over time. Where variation within a species is limited, the degree and rate of change will be slower, which means that the species is less able to cope with environmental changes, or to adapt to changes taking place within species with which it interacts. Therefore, within species variation has great significance as a component of biodiversity, both as an expression of the complexity of the living world and because it is a crucial property of species which enables them to change and respond to their surroundings over time.

3.18 Occasionally, a species will change rapidly over the course of a few generations, due to the success of a new genetic combination, or because a change in the environment increases selection for or against a particular character. These rapid changes have been studied enthusiastically by biologists in order to gain insights into evolutionary processes.

3.19 Geographical variation results from populations of a species having different characteristics over their distribution range. When well developed such variation may be recognised by taxonomists who give formal names to subspecies or races.

3.20 There are many good examples of geographical variation among British plants and animals (see page 28). This variation can be regarded as incipient speciation in extreme cases; it is also another way in which special local characteristics are manifested in our diverse land. Just as local styles of building houses, or of constructing farm gates, contribute to our sense of place, so the outward signs of biological evolution result in the distinctive appearance of species in their typical local settings. Many people value their local wildlife because it represents an essential part of their surroundings, giving both aesthetic pleasure and spiritual refreshment. When they know that this wildlife contains species which are different from those found elsewhere, they have an added reason for pride as well as extra justification for demanding that this wildlife be conserved.

3.21 The important consequence of geographical variation for conserving biodiversity is that a population of a species in one part of its range is not necessarily equivalent to a population elsewhere. While some widespread species which are mobile show little, if any, geographical variation, many species occur as isolated populations with no movement between them. In the second case, geographical variation is likely to occur, particularly where local conditions differ and hence result in contrasting types of selection for alternative characteristics.

Variation in domesticated species

3.22 People have been cultivating plants and domesticating animals since the dawn of civilisation. Prior to cultivation and domestication, wild fruits and seeds were gathered and wild animals were hunted and killed. Then grasses were discovered which provided grain for food; planting grasses and other plants as crops combined with keeping animals for milk, meat and clothing, enabled settlements to be established. This led to the growth of communities and was a major impetus for the development of more sophisticated societies. In pre-historic times, selecting individual plants or animals with preferred characteristics may have led to some improvement in yields or other features for some species. By the eighteenth century in Europe, such selection was becoming sophisticated and more successful. With the recent growth in understanding of genetic mechanisms, very precise selection and control for desired characteristics has become possible.

3.23 In the UK there has been a long and successful history of plant breeding and the selection of domestic animals for preferred characteristics. For more ancient varieties and breeds, the date and circumstances of their discovery are often unrecorded. In some cases the names bestowed upon fruit and vegetable varieties allude to the person or place where they originated; for others the colour or shape are responsible for their epithets. For animal breeds, their names generally reflect their place of origin and predominance. In either case, they have become part of our cultural and social heritage, in orchards, on farms, and at shows.

THE NUMBER OF SPECIES IN THE UK

3.24 Even in a well-studied country such as the UK there is no comprehensive catalogue of our resident plants and animals. Species new to science (hitherto undescribed) and species new to the UK (previously described elsewhere) are discovered every year. Many groups of tiny plants and

VARIATION IN DOMESTICATED SPECIES

Common Ground's first apple day.

APPLES

The wild crab apple of our woods and hedges is the ancestor of the many varieties of cultivated apples. Apple trees have been grown for at least 3,000 years, the variability of the crab apple, and its cultivated descendent giving rise to an immense number of varieties differing in such attributes as hardiness, growth form, seasons of flowering and fruiting, and the sizes, shapes, colours, textures and flavours of their fruit. Apples dating back to the sixteenth century include Nonpareil, Royal Russet and Golden Pippin; the famous Cox's Orange Pippin is thought to have originated about 1850 from the variety Ribstone. For all these varieties, their appearance and flavours at the table are a welcome and familiar part of everyday life.

Soay sheep.

Scottish black-faced sheep.

SHEEP

Well over 40 breeds of sheep occur in the UK, with some found only on islands such as Boreray or North Ronaldsay, the latter feed on seaweed for most of the year. Length and colour of wool, hardiness, presence or horns (the Manx Logthan is exceptional in having up to four or even six horns in some individuals!) and behaviour all vary considerably. Some breeds are now reduced to relatively few individuals and bloodlines where their original farming niche has disappeared. Some primitive breeds, such as the Soay sheep, bear a resemblance to the original Asiatic mouflon domesticated by people and first brought to Britain in Neolithic times, while others have become bulkier and carry a much heavier fleece.

animals are so little known that it is possible to discover new species relatively easily. For better known groups, discovery of new species may be a rare or improbable event, but finding out more about their biology and distribution offers plenty of scope for anyone with an enquiring mind.

THE MAJOR GROUPS OF ORGANISMS IN THE UK

3.25 There are many books on the plants and animals of the UK, particularly dealing with the larger and more conspicuous species. Our knowledge of the major groups of living organisms in the UK is very uneven. Microbial organisms, such as bacteria and protozoa, are much less studied than larger plants and animals. The algae, fungi, bryophytes and lichens are in turn less well known than flowering plants. Nevertheless, the distribution and status of more lower plants are being revealed. New identification guides and recording schemes are enabling more naturalists to work on these groups and pool their knowledge. For flowering plants, the location, and even population size, are known for the most threatened species.

3.26 Invertebrates are generally less well known than vertebrates. This results from fewer investigators tackling more species, which are also often hard to find and identify. The more popular invertebrates have their distribution and status accurately known, though only very few species have their population sizes assessed. For birds, and now increasingly for reptiles, amphibians and mammals, most species have national population estimates. Other aspects of biological knowledge reflect the trends discussed above. Long term trends (over 10 years) in numbers at sample sites are known for a few flowering plants, for butterflies, larger moths, aphids, some mammals, as well as for breeding and wintering birds. Overall, birds are the best known in terms of their ecology, behaviour and changing numbers over time.

EXAMPLES OF GEOGRAPHIC VARIATION AMONG BRITISH PLANTS AND ANIMALS

VASCULAR PLANTS

Vascular plants have received detailed investigation with respect to their variation in colour and structure. Mountain pansy has flowers which vary from purple through intermediates to yellow; some populations are predominately purple, others mainly yellow. The geographical distribution of these variants has not yet been mapped. Grass of Parnassus has a distinctive variety which grows in coastal habitats. This has larger flowers, atop shorter stems, than typical plants. A third example is the leaf colour of Lords-and-Ladies, which has mainly unspotted leaves in north and west Britain and frequently purple spotted leaves elsewhere.

BUTTERFLIES

The Common Blue typically has females with the upper surface of the wings largely brown; in Ireland females are large, heavily marked with blue and have more prominent orange lunules at the wing margins. On the island of Tean in the Scilly Isles, females have extensive pale, silvery-blue scales on the upper surface of the wings instead of the darker blue found in Ireland and elsewhere. The Grayling has a distinctive small subspecies on the limestone of Great Ormes Head, North Wales. This is mirrored by the Silver-studded blue which aslso has a small subspecies at the same place.

Irish female common blue butterfly.

SHREWS AND VOLES

The Common Shrew occurs as a distinctive subspecies on the island of Islay. It is characterised by very grey fur on the flanks and frequent lack of fifth unicuspid teeth.
There are also three races of the Common Shrew, distinguished by different chromosome numbers, which may have originated through successive colonisations at the end of the last glaciation. The Bank Vole has four island subspecies (on Jersey, Skomer, Mull and Raasay) distinguished principally by skeletal features. The Field Vole shows variation between populations on Scottish Islands, the population on Islay being the only one regarded as a distinct subspecies.

SAND LIZARD

The Sand Lizard is now confined to two areas in the UK. The primary areas are the heaths of Dorset, Hampshire and Surrey, with the coastal dunes of Merseyside and the south Lancashire coast also having significant populations. The southern populations are typically darker than those from the north-west and have different markings. The differences may be partly related to the different habitats occupied by the Sand Lizard, rather than the effects of gegraphical separation. Whatever the causes, there is a further good example of substantial within-species variation

Marine organisms occuring within UK waters	
Group	**British species**
Marine algae	840
Invertebrates	Estimated 6,500
Fish	300
Birds	188
Mammals	33
TOTAL	Estimated about 8,000

Endemic species in the UK	
Group	**Number of endemic species**
Lower plants	About 20 bryophyte species
Higher plants	About 43 (excluding microspecies)
Invertebrates	About 9
Vertebrates	One: Scottish crossbill

Numbers of terrestrial and freshwater species in the UK compared with recent global estimates of described species in major groups		
Group	**British species**	**World species**
Bacteria	Unknown	>4,000
Viruses	Unknown	>5,000
Protozoa	>20,000	>40,000
Algae	>20,000	>40,000
Fungi	>15,000	>70,000
Ferns	80	>12,000
Bryophytes	1,000	>14,000
Lichens	1,500	>17,000
Flowering plants	1,400	>250,000
Non-arthropod invertebrates	>3,000	>90,000
Insects	22,500	>1,000,000
Arthropods other than insects	>3,000	>190,000
Freshwater fish	38	>8,500
Amphibians	6	>4,000
Reptiles	6	>6,500
Breeding birds	210	9,881
Wintering birds	180	-
Mammals	48	4,327
TOTAL	88,000	1,770,000

3.27 Many bird species typical of lowland farmland in the UK have undergone pronounced declines since the mid 1970s. These include the well documented declines of the grey partridge, barn owl and lapwing. A large number of other more common farmland bird species have also severely declined over the last two decades. For example, recent research by the British Trust for Ornithology commissioned by JNCC suggested that 10 out of 12 seed-eating birds that are found on farmland showed signs of decline between 1977 and 1991 (although for all other bird species there was a slight increase over the same period). These include linnet (36% decline), reed bunting (−46%), skylark (−53%), corn bunting (−62%) and tree sparrow (−81%). These declines in farmland bird populations have coincided with major changes in agricultural practices in lowland Britain. These include the switch from spring to autumn sowing of arable crops, which also led to the loss of winter stubble, a move away from crop rotations and mixed farming, an increase in the inputs of inorganic fertilisers and pesticides, and the intensification of pasture management.

3.28 There are also differences in our knowledge of terrestrial, freshwater and marine organisms; in general most is known about terrestrial species, least about marine species. This reflects both the numbers of people studying these environments as well as the ease of finding and recording the organisms.

Examples of species where the UK holds a significant proportion of the European or World population	
Species	**Proportion of population**
Bluebell	Unknown: estimated up to 30% of the European/World population
Snail *Leiostyla anglica*	Unknown: estimated 70% of the world range
Grey seal	About half of the world population
Gannet	About 60% of the world population nest in Britain
Pink-footed goose	About 80% of the world population overwinter in Scotland and England

3.29 Countryside Survey 1990 gives information on the more widespread plants using a sample of 11,500 fixed quadrats, designed to be representative of Great Britain. The average number of plant species in each 200 m quadrat varied from 6 in arable fields to 23 in upland grass mosaics.

Changes in species status

3.30 Information on changes in species status can be gleaned from a variety of historical sources as well as from many observations and studies ranging from casual observations to detailed, systematic studies. In some cases

COUNTRYSIDE SURVEY 1990

Countryside Survey 1990 combines state-of-the-art satellite image analysis and detailed ecological field survey in an overview of the fabric of the British countryside.

The survey has achieved its three objectives:
- to record the stock of countryside features in 1990, including information on land cover, habitats and species;
- to measure change by comparison with earier surveys in 1978 and 1984;
- to provide a firm baseline, in the form of a database of countryside information, against which future changes can be assessed.

The detailed ecological field survey covered a random sample of 508 one kilometre squares, stratified by the ITE Land Classes. In each 1 km square details of land cover, field boundaries, habitats and soils were recorded on a map.

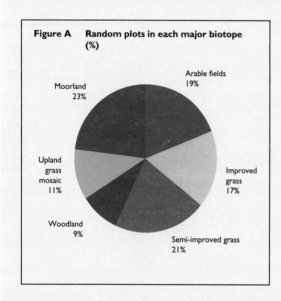

Figure A   Random plots in each major biotope (%)

The plant species composition of 23 vegetation plots (quadrats) was recorded and each plot was permanently marked for future reference. In addition, a sample of freshwater invertebrates was collected from a watercourse in the 361 squares where a suitable site was found.

Countryside Survey 1990 provides national estimates for the stock and change of land cover types, field boundaries and plant species composition and diversity. Because these estimates are based on a national sample they may not always provide reliable figures for smaller areas. To help overcome this problem detailed ecological data from the field survey have been combined with information about the distribution of land cover types obtained from satellite images in the Countryside Information System database.

Countryside Survey 1990 was funded by the Department of the Environment, the National Environment Research Council and the Department of Trade and Industry. The Survey was undertaken by the Institute of Terrestrial Ecology and the Institute of Freshwater Ecology.

CHANGES IN THE SPECIES DIVERSITY

An analysis of changes in plant species richness between vegetation plots surveyed in 1978 and 1990 was included in the Countryside Survey 1990. In 1978 over 1000 vegetation plots (200m^2 quadrats) were located at random within a sample of one kilometre squares representative of Great Britain. The same plots were re-surveyed in 1990. The plots have been grouped in six broad habitat types in Figs B and C.

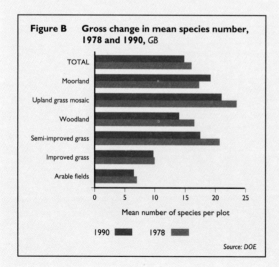

Figure B   Gross change in mean species number, 1978 and 1990, GB

Mean number of species per plot

1990 ■   1978 ■

Source: DOE

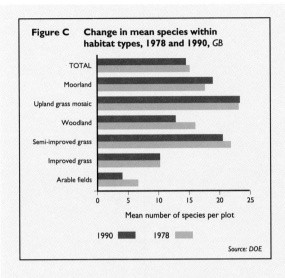

Figure C   Change in mean species within habitat types, 1978 and 1990, GB

Mean number of species per plot

1990 ■   1978 ▨

Source: DOE

Two types of change have been analysed.

Fig B shows the gross change in mean species number for all plots surveyed in both 1978 and 1990, regardless of whether the plots remained in the same broad habitat type. In this analysis there were significant losses of species richness in semi-improved grassland. (–13%), woodland (–14%) and upland grass mosaics (–11%). There was a gain in richness in moorland habitats (+7%).

The second analysis in Fig C shows the change in species numbers just for the plots that remained within the same habitat type in 1978 and 1990. In this analysis there were significant losses of richness in arable fields (–29%) and woodlands (–20%), and a gain in richness in moorland habitats (+8%).

The results show a general trend towards a reduction of plant species richness in the most widely occurring vegetation of fields and woods between 1978 and 1990. In contrast, the plant species richness of moorland habitats has increased but this may be associated with disturbance and the spread of acid grassland in these inherently species-poor habitats.

fossil evidence reveals changes which have occurred prior to historical sources being available.

BRITISH HABITATS

3.31 In the UK we often use the term **habitat** to refer to the major assemblages of plants and animals found together, as in woodland or sand dune habitats. More properly, a habitat is the locality or local area occupied by a species, but in this chapter it is used in its familiar, broader sense.

3.32 Ecologists have described habitats most frequently in terms of their vegetation communities. Plants are easier to sample than mobile and often elusive animals, and many plants tend to occur together consistently as well-defined **communities**. A number of these communities make up each habitat; the **National Vegetation Classification** has described British plant communities in detail. This project has defined semi-natural communities (those modified by human influence to a limited extent only) by recording the occurrence of plants in habitats throughout the UK.

3.33 Although we tend to think of habitats most frequently as aggregations of plant communities, animals from birds to invertebrates are now used more frequently to define communities. This can give us fresh insights into

the classification of habitats because animals respond to different environmental factors compared with plants. For example, areas of bare ground devoid of vegetation are of little concern to those studying plant communities; however, these can be vital breeding or hunting areas for invertebrates and essential feeding grounds for birds.

The effects of human activities on British habitats

3.34 Over much of the UK forest habitats would predominate if human influences had not intervened. Consequently, those plants and animals characteristic of forest conditions are most numerous in terrestrial situations. Where the natural forest cover has been cleared for farming, intensive forestry or urban land use, fewer species will occur. Other species characteristic of open habitats such as grasslands, heathlands and wetlands, will colonise and exploit areas cleared of tree cover. The extent of these open habitats in the absence of human intervention is a matter of dispute. While climate and the exposed conditions will maintain most coastal habitats in a treeless state, inland the effects of grazing mammals may have kept some areas with little or no tree cover. Uplands above the tree line (currently about 700 m in the Highlands of Scotland) also lack trees, and some areas with thin, freely draining soils, or conversely ground which is waterlogged (bog and fen habitats) will not support trees.

ROTHAMSTED INSECT SURVEY LIGHT TRAPS

There have been considerable changes in moth species richness and diversity at Rothamsted since the 1930s. Loss of habitats due to more intensive farming practices has reduced species richness and species diversity of larger moths at Rothamsted. Similar changes are known to have occurred at other trap sites in agricultural locations.

POPULATION TRENDS FOR BRITISH BREEDING BIRDS FROM THE COMMON BIRDS CENSUS (CBC)

The Linnet recovered after the severe winters of 1961/62 and 1962/63 to a peak in the mid 1960s; since then a steady decline has continued so that the species is now at an all time low. The chemical control of weeds in arable crops is thought to be largely responsible. The Nuthatch has increased from the mid 1970s onwards after a period of fluctuating numbers. At the same time it has expanded in the northern parts of its range in the north of England and into Scotland. The reasons for the increase are not well understood.

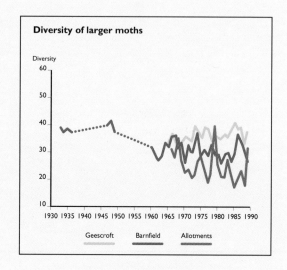
Diversity of larger moths

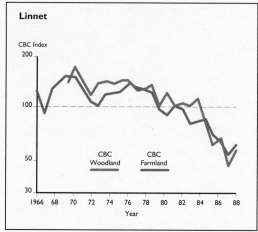
Linnet

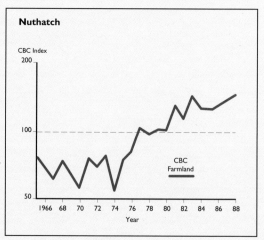
Nuthatch

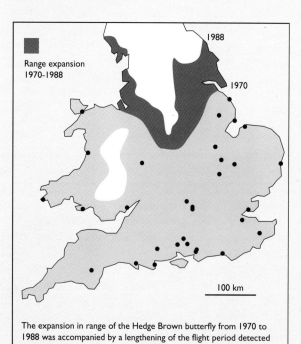
The expansion in range of the Hedge Brown butterfly from 1970 to 1988 was accompanied by a lengthening of the flight period detected by the National Butterfly Monitoring Scheme at the sites marked on the map

3.35 The clearance of perhaps 90% of the UK's forest cover during the past 5,000 years has been detrimental to many species dependent upon forest conditions. These include many plants and invertebrates, with significant extinctions of beetles associated with ancient trees and dead wood. These **saproxylic** (feeding on dead wood) insects have been recorded as fossils from peat deposits. Recent work identifies 17 saproxylic beetles known only as fossils originating since the last glaciation. They no longer occur in the UK due in part to loss of ancient trees from woods and forests. This total is based on records from few sites with fossil remains, so the number of documented extinctions will probably increase substantially when more sites are studied.

Terrestrial and freshwater habitats

3.36 The best and most recent estimates for the land cover of Great Britain, including the more common semi-natural habitats, are provided by Countryside Survey 1990. Semi-natural habitats cover about a third of Great Britain. Between 1984 and 1990 there were minor changes in the net area of some habitat types but no clear trend towards a loss of semi-natural habitat was evident.

Woodland habitats

3.37 The natural **climax vegetation** (the plant communities which would develop and be present in the absence of human intervention) over much of the UK is **broadleaved forest**, dominated by trees such as oak, ash and small-leaved lime. While much of the land surface would have been covered by trees before the first clearances for agriculture took place, there may well have been extensive open areas resulting from grazing or browsing of large herbivores and the succession of ponds, swamps and meadows created by beavers in river valleys. The natural forests have been termed **wildwood** and some of our woods are probably derived directly from these forests, with a continuity of woodland vegetation present (though there may have periods when few, if any, large trees remained). Woodland is termed ancient if it has been continually present since before 1600. Woodland is called recent if it is present on land known not to have been woodland in the historical past.

3.38 Today, forests and woodlands make up about 10% of our land surface. Most of this woodland area has been established relatively recently on sites which have not been wooded for a long time. Some 15% of the woodland area is ancient in origin. Surviving ancient, semi-natural woodlands are, particularly in England, isolated, small areas, surrounded

The majority of lowland woods have had a long history of management as coppice with standards until this century when the practice of coppicing has been largely abandoned.

by intensively farmed land, and are greatly changed in their plants and animals from the ancestral forest cover. These changes have been brought about by many generations of human management, with selective felling, coppicing, and in some cases re-planting, changing the proportions of tree and shrub species. In turn these changes have influenced the ground cover of herbs and lower plants, and there have been profound changes in the assemblages of animals present. The ground flora is important for recognising woodland plant communities, of which 25 have been recognised by the National Vegetation Classification.

3.39 The majority of lowland woods have had a long history of management as **coppice with standards**. This produced large timber from the few trees allowed to grow to maturity as **standards**, together with small wood from cutting shrubs or trees regularly every 10 to 15 years or so, known as **coppicing**. While many native species readily grow again after being cut down to stumps, doubtless some species were encouraged at the expense of others because they were favoured by woodmen. Such coppice with standards woods are very different in appearance from their neglected successors. They have an open, sunny feel, with relatively few large trees (to avoid shading out the coppice re-growth), quite extensive freshly coppiced areas with vernal flowers and insects such as the woodland fritillary butterflies. There are broad trackways, known as **rides**, which are used to extract the timber and wood during winter. There is relatively little mature timber in such woods, particularly in comparison with the primary wildwood, where over half the

Britain's native pine forest is found only in the Highlands of Scotland.

trees can be mature or post-mature. The tradition of managing woodlands as coppice with standards has favoured some wildlife at the expense of others, with early succession species gaining the advantage at the expense of those associated with ancient trees and dead wood.

3.40 Wildlife dependent upon mature timber has persisted in a few places where there has been better continuity of ancient trees. The Royal Forests (places where deer were kept), including Windsor Forest and the New Forest, have a long history of retaining ancient trees. Many of these were managed as **pollards**, essentially coppice set on a bole sufficiently tall to prevent browsing by deer on the fresh re-growth. Trees managed in this way can live for hundreds of

years, well beyond their normal span. In consequence they can build up a rich community of lichens on their bark, invertebrates living in sap runs, with fungi and decaying wood within their massive boles.

3.41 Distinctive **Caledonian Pine Forest** remains in a number of Scottish glens. Extensive felling has reduced its area and removed many of the older trees. Today many remaining areas receive management sympathetic to their wildlife. Our only native conifer forest has birds such as Scottish Crossbill and Crested Tit, with an assemblage of pine-feeding insects.

3.42 The history of woodland management this century has been one of abandonment of coppicing, with increased planting of non-native tree species in many remaining woodland sites. This has resulted in the decline of plants and animals associated with the early successional stages of coppice. There have also been significant losses of ancient woodland to clearance for agriculture. Since the introduction of the Government's broadleaf policy in 1985 losses of ancient woodland due to conversion to agriculture or to conifer forest have ceased. This policy has also encouraged an increasing interest in the re-establishment of coppice working, and in the creation of new native woodlands.

3.43 Because the natural land cover of the UK is principally woodland, we have inherited more woodland species than for any other kind of habitat. The structural complexity of woodland creates a great variety of niches, which are exploited by up to two to three hundred vascular plants and perhaps over 5,000 animals (mostly invertebrates). There is as yet no reasonably complete species inventory for any woodland in the UK, though there are extensive lists for many groups in some well-studied sites such as Wytham Wood, Oxfordshire and Abernethy Forest, Inverness-shire.

3.44 Results from Countryside Survey 1990 show a decrease in plant species diversity within woodlands between 1978 and 1990. There were on average 16 species per 200 m quadrat in woodlands in 1978 compared with 13 species in 1990 in the same quadrat, a 20% reduction.

Grassland habitats

3.45 Keeping livestock has been the major factor behind the creation of grasslands in the UK; **meadows** are cut for hay to feed to stock in winter, while **pastures** are grazed by animals. There are many types of grasslands, which have developed on different soils, influenced by slope, aspect,

Ancient woods in Buckinghamshire

Dot size relates to the actual area of each wood

This is a county of extreme contrast: while the Chilterns and Burnham Beeches are among the most densely wooded parts of England, the Vale of Aylesbury has no ancient woods at all. In the north of the county most ancient woods lie on the poorly drained clays or infertile sands in the former forests of Bernwood, Whittlewood and Whaddon Chase

Based on the Ordnance Survey 1:250,000 map with the permission of The Controller of Her Majesty's Stationery Office. © Crown Copyright

climate and management history. While some grasslands may well have originated naturally before human clearance of shrubs and trees, the great majority owe their existence to farmers in ancient, pre-historic times. In some cases old grasslands contain earthworks made by the first inhabitants, who cleared the drier hills and slopes and thereby established a sward, particularly rich in plants and animals on soils derived from chalk or limestone. Such downlands remained clear of shrubs and trees for hundreds of years until changing farm practice, and loss of rabbits through myxomatosis, allowed taller grasses and scrub to establish from the 1950s onwards. The beautiful Pasque-flower is characteristic of some of the finest ancient downs which have not been ploughed or treated with fertilizers or herbicides. More widespread herbs such as Horseshoe Vetch and Common Rock-rose can form extensive patches amongst fine-leaved grasses. Downs are amongst our richest places for butterflies, with pride of place going to the warmth-demanding species associated with short turf: these include the brilliant Adonis Blue, the Chalkhill Blue and Silver-spotted Skipper.

3.46 Flood-plain meadows in river valleys can be enriched by winter floods which deposit fine silt washed down from higher ground. In some cases irrigated water-meadows were established through construction of an intricate system of water channels. In a few of these meadows the spectacular Fritillary grows, rarely in great abundance. More frequent are plants such as Great Burnet and Common Meadow-rue. When flooded, wintering birds such as Shoveler and Wigeon are attracted to damp meadows; later they are the haunt of breeding waders and other birds. Neutral meadows also occur on clay soils away from river flood-plains, though few have survived agricultural improvement.

3.47 Acid grasslands support fewer plants than calcareous grasslands, and are typical of sandy soils or of soils derived from harder rocks in western Britain. Nevertheless, they have their own characteristic plants such as rushes and Whorled Caraway which thrive in these conditions. As with calcareous grasslands, the wildlife of these areas is best sustained by traditional, low intensity management; for hay on meadows and by grazing animals on pastures. Neglect steadily erodes the richness of grasslands, application of fertilisers or herbicides rapidly eliminates all but a few common, tolerant species.

3.48 Results from Countryside Survey 1990 show that of nearly 7 million ha of managed agricultural grasslands in Great Britain there are less than 0.3 million ha of unimproved and calcareous grasslands. Countryside Survey 1990, and other recent surveys suggest that only a

Peter Wakely, English Nature

Ancient meadows require careful management of their characteristic plants if they are to continue to flower in profusion.

proportion of the remaining unimproved grassland supports its characteristic biodiversity.

Lowland heath habitats

3.49 Heathlands are classic **plagioclimax** habitats: that is human management activities prevent natural successional processes from proceeding through to the creation of woodland. As with grasslands, heaths originated when the natural woodland cover was cleared in prehistoric and historic times. Heathlands are the result of centuries of intensive exploitation, including grazing livestock, cutting vegetation and turves, digging peat from wet heaths and sometimes burning in winter with the intention of improving grazing potential. These processes have produced types of vegetation which are classic deflected climaxes, that is they have a floristic composition far removed from that which can simply be obtained by woodland clearance. However, it is only continued management which prevents natural successional processes from redeveloping woodland cover. Heaths have long been subject to accidental summer fires, which are damaging to wildlife, particularly where neglect has resulted in the development of scrub and the accumulation of plant remains known as litter. These summer fires burn at a higher temperature than winter fires, and at a time of year when many plants and animals are more vulnerable to fire.

3.50 Heaths typically occur on sandy, acid soils which are free-draining and hence dry. In some cases waterlogging in a valley bottom leads to local peat formation and the development of wet heath communities. An obvious impression created by many heaths is that they are dominated by Heather or Heath species. This is particularly so in late summer when their vivid red or pink flowers attract huge numbers of pollinating bees and bumblebees.

Breckland heath. Heathlands are the result of centuries of intensive exploitation.

3.51 Just as with grasslands, a wide variety of heathland types has been recognised; for instance 15 plant communities are recognised by the National Vegetation Classification. Of these, 13 are dry heath types and two are wet heaths, but overlying this vegetation classification are more complex associations of numerous invertebrate assemblages, yet to be formally characterised. The continued management of heaths is essential if their biodiversity is to be sustained. Grazing, cutting and burning can all play their part, with the emphasis being on management of small patches to create a mosaic of different age classes of heather and other heathland plants.

3.52 The loss and fragmentation of Dorset heathlands has been well documented. In the mid eighteenth century there were about 39,960 ha of heaths in Dorset; by 1983 5,670 ha remained, a loss of 86% in area. The remaining patches of heath are naturally smaller than formerly, and they are separated from each other by farmland, plantations or buildings, each of which are inhospitable terrain for most heathland species to cross. In such circumstances local extinction from a patch of heath is unlikely to be made good by a subsequent recolonisation. The likely trend is continued loss of heathland species from many smaller patches unless these can be linked together by reinstated heathland as corridors.

3.53 On hot, dry southern heaths the Sand Lizard and Dartford Warbler are scarce and threatened species requiring a mosaic of heath age classes and sensitive conservation management if they are to survive on the remaining heathland fragments. Plants such as Marsh Gentian and Dorset Heath are confined to heathland, while ground-nesting bees and wasps, spiders and the Silver-studded Blue butterfly are all typical inhabitants of younger heath with bare ground. Heathland ponds and pools are among our richest sites for dragonflies, with over 20 of our 39 species occurring on the best sites.

3.54 There are about 58,000 ha of lowland heathland remaining in Britain. In the south, most heathland remains in Hampshire within the New Forest, followed by Surrey, Dorset, Breckland and the Suffolk Sandlings. There are substantial areas of heathland in northern and western

Golden eagles are only found in the larger upland blocks.

Britain; these are less well known but nevertheless are valuable wildlife habitats.

Upland habitats

3.55 There have been a number of definitions of **upland** habitats, their extent depending on whether the area above enclosed farmland or above a particular altitude is chosen. About 30% of the land surface of Britain is above enclosed farmland, though much of this is farmed as rough grazing (principally for sheep). About 3% of the land surface is **montane**, that is above the potential tree line (at about 700 m). At these high altitudes short, sparse vegetation similar to Arctic tundra is found. Slope and aspect are crucial determinants of the plant communities, with the duration of lying snow setting limits to the growing season and giving rise to distinctive snow-bed communities. The remaining uplands are termed **sub-montane**; originally the lower zones were wooded, but all except a few tiny fragments were lost long ago mainly as a result of grazing and burning, leaving heather moorland and acid grasslands. In poorly drained parts of the sub-montane zone, there are extensive blanket bogs which have developed as a result of peat deposition.

3.56 In addition to a number of plant communities which are well-represented in the UK compared with other countries, our uplands support a unique assemblage of breeding birds. Golden Eagle (which are only found in the larger upland blocks), Peregrine, Raven, Ptarmigan and Red Grouse breed in high numbers.

3.57 Intensive grazing by sheep has reduced the area of dwarf shrubs (notably heather) over much of our uplands, leading to an increase in the amount of acid grasslands. In some areas cessation of cattle grazing has led to the spread of bracken. On heather moorland, where management for Red Grouse remains economically important, patches of heather are burnt on a 10 to 25 year cycle. This creates an intimate mixture of different age classes, with fresh regrowth of heather in the first years after burning.

3.58 Between 1978 and 1990 there was an 8% increase in the plant species diversity within moorland habitats. Moorlands are inherently species-poor habitats and, in this situation, increased plant diversity may be associated with the spread of acid grassland and disturbance.

3.59 Montane vegetation is damaged by burning, and it is easily eroded by trampling or skiing. Many of the summits of our mountains have been adversely affected by increased recreational access, resulting in the loss of typical vegetation cover and the associated invertebrate assemblages. Further down the slopes, conversion of moorland to conifer plantations displaces the existing wildlife and creates a different type of habitat. There has been a trend towards agricultural improvement of moorland since the Second World War, with drainage and re-seeding leading to pastures with high densities of sheep and little wildlife. Where the valleys of enclosed farmland have also seen pasture improvement or conversion to arable, there are further pressures on mobile upland birds such as Golden Plover which utilise lower areas at certain times of the year.

Wetland habitats

3.60 Wetlands can be divided into those where the water arrives only from rainfall, termed bogs, and those where the water also arrives from streams, rivers, springs or seepages, which are fens or mineral marshes. Both are rich in characteristic biological diversity, often including species exploiting associated freshwater pools. Where waterlogged remains of plants accumulate in conditions lacking oxygen, peat is formed. The absence of oxygen prevents organisms such as bacteria and fungi from breaking down dead organic material, and recycling the nutrients as happens in most habitats. The accumulation of peat over time raises the land surface, so that eventually a domed bog surface is created (a **raised bog**). The only water which reaches the peat surface under these conditions will come from rainfall, so that the nutrients available from groundwater are absent. Therefore, bog plants are adapted to cope with low nutrient levels, and with the acid conditions which prevail in waterlogged peat soil. In addition to the preserved remains of plants in peat, plant pollen and remains of insect cuticle (notably of

beetles) are also preserved. The study of such remains has revealed much about the history of our vegetation and climate, particularly now that precise absolute dates can be found from radiocarbon dating.

3.61 On an actively growing bog, *Sphagnum* mosses are responsible for much of the peat accumulated. The more intact bogs, which have not been burnt or cut-over, and where the water remains held at the bog surface, support the greatest range of Sphagnum species growing in a complex pattern of hummocks and hollows. Shallow pool systems are also characteristic of intact bogs, the shapes and patterns of the pools (best observed from the air) changing in different areas according to the local climate. In addition to *Sphagnum* mosses, attractive plants such as Bog Rosemary, Cranberry and Sundews are typical inhabitants of the bog surface.

3.62 In upland areas of high rainfall, blanket peat forms on all but the steepest slopes. On upland slopes nutrients from **springs** and **flushes** can increase the variety of plants over a range of a few metres, with richer assemblages of insects such as craneflies, whose early stages are spent in the soil, being hunted by waders and other birds.

3.63 The remaining large areas of lowland bogs, notably the Flow Country in northern Scotland, and open moorland, are important habitats for breeding birds. These are considered to be of international importance in their own right, with species such as Dunlin, Greenshank, Red-throated Diver and Wood Sandpiper. Many water beetles and dragonflies breed in the acid pools on bogs where water levels have not been lowered by peat extraction. Bogs do not need specific management unless they have been damaged, when remedial treatment is needed to raise and restore water levels.

The Flow Country in northern Scotland, one of the few large areas of lowland bog remaining.

3.64 Fens are widely distributed in the UK, with many small sites in comparison with bogs. The larger fens, for example in East Anglia to the south-west of the Wash, have a long history of drainage for agriculture. Here an area of about 25,000 ha has been reduced to four small sites of less than 500 ha, with the loss of many typical fenland species over this part of their range. The Large Copper butterfly was known from the East Anglian Fens and the Norfolk Broads, until in the middle of the last century when its last stronghold at Whittlesey Mere was drained.

3.65 Large fens remain in the shallow valleys of Broadland in East Anglia, and in Strathspey in Scotland (the Insh Marshes), with many smaller sites in Wales, Scotland and some in England. Frequently, fens occur alongside other habitats, especially carr woodland dominated by alder and birch, which can invade fens which are drying out naturally or due to drainage and water extraction. Unlike bogs, many fens have long-established management regimes which can sustain many aspects of their biodiversity. Cutting reeds or sedge for thatching are still important land uses within the Norfolk Broads, where they maintain rich fen plant communities with plants such as Common Reed, Saw-sedge, several sedges (Carex species) Milk Parsley, Bog Myrtle (in areas with groundwater movement), and Grass of Parnassus.

Freshwater habitats

Physalia

An acid moorland stream in Exmoor, supporting a sensitive and characteristic assemblage of animals and plants.

3.66 Freshwater habitats are conventionally separated into standing waters (lakes, ponds and pools) and running waters (rivers, streams and springs). In addition to the plants and animals which spend most or all of their lives in water, many others live at the water edge. Thus fringing habitats are important in their own right as well as contributing to the wildlife and appearance of freshwaters. Because the quality of water in standing and running waters depends upon land use in the surrounding catchment, it is essential to take a broad view of the needs of freshwater habitats and species. Treatment of sewage, disposal of farm wastes, levels of fertilizer use by farmers, discharges of industrial effluents, all impact upon the biodiversity of our freshwaters. The site-based approach to sustaining biodiversity has very limited returns when tackling such broad issues. Policies which seek higher overall standards for water quality (and water availability for areas with falling water tables) are essential for future progress.

3.67 Because of continuing concerns over water quality, there is extensive monitoring of freshwater itself (mainly of rivers and streams) and of species sensitive to various types of pollution (particularly insect larvae). There have also been extensive surveys of water plants and some groups of invertebrates, which have identified typical communities associated with different freshwater situations. The response of these communities to different levels of pollution now allows the recovery or deterioration of water quality to measured with precision. Recently, the acidification of catchments resulting from atmospheric pollution has become of increasing concern for the effects on wildlife.

3.68 Britain has a large number of ponds and lakes; estimates vary widely for smaller ponds, but for water bodies larger than 4 ha over 5,500 have been recorded. Countryside Survey 1990 produced an estimate of around 300,000 ponds under 1 ha in Great Britain.

3.69 It has been estimated that we have about 10,000 river systems in Britain, with over 109,000 associated streams. In addition there are many gently flowing ditches in grazing marshes within the approximately 500,000 ha of this habitat in England and Wales. Rivers are dynamic systems, which change their courses and profile through erosion and deposition, particularly when in flood. Pools and riffles, steep banks, sand and shingle bars and old cut-off channels, all create a variety of niches which are exploited by specialist plants and animals.

3.70 Introduced species have spread rapidly in some freshwater habitats. Exotic fish have displaced native species in many rivers and lakes, while the spread of plants such as Canadian Pondweed and Australian Swamp Stonecrop have caused problems for native plants in many lakes and ponds.

Coastal habitats

3.71 The UK has a long coastline in relation to its land area. Our coastal habitats are exceptional for their variety and extent in a north-west European context. The best examples of some coastal habitats have been little modified by human activities; for example, hard-rock cliff ledges, soft-rock cliffs and ungrazed saltmarshes. Many of the other habitats have been considerably altered; for instance, sand dunes have frequently been grazed or have been stabilised through erecting fences or planting conifers, and estuaries have typically been developed from their landward margins.

3.72 Cliffs are familiar and well-loved features of many parts of our coast. From the White Cliffs of Dover to the Old Man of Hoy and Harma Ness on Unst in Shetland, spectacular cliffs and stacks dropping down to a foaming sea are recognised as a special part of our coastal heritage.

Plants that grow on hard rock cliffs need to be tolerant to salt spray and be able to persist on thin scraps of soil clinging to narrow ledges.

Slowly eroding cliffs are characteristic of northern and western Britain, with isolated examples elsewhere. Cliffs formed from hard rocks support a community of plants which are tolerant of salt spray and can persist even on thin scraps of soil clinging to narrow ledges and clefts in the rock. Rock Sea-lavender and Thrift grow here, often adjacent to massive colonies of sea birds which nest safe from mammalian predators on the tallest and most inaccessible cliffs. Gannet, Razorbill and Guillemot are just three examples of birds which can be seen nesting and wheeling around such cliffs.

3.73 Eroding cliffs formed from the softer rocks found in southern and eastern England can retreat by several metres each year. The pebbles, sand and silt washed away by the sea can be deposited further along the coast to form shingle beaches, spits and build up the front of sand dunes. Plants characteristic of disturbed ground (including some species thought of as 'weeds') flourish where fresh soil is regularly exposed for colonisation by seeds. Where water trickles down and forms seepages, plants such as Common Reed and Horsetails Equisetum species thrive. Areas of bare ground warm up quickly on south-facing slopes, providing nesting sites for solitary bees and wasps and hunting arenas for predatory ground beetles. Many rare and threatened invertebrates are associated with soft-rock cliffs.

3.74 While **shingle beaches** are found extensively around our coastline, larger **shingle features** are rare, just as they are elsewhere in Europe and the rest of the world. The largest example, and the most significant for its plants and animals is Dungeness, Kent. Here the shingle has built up in narrow ridges to form a structure known as a **cuspate foreland** which has been colonised by a fascinating assemblage of wildlife, much of which remains despite considerable damage due to many piecemeal developments. In addition to plants such as Yellow Horned-poppy and Sea-kale which are typical inhabitants of shingle, other plants have developed distinctive forms, such as the prostrate Blackthorn and Broom bushes. There is a rich invertebrate fauna, including the largest assemblage of bumblebees in Britain, an endemic leafhopper, and several distinctively pale subspecies of moths found nowhere else in the world.

3.75 **Sand dunes** and their fringing beaches epitomize seaside holidays and coastal recreation for many people. Dunes have often been modified by developments as diverse as golf courses and pine plantations, and the tensions between allowing increased access and sustaining their characteristic wildlife have proved hard to resolve. There is typical sequence of plants, from the colonisers and stabilisers found along fore-dunes (mainly Lyme Grass and Marram Grass), through the inhabitants of the main ridges and hollows (often dominated by Marram Grass, but with carpets of orchids, such as Pyramidal Orchid in calcareous dune hollows), the deeper hollows, often flooded with temporary pools (called **slacks**) where

There are about 56,000 ha of sand dunes around the coast of Great Britain.

rushes and water plants may persist, finally ending with a landward transition to grassland, heath or other terrestrial habitats. Some of the most spectacular dunes in Britain are the sandy plains, called machair, of the Outer Hebrides, where grazing and periodic cultivation maintains short grasslands rich in wild flowers and breeding waders. Britain's sand and shingle structures support internationally important numbers of breeding Roseate, Arctic, Sandwich and Little Terns. The Natterjack Toad breeds in temporary pools in a few dune slacks, where it avoids predators found in permanent ponds, and develops rapidly in warm, shallow water. Dune insects and other invertebrates have various adaptations to enable them to deal with the hot, arid environment. They include a substantial proportion of species not found in other habitats, some of which are yellow or silvery in colour for effective camouflage against the sandy ground.

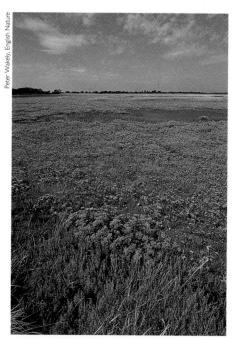

Saltmarshes develop principally around our major estuaries, where fine silt and other sediments are trapped.

3.76 There are about 56,000 ha of sand dunes in Great Britain, widely distributed around our coast where there is a supply of sandy sediments which can be blown inland from shoreline deposits.

3.77 Saltmarshes develop principally around our major estuaries, where fine silt and other sediments are trapped by salt-tolerant plants such as the Glassworts species, Saltmarsh grasses species and Annual Sea-blight. As with sand dunes there is a marked zonation of plants from the young saltmarsh at the lower seaward margin, through the middle marsh where creeks intersect richer plant assemblages, including Sea Lavender and Sea Aster with increasing frequency of the fine-leaved Red Fescue grass, to the upper marsh where more shrubby species appear such as Sea-purslane and Sea Wormwood. The landward transitions to other habitats have often been lost or are truncated through construction of sea walls for protection against tidal inundation. The most species-rich upper zones have also suffered most from reclamation for agriculture and industry.

3.78 Many saltmarsh plants, with the exception of grasses, are intolerant of grazing. For those marshes with established cattle grazing (for instance around Morecombe Bay) a short, species-poor sward is created. This is exploited by feeding ducks and geese in winter, but is otherwise poor in wildlife. The more diverse structure and richer assemblages of plants and animals found in ungrazed saltmarshes are greatly prized, particularly where these communities grade naturally into sand dune or other semi-natural habitats.

3.79 There are about 44,000 ha of saltmarshes around the coast of Great Britain, with the largest examples within major estuaries such as the Wash, Thames, Mersey and Solway Firth.

3.80 Britain has an internationally important suite of estuaries, with a total area of about 530,000 ha of which over 300,000 ha is intertidal habitats. This represents over a quarter of the estuarine area of the Atlantic coast for north-west Europe (excluding Scandinavia).

3.81 Estuaries are notable for their range of habitats, with tidal flats, saltmarsh, sand dune and shingle often occurring in close proximity. Rocky shores and cliffs are more frequent in northern and western Britain, while saline lagoons (with their small but distinctive assemblage of threatened species) are found more in the south. Associated habitats include coastal grazing marshes, usually reclaimed from saltmarsh, but with their complex ditch systems and if left unimproved agriculturally, they are often important for their aquatic plants and invertebrates, as well as for wintering and breeding birds.

Estuaries are vulnerable to developments for housing, industry, transport and recreation and from the effects of pollution.

3.82 Estuaries are highly productive habitats, with high densities of invertebrates present in the fine sediments of intertidal flats. These provide abundant food for fish at high tide and for migrant and wintering waterfowl at low tide. The geographical position of the United Kingdom, at the meeting point of several routes used by migrating birds, combined with the large number and area of estuaries, results in their use by huge numbers of migrants. The number and distribution of wintering birds is greatly affected by weather conditions here and in adjacent countries. Because of the mild Atlantic influence on our shores, winters are typically warmer than for other European estuaries of comparable latitude, favouring birds which cannot feed adequately during periods with freezing temperatures.

3.83 Estuaries are naturally dynamic and often rapidly changing systems. This is a function of the tidal cycle interacting with the inputs from major rivers flowing down to the sea. However, they are vulnerable to developments for housing, industry, transport and recreation, both for direct land take and from indirect effects such as pollution. Their position at the outfall of rivers into the sea has led to the growth of many nearby towns and cities with harbours and links into road and rail networks. There are continuing development pressures for urban, industrial and transport facilities. The future of the biodiversity of our estuaries depends upon their core habitats being sustained intact, with development in other areas being compensated for by provision of new habitats from the release of land into positive and sympathetic management for wildlife.

Marine habitats

3.84 Marine life is less familiar to most people than life on land or in freshwaters. This is mainly the result of the inaccessibility of life in the sea. Apart from marine life in rock pools which offers a glimpse to many children, only qualified divers are able to experience the habitats and species at first hand. Some new displays of marine life, coupled with high quality television documentaries, are now opening up new horizons for many people. This is important for raising understanding of the issues surrounding marine biodiversity, particularly in the context of marine pollution and the harvesting of fish and other marine species.

3.85 Within United Kingdom territorial waters we have a wide range of marine habitats, whose nature is defined by the nature of the substrates and the temperature and quality of the water. Intertidal habitats and the sea floor may comprise hard bedrock (particularly on western and northern coasts), boulders, shingle, sand and mud. Each supports its own typical

Male cuckoo wrasse and sea fern.

assemblages of plants and animals, adapted to cope with the tidal cycle near the shore or to exploit the darker waters at greater depths. Soft sediments can contain a wealth of burrowing species, adapted to filtering out fine particles of food, while dwellers on rocky surfaces cling on tight to flat surfaces or seek shelter in cracks and crevices to escape predators or to survive the pounding of waves on windswept shores.

3.86 Within our 12 mile limit is an area equivalent to 70% of the land surface of the UK. There is insufficient space here to give accounts of even the major sections of coast and their associated communities of plants

There is a wide range of marine habitats within UK territorial waters. Here, a kelp forest with urchins and soft corals in the Outer Hebrides.

and animals. In general, western coasts enjoy warm water as a result of the North Atlantic Drift, while on North Sea coasts the water temperature fluctuates much more. Enclosed, shallow inlets also tend to warm up more rapidly in summer, enabling faster growth by some species. There is also a trend towards a greater richness of marine life along the warmer south-west coast of the English Channel; the Irish Sea is relatively cold in winter, limiting the northward range of southern elements in the plants and animals.

3.87 Birds, cetaceans (whales, dolphins, seals and porpoises) and fish are generally highly mobile, ranging widely during the course of each year as they exploit different habitats and opportunities during their life cycles. Many plants and invertebrates are relatively sedentary once they have settled out and become attached to their preferred substrate. At the early stages of their life history, however, they can be dispersed widely by currents as tiny plankton. The large marine algae, known as seaweeds, are abundant along many coasts. Their numbers decline rapidly in deeper, darker waters, but where they colonise rocks and other substrates they form the basis of an important food chain, as well as creating a more complex range of structures which in turn are homes and habitats to many invertebrate and vertebrate animals.

3.88 While marine habitats have not been changed by human activities to the extent of their terrestrial and freshwater counterparts, nevertheless they have been considerably modified in some respects. Dredging and

An example of intertidal habitat at Lochcarron District.

people live, and where there is the biggest likelihood that wildlife can be seen each day. Making room for biodiversity to increase within remaining greenspace is a priority for many people, to create better living conditions and to allow the stimulus of the natural world to touch those living even in the middle of our largest cities.

3.90 Within open areas in towns and cities, there is often considerable potential for restoring remnant habitats, or creating new ones. The designation of **wildlife corridors**, as routes along which wildlife may disperse, has already taken place in some urban areas. Habitats where there are a significant numbers of species with good powers of dispersal (often species which are pioneers colonising young or ephemeral habitats) are easiest to restore or establish. Grasslands and ponds are popular choices, where encouraging results can be achieved rapidly.

Within open areas in towns and cities, there is often considerable potential for restoring remnant habitats, or creating new ones.

dumping of sediments from estuaries has altered the sea floor considerably in some places. The effects of oil pollution on seabirds and shore communities have been well documented following the wrecking of the Torrey Canyon and Braer. Given time, recovery will take place, though much loss of marine and coastal life occurs in the meantime. The harvesting of fish stocks, an important industry in the United Kingdom and the European Community, remains a contentious issue. For many species, fishermen must now sail further because inshore and nearby fish stocks have become so depleted. Given careful treatment, many fish can be harvested on a sustainable basis over a long timescale. Gaining agreement over the future wise use of marine life is a high priority for the United Kingdom, Europe and the rest of the world.

Urban and new habitats

3.89 While built land has only tiny biodiversity remaining, fragments of ancient habitats can persist with significant wildlife interest, even when surrounded by urban land. Gardens can also support an interesting array of the more common and adaptable plants and animals, particularly when they are larger and contain patches which are not regularly mown or cultivated. Also, many cultivated and introduced plants grow in gardens and other urban habitats. Urban landscapes are where the great majority of

3.91 Some new, artificial habitats can acquire rich assemblages of certain groups. The lakes created after gravel workings are a good example, where waterfowl and dragonflies can quickly establish breeding populations. However, there is no shortage of such new habitats, and in many cases ancient habitats of greater biological diversity will have been destroyed prior to their creation. Ancient habitats, which are not re-creatable once lost, should be sustained in preference to creating new, artificial habitats.

Cultural landscapes

3.92 The United Kingdom is rich in historical remains spanning the last 10,000 years. These remains tell us much about past human occupation and land use, including traditional land management practices. These are often well-documented in ancient manuscripts and in modern publications. When ecological knowledge is combined with detailed historical analyses in studying the origin and development of our landscapes, many strands of evidence come together to reveal how the patterns of fields, hedges and woods have developed around each village settlement. In 'The History of the Countryside' Rackham (1986) has shown both how some landscapes have changed and, conversely, how many features are of considerable antiquity, and have remained remarkably constant over the last five or six centuries.

3.93 In addition to being a subject of great interest in its own right, historical ecology and the investigation of cultural landscapes (landscapes created by a long history of traditional management practices) can shed light on how biodiversity has changed over recent centuries. If we wish to understand why Cornwall is different from Cambridgeshire or Argyll, then an examination of historical as well as natural processes is essential.

3.94 Almost 77% of the UK is farmed, and agricultural practices will continue to have a significant effect on the cultural landscape. Modern machinery, which is now abundant in Britain, can drain or modify the land much more rapidly and cheaply than previously. This makes many small features and habitats, of great local interest, much more vulnerable to being tidied up or removed, especially when this may only take a day or two to accomplish. The work of Farming and Wildlife Advisory Groups (FWAG) in particular has concentrated on helping farmers to conserve landscape features, including those of historic interest and to find a place for existing habitats, restoring and creating new opportunities for wildlife where possible.

Habitat conservation and re-creation

3.95 The preceding brief accounts of our habitats and cultural landscapes can do no more than introduce the richness of our biological diversity. While it is quite easy to relate to the plight of an endangered species, the concept of an endangered habitat may seem remote and abstract to many people. Nevertheless, habitats are of great significance in their own right, having developed initially through the colonisation of the UK from the rest of north-west Europe after the last glaciation, and then subsequently under the direction and influence of traditional human land management activities. The results of these long historical processes, are not reproducible over short timescales, and indeed like the individual species themselves, are a product of evolution combined with chance events, which cannot be re-run the same a second time.

3.96 While some simple habitats, particularly those populated by mobile species which are good colonisers, have some

potential for re-creation, the majority of terrestrial habitats are the result of complex events spanning many centuries which defy re-creation over decades. Therefore, the priority must be to sustain the best examples of native habitats where they have survived, rather than attempting to move them or re-create them elsewhere when their present location is inconvenient because of immediate development proposals.

3.97 The prospects for habitat re-creation are best when land of greatest potential is

Pevensey Levels and Mynydd Y Cemaes; landscapes created by a long history of traditional management.

selected; this will generally be where some semi-natural vegetation remains, where the soil has not been enriched through use of fertilizers, and where nearby sites (notably SSSIs) can act as colonisation sources to speed the establishment of characteristic native species. Duplicating habitats around SSSIs and linking isolated sites together through the maintenance of appropriate landscape features have much to recommend them as positive measures to sustain biodiversity. They complement the more traditional site-based approach to wildlife conservation, though they are no substitute for retaining the best examples of habitats through appropriate management in cooperation with their owners.

NATIONAL BIODIVERSITY PATTERNS

3.98 At the scale of the United Kingdom there are patterns and trends in biodiversity due to the influence of climate, geology and human activities. Describing and analysing these patterns is at a relatively early stage of development, with the Institute of Terrestrial Ecology (Merlewood and the Biological Records Centre

1

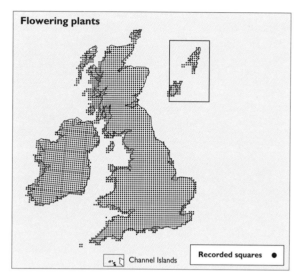

Flowering plants

Channel Islands
Recorded squares ●

2

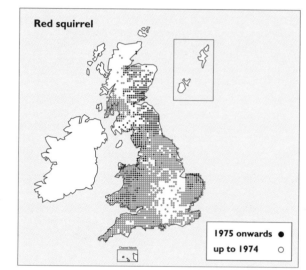

Red squirrel

1975 onwards ●
up to 1974 ○

Channel Islands

3

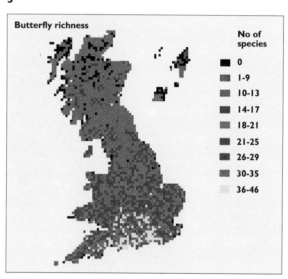

Butterfly richness

No of species

0
1-9
10-13
14-17
18-21
21-25
26-29
30-35
36-46

4

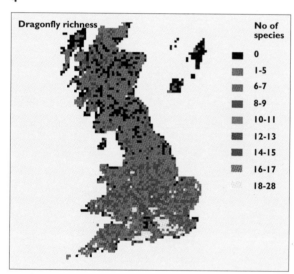

Dragonfly richness

No of species

0
1-5
6-7
8-9
10-11
12-13
14-15
16-17
18-28

5

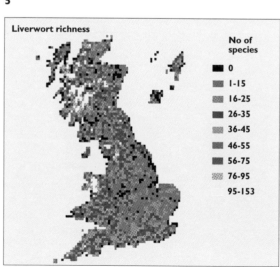

Liverwort richness

No of species

0
1-15
16-25
26-35
36-45
46-55
56-75
76-95
95-153

6

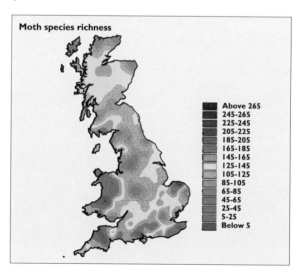

Moth species richness

Above 265
245-265
225-245
205-225
185-205
165-185
145-165
125-145
105-125
85-105
65-85
45-65
25-45
5-25
Below 5

7

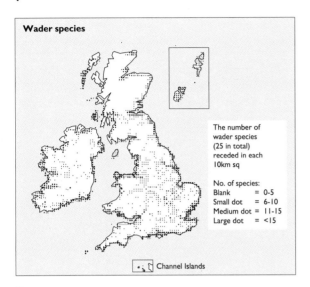

Wader species

The number of wader species (25 in total) receded in each 10km sq

No. of species:
Blank = 0-5
Small dot = 6-10
Medium dot = 11-15
Large dot = <15

Channel Islands

8

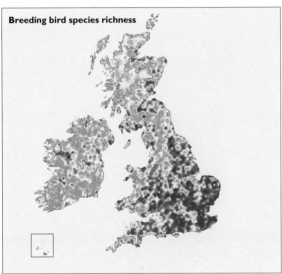

Breeding bird species richness

8

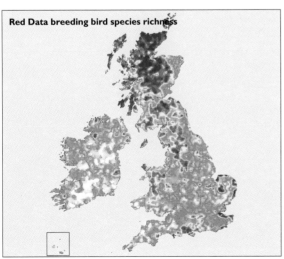

Red Data breeding bird species richness

KEY TO MAPS

1 Flowering plants coverage map
The coverage for flowering plants show what can be achieved by dedicated volunteers recording a popular group in the UK. Such well-coordinated schemes capture many records and observations to give an accurate account of the status and distribution of our wildlife. Map from the Biological Records Centre.

2 Red squirrel coverage
The decline of the red squirrel to isolated enclaves during this century is shown in this Biological Records Centre distribution map. Documenting such large changes in the range occupied by a species is essential before deciding what conservation action is needed.

3 Butterfly species richness
There are more butterfly species in southern Britain than in the North, though there are also a few northern species not found in the South. Most butterflies select hostplants growing in warm, sunny conditions; areas with higher average temperatures and sunshine totals are favoured. With their sensitivity to weather factors, butterflies are a group which will respond rapidly to any future climate changes. Analysis and map from the Biological Records Centre.

4 Dragonfly species richness
Although their aquatic larvae contrast with the plant feeding caterpillars of butterflies, the species richness trends for dragonflies are similar to butterflies. More species are found in the South, though with a different pattern of the richest areas linked to the presence of suitable water bodies. Analysis and map from the Biological Records Centre.

5 Liverwort species richness
The liverworts provide a contrast to the butterflies and dragonflies in that more species occur in North-West Britain. These areas have higher average rainfall than in the South and East, thereby creating humid conditions favoured by these plants. Analysis and map from the Biological Records Centre.

6 Moth species richness map
The mean species richness for larger moths over Great Britain has been assessed by a network of light traps run as part of the Rothamsted Insect Survey. These traps have been operated at a total of 369 sites up to 1992, giving extensive national coverage. The map shows the average number of larger moth species sampled by a Rothamsted light trap in a year for different areas of Britain.

7 Wintering wader species richness
The UK is visited by many migratory waders. These birds congregate particularly in major estuaries to feed on invertebrates, mainly on intertidal mudflats. These areas are of international importance for the survival of these species during often harsh winter weather.

8 Breeding bird species richness
There is considerable geographical variation in the number of breeding birds across the UK (light blue equals least species deep red most). There is also a contrast between the higher total species richness found in the South and East, and the greater richness of Red Data Birds in the North and West. Data collected as part of the British Trust for Ornithology/Scottish Ornithologists' Club/Irish Wildbird Conservancy 1988-1991 breeding bird atlas.

One of the UK's few endemic plants: the Lundy cabbage.

at Monks Wood), the Unit of Comparative Plant Ecology (UCPE, University of Sheffield) and the British Trust for Ornithology (BTO) pioneering the use of information obtained through traditional biological recording techniques for these novel analyses.

3.99 Prior to the 1950s, biological recording concentrated on defining the status of species within the boundaries of counties, formalised within the Vice-Counties system. In 1950, a conference of the Botanical

An endemic invertebrate: Procas granlicollis

Society of the British Isles (BSBI) agreed to map the distribution of British plants using the 10km squares of the national grid. This initiative culminated in the publication of the 'Atlas of the British Flora' after five years of fieldwork covering approximately 3,500 squares. This atlas mapped 1,700 flowering plants and ferns with hitherto unrivalled precision. National recording schemes were established for other plants and animals.

3.100 The BTO initiated a national survey of breeding birds from 1968 to 1972, which was repeated from 1988 to 1991, using both 10km squares and tetrads of the national grid. An equivalent survey of wintering birds was conducted from 1981 to 1984. These standardised surveys generated the data analysed to produce the species richness maps.

3.101 Studies of animal and plant distributions at the national and local scale will be greatly helped by the recent completion of the ITE Land Cover Map of Great Britain. The map uses satellite images to show the distribution and detailed patterning of land cover across Britain at a field-by-field scale.

UK BIODIVERSITY IN RELATION TO THE REST OF THE WORLD

Resident species of international importance

3.102 The UK has relatively few endemic species due to the relatively short period since recolonisation after the last glaciation. We have other species for which we hold a significant proportion of the world population. For both of these categories of species we have a special responsibility, as their survival depends to a great extent upon the care with which we sustain their critical habitats. Of particular note, therefore, is the relative diversity of our marine habitats, and the importance of marine conservation around our shores, the wetlands of northern Scotland in the Flow country and the areas that have been in continuous woodland for a long period such as the New Forest.

Conservation of mobile species

3.103 Many important elements of the UK's biodiversity are interlinked with biodiversity elsewhere, most notably for migratory birds, sea mammals and fish. Our actions concerning these species contribute to their survival and success overall; by exercising responsible stewardship on their behalf we can help to sustain species for which we share responsibility with other nations.

3.104 For its size, the UK is of outstanding importance for migratory birds which breed or winter on terrestrial and

A common dolphin off Eigg, Inverness-shire.

estuarine habitats. This is the consequence of our geographical position at the junction of a number of migration routes, or flyways. The success of these highly mobile species depends upon continuity of suitable habitats being present throughout the year (for feeding, resting and nesting), in each of the countries visited by each species. By conserving sites with internationally important populations of migratory birds, the UK makes a substantial contribution to the survival of these species.

Mobile sea mammals

3.105 The UK has an internationally important population of the Grey Seal, with about 100,000 out of a total of around 120,000 in the East Atlantic stock; the other stocks are reproductively isolated from the East Atlantic stock, in the West Atlantic (71,000 to 125,000) and the Baltic (1,200). The Harbour Porpoise, Common Dolphin and the Bottle-nosed Dolphin are three cetaceans which occur frequently in our inshore waters. The Harbour Porpoise and Bottle-nosed Dolphin have apparently declined significantly in recent decades within British waters. Cetaceans are capable of long distance movements, as well as showing fidelity to particular feeding and breeding areas.

Sustainable use of wide-ranging species

3.106 Harvesting fish, shooting red deer and collecting seabirds such as Fulmars and Gannets are just three examples of long-established exploitation of wild species in the UK (although the last practice is almost extinct). Such use is sustainable only if the population of the exploited species does not continue to decrease significantly as a consequence of harvesting. The ecology of harvesting has been investigated by ecologists in order to discover what regulatory rules and strategies will enable sustainable harvesting to continue

without the exploited populations being brought to the brink of collapse. In some well-known cases exploited populations have been brought to the edge of extinction, for example, the dramatic losses of whales from the oceans of the world.

Why the UK's Biodiversity Is Special and Significant

3.107 The UK has a rich and characteristic biological diversity for an island of its size, isolation and geographical position. Although the short period of time since the last glaciation has allowed relatively few endemic species and sub-species to evolve, there is considerable potential for more to appear given sufficient time and space in the future. The high human population and long history of intensive land use have resulted in many forest species disappearing, or becoming restricted to small areas, rather than occurring widely over the country as a whole. Species associated with other habitats may have extended their range as a result of agricultural and other human activities, until more intensive land use this century has generally reduced species richness and the abundance of more specialised species.

3.108 The special features of the UK's biodiversity are the consequence of evolutionary processes modifying species which have colonised this country over the last 10,000 years. The development of distinctive assemblages of plants and animals within British habitats, in most cases shaped by traditional countryside management practices,

Great Britain has a rich and characteristic biodiversity for an island of its size, isolation and geographical position.

LAND COVER MAP OF GREAT BRITAIN

A unique land cover map of Britain has been developed from high resolution satellite images. This is the first time since the 1960s that the land cover has been mapped in full. The map shows detail of villages, woods and farmland at a field-by-field scale.

The land cover map shows the dominant land cover for each 25 metre by 25 metre area (pixel) of Great Britain. Land cover was classified into 17 key types. It was produced using cloud-free images from the Landsat satellite, between 1988 and 1991. Summer and winter satellite data were combined to enhance the seasonal differences in various cover types, such as deciduous and evergreen trees.

The land cover map has been inter-calibrated with the Countryside Survey 1990 field work and the data is integrated in the Countryside Information System. Digital data are available for any part of Britain.

Inland water
Bare ground
Beach/mudflat
Saltmarsh
Bog
Rough grass/marsh
Bracken
Moorland grass
Open shrub heath/moor
Dense shrub heath/moor
Broadleaved/mixed wood
Coniferous wood
Tilled land
Managed grassland
Suburban
Urban

has resulted in a countryside which tells the story of our changing relationships with other species, if we take the trouble to find and interpret the clues.

3.109 Moreover, the true significance of biological diversity in the UK is even greater than the number of species present and their intrinsic value, or their value to us as a nation. Because our plants and animals are in a constant state of evolutionary change, we may view much of their significance as being the **evolutionary potential** they represent. If our plants and animals can be sustained in their full variety, with species extending over extensive ranges rather than being confined to tiny enclaves, and with each species containing a broad base of genetic variation rather than a few very similar individuals, then we can anticipate that they will give rise to new species in future. Some of these will remain as island endemics confined to this country; others may be successful on a wider stage. Either way our biodiversity has an evolutionary future. The choice of whether this future is indeed realised, or is truncated by accelerated extinctions, is ours.

SECTION 2

CHAPTER 4

CONSERVATION WITHIN HABITATS

INTRODUCTION

4.1 This chapter explains how the United Kingdom addresses its responsibilities under Article 8 of the Convention on '*in situ*' conservation. '*In situ*' refers to conservation of plants and animals in the wild state, in contrast to '*ex situ*' conservation in zoos or collections. UK habitats are rarely wild or natural since they bear the marks of man's impact over many centuries. Some, such as parks and gardens, are very far from being so.

Key players

4.2 National boundaries are irrelevant to wildlife. The conservation of plants and animals over their natural range and the maintenance of the influences that may in the long term support the distribution and abundance of wildlife populations depend, to an increasing extent, on international co-operation to implement coherent policies over the whole of the relevant areas. Key partners in sustaining and enriching the UK's biodiversity are landowners, occupiers and managers, planners, regulatory bodies, conservation organisations (voluntary and statutory) and those who set the economic and political framework within which these people make decisions. These people will be responsible for ensuring that the requirements of Article 8 of the Convention on Biodiversity are met (see box).

The overall goal and objectives

4.3 The overall goal, principles and objectives for UK policy towards biodiversity are set out in Chapter 1. They have especial relevance to geological and landscape conservation and the conservation of wildlife in its natural habitats. Some have underlain policies and programmes for many years.

4.4 The government seeks to ensure that its legislation, policies and practices underpin the conservation of the abundance and diversity of wildlife and their habitats and minimise the effects on wildlife where conflicts of interest are inevitable. The importance of these objectives is reflected in the international obligations the UK government has recognised, together with other countries, to achieve appropriate action over the natural range of endangered species and wildlife habitats. These international obligations underlie much of the UK's legislative framework for conservation.

Commitment to action

4.5 Numerous mechanisms are in place to help meet these goals. The UK has a statutory framework of protection for specially important sites and threatened species; there are planning policy guidelines setting the framework for positive land use planning decisions; there is a regulatory framework of standards and limits governing emissions to the air, land, freshwater and sea; quality objectives are beginning to be set, such as for water quality; incentives schemes are available to encourage landowners and managers to manage their land in environmentally sensitive ways. Increasingly wildlife and beautiful landscapes are being regarded as explicit products of land management to be sought directly rather than expecting them to emerge as a by-product of other goals such as food production. Programmes of action, devised as a partnership between key players, are vital in addressing the key threats to biodiversity.

4.6 Partnership and sensitivity to the economic, and social context of decision making are important as we enter the final years of the century. The threat is that decline in numbers and genetic variation of some species will continue and artificiality will further displace naturalness, this will impoverish us all. The goal of this plan is to galvanise and focus action by everybody involved in land and water use and management decisions in support of wildlife richness thus safeguarding this key aspect of our quality of life.

The main threats to UK Biological Diversity

4.7 During this century some species have become extinct, many have suffered significant population declines, natural or semi-habitats have declined markedly in extent and some are now only found in fragments. Water and soil quality has declined (although improvement in recent years is encouraging), air quality has fluctuated, our softer coastlines have been modified in many places by hard defences and the natural processes of sedimentation and erosion have been interrupted. The main factors effecting these wildlife and landscape changes have been agricultural intensification particularly in the last 50 years, built development – houses and roads, industry and minerals extraction and commercial forestry. The Sustainable Development Strategy reviews the impacts on the environment of the key sectors, including road transport, agriculture, forestry, energy, minerals and fishing and how these land and water uses can be managed and modified to make them more environmentally sustainable.

The large copper butterfly has been extinct in Britain since 1865.

Natural History Museum

ARTICLE 8 OF THE BIODIVERSITY CONVENTION: *IN SITU* CONSERVATION

Each Contracting Party shall, as far as possible and as appropriate:

a) establish a system of protected areas or areas where special measures need to be taken to conserve biological diversity;

b) develop, where necessary, guidelines for the selection, establishment and management of protected areas or areas where special measures need to be taken to conserve biological diversity;

c) regulate or manage biological resources important for the conservation of biological diversity whether within or outside protected areas, with a view to ensuring their conservation and sustainable use;

d) promote the protection of ecosystems, natural habitats and the maintenance of viable populations of species in natural surroundings;

e) promote environmentally sound and sustainable development in areas adjacent to protected areas with a view to furthering protection of these areas;

f) rehabilitate and restore degraded ecosystems and promote the recovery of threatened species, inter alia, through the development and implementation of plans or other management strategies;

g) establish or maintain means to regulate, manage or control the risks associated with the use and release of living modified organisms resulting from biotechnology which are likely to have adverse environmental impacts that could affect the conservation and sustainable use of biological diversity, taking also into account the risks to human health;

h) prevent the introduction of, control or eradicate those alien species which threaten ecosystems, habitats or species;

i) endeavour to provide the conditions needed for compatibility between present uses and the conservation of biological diversity and the sustainable use of its components;

j) subject to its national legislation, respect, preserve and maintain knowledge, innovations and practices of indigenous and local communities embodying traditional lifestyles relevant for the conservation and sustainable use of biological diversity and promote their wider application with the approval and involvement of the holders of such knowledge, innovations and practices and encourage the equitable sharing of the benefits arising from the utilization of such knowledge, innovations and practices;

k) develop or maintain necessary legislation and/or other regulatory provisions for the protection of threatened species and populations;

l) where a significant adverse effect on biological diversity has been determined pursuant to Article 7, regulate or manage the relevant processes and categories of activities; and

m) co-operate in providing financial and other support for in situ conservation outlined in subparagraphs (a) to (l) above, particularly to developing countries.

Key international obligations

4.8 The UK Government has played an active part in negotiating and then signing up to a number of important international conservation conventions. These include:

- **The "Bern" Convention on the Conservation of European Wildlife and Natural Habitats** which imposes obligations to conserve wild plants, birds and other animals, with particular emphasis on endangered and vulnerable species and their habitats. The provisions of the Convention underlie the EC Habitats Directive (see below) as well as the UK's wildlife legislation.

- **EC Council Directive on the Conservation of Wild Birds – the Birds Directive (79/409/EEC)** applies to birds, their eggs, nests and habitats; provides for the protection, management and control of all species of naturally occurring wild birds in the European territory of Member States (Article 1); requires Member States to take measures to preserve a sufficient diversity of habitats for all species of wild birds naturally occurring within their territories (Articles 2 and 3) in order to maintain populations at ecologically and scientifically sound levels, and requires Member States to take special measures to conserve the habitat of certain particularly rare species and of migratory species (Article 4).

- **EC Council Directive on the Conservation of Natural Habitats of Wild Fauna and Flora, adopted by the Council in May 1992 – the Habitats and Species Directive (92/43/EEC)** contributes to the conservation of biodiversity by requiring Member States to take measure to maintain or restore natural habitats and wild species at a favourable conservation status in the Community, giving effect to both site and species protection objectives. Following a period of consultation, sites to be designated as Special Areas of Conservation (SACs) must

Agricultural intensification is one of the main factors effecting wildlife and landscape changes in the last 50 years.

be agreed with the EC Commission by June 1998.

- **EC Council Directive on the Assessment of the Effects of Certain Public and Private Projects on the Environment (Directive 85/337/EEC)** requires environmental assessment to be carried out, before a decision is taken on whether development consent should be granted for certain types of project which are likely to have significant environmental effects.
- **The "Ramsar" Convention on Wetlands of International Importance especially as Waterfowl Habitat (Command 6464)** requires signatories to protect wetlands of international importance, to promote wetlands generally and to foster the wise use of wetland areas. At least one site in each country must be designated for inclusion in the Ramsar List.
- **The "Bonn" Convention on the Conservation of Migratory Species of Wild Animals** requires the protection of listed endangered migratory species, and encourages separate international agreements covering these and other threatened species. An agreement covering the Conservation of Bats in Europe was ratified by the UK in September 1992 and will come into force in January 1994. An Agreement on the Conservation of Small Cetaceans of the Baltic and North Seas ("ASCOBANS") was ratified by the UK in July 1993, and is also expected to come into force early in 1994.

- **The Convention on International Trade in Endangered Species (CITES)** prohibits or regulates international trade in species which are threatened with extinction or likely to become so and are subject to significant trade.
- **The International Convention for the Regulation of Whaling** (1946), on which the work of the International Whaling Commission is based. The Commission is responsible for the management and conservation of whale stocks on a world-wide basis.

UK statutes

4.9 The UK has a long tradition of conservation which predates these international instruments. The Protection of Wild Birds Act 1880 was followed by a further legislation during the later 19th and early 20th centuries to support a growing concern to protect bird species from decline. This legislation was consolidated and strengthened to protect all bird species in 1954, while 1949 saw the establishment of a statutory framework for the protection of wildlife habitat, geological and landscape features in the form of the National Parks and Access to the Countryside Act, followed by the Countryside Act 1968 and the Countryside (Scotland) Act 1967. The 1949 Act gave statutory powers to the Nature Conservancy which thus became the first official body in the world solely devoted to wildlife conservation at the national level. The Nature Conservancy Council Act 1973 established the Nature Conservancy Council to replace the committee of the Natural Environment Research Council known as the Nature Conservancy.

4.10 These threads of long established national tradition and the growing awareness of the need for international co-operation were effectively brought together in statutory terms in the Wildlife and Countryside Act 1981 and the Nature Conservation and Amenity Lands (Northern Ireland) Order 1985. The Environmental Protection Act 1990 and Natural Heritage (Scotland) Act 1991 reorganised the way nature conservation was administered by creating separate agencies for England, Scotland and Wales and a Joint Nature Conservation Committee to co-ordinate UK and international functions. The Wildlife and Countryside (Amendment) Act 1991 further strengthened the protection to wildlife afforded by the 1981 Act.

4.11 The 1981 Act and 1985 Order are the bedrock of nature conservation in this country; they established a statutory framework for the conservation of land important for wildlife and natural features and the protection of birds and other endangered wild plants and animals. They enable the UK to meet its international obligations, supported by other regulations governing emissions to the air and freshwater, providing for the setting of statutory water quality objectives and by the planning and development control system. The need for legislative changes is kept under review. New regulations are proposed to give effect to the EC Habitats Directive. These will recognise the importance of preventing the deterioration of key sites. They will also provide a statutory basis for the protection of key sites and species in the marine environment. A statutory framework can, however, only achieve so much. It must be bolstered and enhanced by appropriate incentives, policies and actions.

The Statutory Agencies

4.12 The three country agencies, English Nature, Scottish Natural Heritage and the Countryside Council for Wales, together with the Environment Service of the Department of Environment for Northern Ireland, are responsible for providing advice to the government on policies for or affecting nature conservation; for notifying land of special interest for its wildlife, geological and natural features; for establishing and managing National Nature Reserves; for disseminating information about nature conservation and

advising on the effects of ecological change and for carrying out or commissioning research in support of these duties. Through their Joint Nature Conservation Committee they discharge their special functions for nature conservation throughout the UK, and provide a collective view on international matters and those questions which affect the UK as a whole. They receive grant in aid to carry out their work, from Government. See table for details of the size of this grant which has grown in cash terms from some £18 million in 1981 to £138 million in the current year. (NB: In order to make comparisons expenditure by the Countryside Commission is included since from 1991 its functions in Scotland and Wales have been merged with those of the former Nature Conservancy Council).

4.13 The Countryside Commission, established by the 1968 Countryside Act, has the twin objectives of conserving and enhancing the beauty of the English countryside and improving and extending opportunities for people to enjoy it. Many of these concerns centre on human interaction with the natural world.

4.14 All the nature conservation agencies promote environmentally sensitive development patterns and land

Grants in aid to countryside and nature conservation agencies 1980/81 to 1993/94 (£ thousand)

	Countryside Commission	Nature Conservancy Council	Countryside Commission for Scotland			Total	Total corrected for 1993/94 prices
1980/81	7,620[1,2]	9,400	1,068			18,088	37,665
1981/82	8,320[1,2]	10,200	1,343			19,863	37,719
1982/83	11,200[2]	11,400	3,545			26,145	46,346
1983/84	12,600[2]	12,800	4,307			29,707	50,332
1984/85	12,800[2]	18,100	4,399			35,299	56,918
1985/86	15,200[2,3]	22,700	4,557			42,457	64,917
1986/87	17,900[2,3]	32,100	4,800			54,800	81,178
1987/88	22,800[2,3]	36,250	5,113			64,163	90,096
1988/89	21,100[2,3]	38,950	5,460			65,510	85,744
1989/90	22,200[2,3]	40,150	5,780			68,130	83,673
1990/91	24,500	44,819	6,688			76,007	86,428

	Countryside Commission	English Nature[4]	Countryside Commission for Scotland	NCC for Scotland[4]	Countryside Council for Wales[4]		
1991/92	29,647	32,416	7,700	17,624	14,554	101,941	108,674

	Countryside Commission	English Nature[4]	Scottish Natural Heritage[4]		Countryside Council for Wales[4]		
1992/93	42,553	38,130	33,500		17,305	131,488	135,233
1993/94	44,066	37,919	36,142		19,841	137,968	

Note: [1] At this time the Countryside Commission was not a grant aided body. Figures represent actual spend
[2] These figures include funds for Broads level authorities
[3] These figures include an allowance for Groundwork
[4] These figures include funds for the Joint Nature Conservation Committee

management practices. They also work in partnership with a wide variety of environmental organisations, farmers and land managers, to assist the public to experience the countryside and its different qualities.

The voluntary movement

4.15 The voluntary movement continues to play a conspicuous part, often owning and managing both Nature Reserves and other areas of wildlife importance. Wildlife protection remains a key objective of the National Trust, which has become the largest private landowner in Britain with an estate of over 240,000 hectares. The Royal Society for the Protection of Birds was founded in 1889, and acquired its first reserve in 1931. It is now the largest voluntary wildlife-conservation body in Europe, with some 850,000 members, and a research department of over a dozen scientists. Its 120 nature reserves cover 76,000 hectares. The Society for the Promotion of Nature Reserves evolved over the years, through the Royal Society for Nature Conservation (RSNC), into the RSNC Wildlife Trust Partnership, the major voluntary organisation in the UK concerned with all aspects of wildlife protection. At its core are 47 County Wildlife Trusts and 50 Urban Wildlife Groups. With a total membership of over 250,000, they own or manage over 2,000 nature reserves.

Research expenditure

4.16 Research relating to biodiversity is carried out by a wide range of Government Departments, including DOE, MAFF, the Forestry Commission, the Scottish and Welsh Offices, Northern Ireland Departments and Overseas Development Administration, Research Councils (NERC, the Biotechnology and Biological Sciences Research Council, – which will succeed the Agricultural Research Council on 1 April 1994 – Economic and Social Research Council and others) the statutory conservation agencies, universities, museums, botanic gardens and the private sector.

4.17 In 1991, the House of Lords Select Committee on Science and Technology estimated that £16.5 million was allocated to research in systematic biology. But this is only one element of biodiversity research. As there is no single register of research projects relevant to biodiversity, it is difficult to give precise figures on expenditure. For example, research expenditure by the Department of the Environment on projects relating to biodiversity includes work carried out under the air quality, global atmosphere, environmental protection, water and countryside research programmes, as well as by the statutory conservation agencies and National Rivers Authority.

4.18 The Natural Environment Research Council has estimated research spending of £23.3m (in 1991-2) of direct relevance to marine, terrestrial, freshwater and polar biodiversity, although much of its other research will also have a more indirect bearing. The Ministry of Agriculture, Fisheries and Food spent £16.4m of its 1991–2 Research and Development budget in the rural environment, which includes research on the impact on wildlife of different agricultural practices. For example it is funding R & D at the ADAS Research centres, Redesdale in Northumberland and Pwllpeiron in Dyfed, into developing systems of hill pasture management for sheep that conserve and enhance the structure and dynamics of the native plant and invertebrate communities. In addition, MAFF also carries out detailed ecological monitoring of ESAs and other incentive schemes, which do not appear in the research budget. MAFF also organises a register of agri-environment R & D on behalf of the Priorities Board for research and development in agriculture and food. This sets out the expenditure of a number of public sector research funding bodies, much of which impinges on biodiversity.

4.19 The Forestry Commission spent an estimated £2.3m on environmental research in 1992–3 and has recently launched a multi-disciplinary project team to undertake research on biodiversity in forests. FC also produces, through the Forestry Research Coordination Committee, a collation of publicly funded research into forestry, much of which is relevant to biodiversity. Much research in the environment sector has multiple objectives and multiple uses – for example, Countryside Survey 1990 and climate change modelling work – often with a direct or indirect bearing on biodiversity.

4.20 In order to achieve the overall objective of maintaining and, where possible, enhancing our biodiversity across its natural ranges, the UK government and its conservation agencies have determined that:

- Sustainability will be the guiding principle underlying their actions.
- Major conservation targets will be set for the year 2000 and later which will be used to focus their actions and priorities.
- Nature conservation objectives will be drawn up for manageable sections of the countryside, working with other organisations as necessary to achieve them.
- Help and advice is provided for partners of the conservation agencies so they take positive action for nature beyond the protection of statutory sites.
- Monitoring systems will be established which are integral to all the agencies work, and focus on the effectiveness of their actions in delivering their objectives.
- Initiatives will be integrated and focus on species. The

approach should deliver appropriate positive management to maintain and enhance the interest of all special sites.

- Much greater involvement will be sought from the community at large.
- The agencies will improve their understanding of the social, economic and political factors driving the broad environment in which they operate, and will seek to influence them for the benefit of biodiversity.

To maintain and enhance biodiversity the UK Government and its conservation agencies will seek greater involvement from the community at large.

How the conservation agencies implement their strategy

4.21 The nature conservation agencies work to achieve a single aim – to sustain and enrich the natural heritage of the UK for all to enjoy now and in the future. In this they are supported by many organisations, land owners and managers and members of the public. Common themes run throughout the day to day work of the agencies – habitat protection and management, the provision of advice, working through others, encouraging enjoyment of the countryside, maintaining and enhancing characteristic species.

4.22 Each agency has statutory responsibilities in respect of the selection, designation and management of special sites of national and international importance the vast majority of which remain in private ownership. In order to maintain the special interest, appropriate management of the varying habitats is essential. Partnerships with land managers are emphasised with recognition for the stewardship and practical management they and their predecessors have carried out on

their land over the years. Grant schemes such as the Wildlife Enhancement Scheme and Tir Cymen support farmers to do work which is of a positive benefit to nature conservation. The agencies work closely with government departments to ensure that their respective land management grant schemes are complementary. Outside designated sites the agencies advance nature conservation interests by influencing the policies and programmes of other governmental organisations and agencies.

4.23 The agencies' advice to central and local government is based on the view that conservation needs should be integrated into all aspects of policy. Agency staff are frequently consulted by local planning authorities about planning applications for housing and industrial development, drainage schemes, road building and energy generation. Industry, voluntary conservation organisations, members of the public, amateur naturalists and students seek to benefit from the knowledge and experience of the agencies, much of which is gained from managing nature reserves and scientific research. Conserving the diversity of wildlife in the UK is a huge task and the agencies can only achieve part of what is required. In recent years relationships with many organisations and groups have been renewed and strengthened, opportunities sought to harness the innovation, energy and commitment of others. Fundamental to this activity is the grants programme, with schemes such as countryside stewardship and the hedgerow incentive scheme designed to help either individuals or organisations to carry out nature conservation work which complements that of the agencies. The agencies wish to try to persuade every community to develop a pride in the biodiversity of its locality as great as its pride in community property and the appearance of its towns and villages.

4.24 Renewed efforts are being made to inform the public of the needs of wildlife and increase their enjoyment of the

Grant schemes support farmers to do work which is of positive benefit to nature conservation.

Conservation projects in schools and tours of reserves stimulate interest in nature conservation

countryside including geological features. Conservation projects in schools, tours of reserves, increased media involvement, information signs on nature reserves, leaflets and magazines which interpret the countryside or give specific advice on species or land management are some of the ways in which the agencies are stimulating public interest. Policies on access to the countryside have been reviewed and facilities provided for informal recreation. The growth of local nature reserves is providing opportunities for people in urban areas to enjoy and understand the natural world. Monitoring habitats and species to follow decline and increase is a prominent element of the scientific work, which together with specific scientific research, underpins the activities of the agencies by providing a solid information base. Programmes to aid the recovery of especially rare and threatened species and habitats under pressure are an increasingly important feature of the agencies' strategy for maintaining the unique diversity of wildlife in the UK.

METHODS USED FOR THE CONSERVATION OF BIODIVERSITY IN THE UNITED KINGDOM

Species conservation

4.25 A variety of actions are needed for the effective conservation of species. Concentrating on the conservation of habitats and sites will address the needs of many species concentrated within particular areas. Many plants and animals have widely dispersed populations. They are not generally amenable to site based conservation initiatives but instead require the retention of such features of the wider countryside as hedges and copses, ponds and flushes. The conservation of species where individuals are small or difficult to identify, or where the population inhabits a very small area (eg a lichen on a tree trunk), and is non-mobile, presents special problems.

4.26 Rare and vulnerable species require more specific action. Many of these have been protected under the legislation already mentioned. The Wildlife and Countryside Act gives specific protection to all whales, porpoises, dolphins and bats, six other mammals, all species of reptiles and amphibians, five

Concentrating on the conservation of habitats and sites will address the needs of many species concentrated within particular areas.

species of fish and 64 invertebrates, and for 168 species of plant as well as all birds. Arrangements are made to permit the killing of game birds in season and pest birds.

The Red Data Books

4.27 The need to concentrate action on individual species usually arises once the species has been classified as threatened. While the key words rare, vulnerable and endangered, which are covered by the term 'threatened', are defined by the International Union for the Conservation of Nature and Natural Resources (!UCN), the scope of these definitions has been extended in a series of Red Data Books dealing with different taxonomic groups and listing the species involved in the different categories. The Bird Red Data Book focuses on threatened birds of Great Britain but also includes species for which Britain has an international responsibility. The Red Data Books produced so far are listed in (see box overleaf).

4.28 National Red Data Books should not just be about those species which are rare and threatened in particular

The conservation of species where individuals are small or difficult to identify or where the population inhabits a very small area presents special problems.

countries, they must also include those species which are not threatened but are of international importance. If all countries dealt effectively with those species for which they had an internationally important population then none of those species would be in danger of becoming extinct.

4.29 The Red Data Books are a key source of guidance in identifying priorities for action but there are many taxonomic groupings for which no such books have been prepared. Priorities for further work in this field are being addressed. It is important for the conservation of biodiversity within the UK that both national and local government have a clear picture of the species which are 'threatened' at their level of responsibility. This has major implications for data collection and manipulation (see Chapter 9).

Species recovery and species action plans

4.30 In 1990 the Nature Conservancy Council produced a report, *Recovery: a proposed programme for Britain's protected species*, explaining the action required to achieve a return to a more favourable status of all the UK species other than birds protected under the Wildlife and Countryside Act 1981. The programme was formulated for a minimum period of 15 years, and the report is one source used to select species needing help. In 1991 English Nature launched an innovative Species Recovery Programme to assist specific endangered native plants and animals. Species are selected because they can benefit from targeted help. Each is tackled through its own costed plan and English Nature work in partnership with landowners and voluntary bodies. The

Royal Society for the Protection of Birds has launched an initiative under which they, in conjunction with the country agencies and other relevant organisations, will prepare an action plan for each of the 117 species listed in the Red Data Book on birds. See boxes for the layout of a species action plan and details of how landowners and government departments can help with a plan for the stone curlew.

4.31 Habitat strategies and action plans are complementary to species action plans. Habitats provide the vital life support systems. Many species are threatened by land use changes which can be addressed through habitat conservation action. Species action plans are used to ensure that the individual species targets are addressed within the habitat action plans.

The dormouse is one of the endangered native animals included in English Nature's Species Recovery Programme.

4.32 In summary, species and habitat action plans serve the following purposes:

- to identify practical actions for conserving priority species and habitats, through detailed examination of current research material;
- to provide a strong scientific basis for, and widespread agreement amongst all concerned, to the actions needed;
- to set objectives and targets against which the success of action can be measured;
- to assign actions for determining work programming and budgetary requirements.

4.33 Scottish Natural Heritage are considering a similar approach for selected species of other groups of organisms in respect of land within their influence. In addition, they have work in progress on a list of 22 rare plants which will produce action plans for the recovery of the species in Scotland. Plantlife (a voluntary body) is running a 'Back from the Brink' campaign to save threatened plants. There is a clear need for greater integration of efforts by the nature conservation agencies and the voluntary sector in this field.

SPECIES ACTION PLAN FORMAT

Title page

Title *Species Action Plan*, Euring Code Number, a unique code number for each species; Species Name; Class of Plan (ie Red Data Bird, Candidate RDB Species, Problem Species, Generic Action Plan); Date; Sponsoring Organisations (ie the Nature Conservation Agencies, RSPB, WWT as appropriate).

Inside cover

Authorship, including all contributors/pathfinder meeting participants. Date of production.

Contents

Part 1: Summary

1.1   Conservation Status: Reason for inclusion in Action Plan process. Population numbers, range, trends and conservation importance. Threats/limiting factors. A standard table is used to summarise information about the status of each species and the quality of biological knowledge about it.

1.2   Legal Status: Status in national (British & NI, and where relevant Isle of Man and Channel Isles), and international law.

1.3   Priority Statement: Overall importance attached to actions for this species (in terms of 'high' 'medium' and 'low'), and headline objective.

1.4   Objectives: for conservation of the species.

1.5   Broad Policies: As to how the objectives in 1.3 will be achieved.

1.6   Actions: Titles of Actions proposed in Part 3 with priority and implementing departments and offices.

1.7   Review: Timetable for monitoring of Actions and reviews of the Plan itself.

Part 2: Biological Assessment

2.1–3 'Introduction', 'Ecology' and 'Distribution and Population' sections from the Red Data Book, updated and amended to take account of new information and Northern Ireland, Channel Isles and Isle of Man as necessary.

2.4 Limiting Factors: Individual discussion of factors affecting population numbers and distribution with weighting as to their respective importance. This expands the 'Threats' section of the Red Data Book. Each is cross-referenced to proposed actions by the Action number.

2.5 Resume of Conservation Action Undertaken to date. Expands the 'Conservation' section of the Red Data Book.

Part 3: Actions and Work Programme

Proposed actions listed under standard headings, each individually identified by BTO species code and the number in which it occurs. The standard headings are:

- Policy and Legislation
- Advisory
- Site Safeguard
- International
- Land Acquisition and Reserve Management
- Future Research & Monitoring
- Species Management and Protection
- Communications & Publicity

Re-establishment

4.34 There has been work on re-establishing species which have become extinct in the UK. This work has been undertaken in line with the criteria set out by IUCN. A further development of these criteria in a UK context is contained in reports published in 1979 by the Nature Conservancy Council on behalf of the UK Committee for International Nature Conservation entitled *Wildlife introductions to Great Britain* and in 1988 by Wildlife Link and entitled *Towards an introduction policy*. These reports also deal with the practices of 're-stocking', that is augmenting the population of a species within an area where it already exists and 'introduction', ie release into an area where the species has not existed in historical times. The agencies recognise the need for clearer, more succinct and widely available statements on the topics of criteria for considering introductions, reintroductions and re-stocking to ensure any action is well organised, cost effective and worthwhile.

4.35 The UK is taking an active part in international efforts to develop practical guidelines and co-operation both to encourage re-establishment projects which benefit wildlife, and prevent the release of alien species which can cause major damage to native fauna and flora.

Re-establishment programme

4.36 Two current re-establishment programmes in the UK are those for the white-tailed sea eagle and the large blue butterfly. Another major and highly successful initiative has been the reintroduction of red kites, a globally threatened species, into England and Scotland from continental stock since 1989. Young red kites have been brought in from Spain

Red kites, a globally threatened species, have been reintroduced into England and Scotland from continental stock since 1989.

and Sweden and from these introductions five pairs produced 10 young in 1992 and 14 pairs produced 21 young in 1993. Meanwhile in mid-Wales a remnant population of red kites which was reduced to five pairs has now been restored to 100 pairs through intensive protection of nest sites and the curbing of illegal poisoning.

Genetic diversity within species

4.37 In carrying out work on a species it is important to consider its genetics. At present there are major gaps in our knowledge about within-species genetic variations or the genetic diversity of remaining threatened populations. The Countryside Council for Wales are working on the genetics of grassland plant species that are either scarce or in decline in order to check the effectiveness of site protection

OTTERS

In 1978 it looked as if the otter was on its way to extinction in England. Of 3,200 stretches of river studied only one in sixteen were found to support this once common creature. Pesticides, pollution and hunting were blamed for the decline.

Fifteen years on a survey funded by the Vincent Wildlife Trust has shown a very different picture; otters were found at one in six sites studied including the Thames. Improvement in the quality of river water, the ban on the use of pesticides such as DDT and the ban on otter hunting has permitted otters to spread from existing populations in England and from Scotland and Wales. Nature conservation agencies and the National Rivers Authority have helped the recovery by encouraging suitable management of river banks and by introducing young otters to rivers where the original populations had died out or where the existing population was so small it was unlikely to recover without new recruits.

We should not be complacent about the otter. It is still threatened by urban sprawl, pollution, loss of habitat and road traffic but thanks to the work of organisations such as the Vincent Wildlife Trust and the NRA who have programmes to monitor, protect and reintroduce otters the future of these creatures in England looks more certain.

ACTION FOR THE STONE CURLEW: AN EXAMPLE OF THE ROLE OF GOVERNMENT DEPARTMENTS AND LANDOWNERS IN BIODIVERSITY ACTION.

The stone curlew provides an example of how national priorities for species should be translated into specific action within targeted areas, and of how Government itself, as a landowner and policy-maker, has a major role to play in sustaining and enhancing the country's biodiversity.

The Stone Curlew Action Plan aims to increase the breeding stone curlew population in England from around 160 pairs to 200 pairs by the year 2000 within their present distribution, while encouraging recolonisation of sites within the past breeding range, and increasing the proportion of the population breeding on semi-natural grassland habitats.

The stone curlew is a rare migrant breeder, mainly confined to the Breckland of East Anglia, and the Wessex downlands. The species traditionally nested on short-cropped turf containing areas of bare ground. Their conversion to arable use as afforestation, together with a relaxation or cessation of grazing pressure on the remaining grasslands, has significantly reduced the extent of suitable habitats across the traditional range of the stone curlew. A high proportion of nests are now found within arable crops, especially sugar beet, where the nests and chicks are highly vulnerable.

Stone curlew.

The main objective of the Plan is to secure the long-term future of stone curlew in its principal population cores by firstly, enhancing the management of existing semi-natural grasslands, and secondly, recreating habitats suitable for colonisation. This involves a wide range of action promoting the sympathetic management of land for stone curlews. They include influencing agricultural policy, including ESA management prescriptions and designations, cereal extensification and set-aside, and encouraging positive management of SSSIs supporting breeding stone curlew through advice to landowners and management entering into agreements with English Nature.

As major landowners within Breckland and Wessex, the MoD and the Forestry Commission must play a major role in re-establishing appropriately managed areas for recolonisation by stone curlew. MoD training ranges on Thetford and Salisbury Plain already hold important stone curlew populations. The Ministry are already involved in management experiments on their ranges, leaving bare soil areas for nesting and feeding. Achieving suitably high levels of grazing, by sheep or rabbits is another issue under consideration. In addition, forest restructuring plans in the Forestry Commission Thetford Forest are an opportunity for re-creating areas of grassy heath suitable for stone curlew.

The policies of the Ministry of Agriculture, Fisheries and Food are key to the future of the stone curlew on existing farmland. The Brecklands Environmentally Sensitive Area includes prescriptions aimed at re-establishing grass heaths. The Arable Set-Aside scheme will allow large areas of former cropland in both Breckland and Wessex to be left bare in the spring which could provide ideal nesting conditions. In the longer term, a carefully targeted Habitat Scheme may create new grass heath areas, helping to link existing, fragmented heaths.

measures in respect of small populations of isolated species. Scottish Natural Heritage are also studying some rare plant species due to concern about possible 'genetic drift' or 'genetic bottlenecks'. The former occurs in small isolated populations and is the process whereby certain parts of the full range of variation are lost. The latter is a single event in time when there is a rapid reduction in the numbers in a population. Even if it is possible to increase the number of individuals it is not possible to regain the lost genetic variation. These concerns are relevant to the contributions made to

recovery programmes by such organisations as the Royal Botanic Gardens at Kew and Edinburgh in the rearing of stock from wild populations. The agencies recognise the need both to collate existing knowledge on within-species variation in the UK and to prioritise and carry out further work.

Introduced species

4.38 Many of the species introduced to Britain since the last ice age are now so familiar as to be regarded as native. These long-

RE-ESTABLISHMENT OF THE LARGE BLUE BUTTERFLY

The large blue butterfly is the rarest of the British blue butterflies.

In England it was formerly found in some ninety sites in the Midlands and South West and it finally became extinct in Devon in 1979.

The demise of the butterfly was caused particularly by the loss of its habitat. It needs very closely grazed grassland, often on steep sided chalk valleys containing patches of wild thyme on which the females lay their eggs.

The caterpillars feed on the thyme and after three weeks flick themselves on to the ground where they wait to be found by one species of red ant attracted by a secretion from the caterpillar. Within four hours the caterpillar mimics an ant grub by inflating the skin behind its head. Believing it to be an ant grub the ant carries it back to its nest where the caterpillar feeds on the grubs before and after hibernating in the nest until it emerges from the ground as an adult the next June.

Scrub encroachment and lack of traditional grazing on original sites have eliminated the ants and the thyme crucial to the existence of the large blue.

Experiments to re-establish the butterfly have been ongoing since 1983. In 1991, a five year programme was initiated as a partnership between English Nature's Species Recovery Programme, the Institute of Terrestrial Ecology and the British Butterfly Conservation Society, with support from the National Trust, the County Wildlife Trusts and other landowners at the sites concerned.

Large blue butterfly.

Key objectives of the programme are to recreate the habitat on at least six sites and establish viable self sustaining populations of 400–5000 on each. Traditional grazing levels are being re-established and the levels of thyme and red ants are being carefully managed and monitored to achieve a favourable balance in the overall species composition and vegetation structure. Five sites have already been restored.

Caterpillars from Sweden have been reared to the stage that they can be released on site to be transported by ants to their nests. The numbers of those reaching maturity and the quantity and distribution of their eggs are being carefully monitored. The butterflies have been successfully introduced to four of the sites. Early results of the breeding and egg laying on two of these are promising. An important feature of the project is the benefit to other species in the habitats concerned, many of which are themselves rare or uncommon.

Other butterfly species which have increased as a result of this project are high brown and small pearl bordered fritillary.

standing introductions include rabbit and fallow deer. Others such as the grey squirrel are regarded as serious threats to native species. Some introductions appear to have very little impact on the native flora and fauna since they find a niche in which they avoid competition. The New Zealand willow herb is possibly in this category. Where a species has a capacity to spread rapidly and where it is likely to oust native species it is generally regarded as undesirable from the standpoint of conserving biodiversity. The species which has made the widest impact has been the common Rhododendron which has proved extremely difficult to eradicate from nature reserves and which is rapidly invading mature woodlands and peat bogs. The control of long established

introduced species such as rabbit, whose population was considerably reduced by the deliberate introduction of Myxomatosis, can have major repercussions (see box page 64).

4.39 Comprehensive statutory controls over the unauthorised release of non-native animal and plant species were introduced as part of the Wildlife and Countryside Act 1981. The controls have since been strengthened by the inclusion of further species. However the Act cannot deal with the problems caused by species introduced before 1981 (such as the mink) which have become well established to the detriment of other wildlife.

RE-ESTABLISHMENT OF THE SEA EAGLE

The sea eagle is one of our rarest birds of prey and is one of only three birds in the UK that is considered to be threatened in world terms.

Formerly widespread throughout Britain, around 200 pairs of sea eagles were estimated to have persisted into the 19th century along the north and west coasts of Britain and Ireland. They were eliminated entirely by persecution; the last breeding attempt being recorded from Skye in 1916.

No natural recolonisation has taken place since then nor was it likely to occur both because of a contraction in the rest of the species range in Europe and because of the general sedentary nature of sea eagles.

Early unsuccessful attempts to re-establish the species were undertaken in 1959 (Argyll) and 1968 (Fair Isle) but it was not until 1975 that the Nature Conservancy Council considered and approved a larger scale and sustained programme to re-establish these birds in the wild in Scotland. The project has been continued by SNH in partnership with RSPB.

Eaglets were taken, under licence, from the healthy population in north Norway (>600 pairs) and flown to Scotland before being transferred to enclosures on Rhum National Nature Reserve, the chosen release site. The birds were kept in quarantine and for acclimatisation before their release; supplementary feeding continued for some time thereafter to aid survival before the birds were able to fend for themselves.

A total of 82 sea eagles were released between 1975 and 1985; survival has been high (60–89%) and first attempts at breeding took place in 1983 with first fledging success 2 years later.

Ten territorial pairs are now established and 34 young in total have been reared in the wild by five of the pairs. Nevertheless, the population is still a small one and population modelling

White-tailed sea eagle.

suggested that further releases were necessary to secure a viable, self-sustaining population. Accordingly, ten further eaglets were released in 1993, with the continuing co-operation of the Norwegian authorities. Further releases are proposed in 1994 and 1995.

4.40 The UK's island status provides a degree of natural protection against certain harmful pests and diseases which exist on mainland Europe and elsewhere in the world. The accidental introduction of organisms, such as Dutch Elm disease, can have a significant impact on UK biodiversity. The UK therefore applies rigorous controls over the standard of imported biological material which is a potential host to pests and diseases. Various statutory instruments, many of which reflect EC legislation, exist for this purpose.

Enforcement of species legislation

4.41 The legislation provides for penalties against those who kill or take protected species from the wild. There have been some prosecutions for such breaches. The RSPB and the conservation agencies work to achieve compliance with the legislation based on an understanding of its objectives. An example of the voluntary approach is a coordinated campaign spearheaded by the Ministry of Agriculture to stop the illegal poisoning of wildlife.

Some police forces have appointed specialist officers for wildlife offences and there is regular liaison between Departments, nature conservation agencies and the police.

4.42 Action planned for species
● The nature conservation agencies and the Joint Nature Conservation Committee working with the voluntary sector will prepare species action plans for the following types of species in priority order:
  – Globally threatened
  – Threatened endemics in the UK
  – Of international importance
  – Occur in a Red Data Book and are declining
  – Occur in a Red Data Book
● Aim to complete and put into implementation plans for at least 90% of the presently known globally threatened and threatened endemic species within the next ten years.
● Continue with species recovery programmes for selected vulnerable species.

- Establish priority red data books for the main taxonomic groups without them.
- Update and publicise guidelines on translocations, re-establishments, introductions and re-stocking.

Protected areas:

4.43 Since the Nature Conservancy was established in 1949 as a government sponsored nature conservation organisation in the UK the main thrust of policies and programmes has been to protect an adequate amount of good quality habitat to ensure core areas for the survival of healthy populations of the native plants and animals and the conservation of geological features. The view was that if the habitat was protected the species would look after themselves. In recent years it has been recognised that additional measures are required to ensure that as wide a range of species as possible survive throughout their natural range. In this connection the fragmentation and subsequent gradual reduction in size of certain habitats, such as heathland, is a major concern.

Sites of Special Scientific Interest

4.44 The basic importance of the protected area system remains and will continue. The key designation used in Britain is Site of Special Scientific Interest (SSSI) and Area of Special Scientific Interest (ASSI) in Northern Ireland. Guidelines for selection of biological sites have been developed over the years and have been formally published by the Nature Conservancy Council in 1989 under the title *Guidelines for selection of biological SSSIs*. The guidelines aim to safeguard best examples of habitat types and sites with notable species or groups of species. The country is divided into areas of search generally corresponding to counties. The following attributes are used in selection:

1 Naturalness – associated with lack of human modification
2 Diversity – measure of the range and richness of species present
3 Typicalness – how well the site typifies the main characteristics of the habitat type
4 Size – associated with the ability of the site to sustain a viable population of the characteristic species
5 Rarity – measure of the scarcity of species or the habitat type.

4.45 The extent to which the site meets the need to conserve nationally rare species contains unusually large numbers of nationally scarce species or contains a large proportion of the countrywide population are also taken into consideration.

RABBITS AND MYXOMATOSIS

The introduction and spread of the Myxoma virus in the UK had many indirect environmental effects because rabbit populations interact strongly with their food plants. The removal of rabbits markedly changed the structure and composition of vegetation, with a wide variety of effects on other species. Some of the examples are anecdotal but serve to illustrate the kind of complex and unexpected things that can happen. As grassland sward became taller and thicker, ant populations declined. These ants are important prey for green woodpeckers, and a decline in green woodpecker numbers has been attributed, at least in part, to the effects of removing rabbits. It is not known whether any prey of green woodpeckers such as wood-boring beetles then increased but it is possible that some did. It would not have been easy, prior to the release of Myxoma virus in Britain, to predict the consequences for woodpeckers or indeed for the wood-boring beetles.

Forest Life Picture Library

Better documented examples include the decline of open country or heathland species of high conservation importance, such as stone curlews and the large blue butterfly, in both cases attributable at least in part to changes in the vegetation. As rabbit populations collapsed predators, such as buzzards and foxes, turned to alternative prey, for example mice and voles. The indirect effects on other organisms of this increased predation on rodents is unknown. In woodlands, due to the lack of rabbits, sycamore seedlings survived in unprecedented numbers. The first few years after the introduction of the Myxoma virus saw a whole generation of this introduced tree dominating in woodland glades and shading out the existing plants.

Rabbit.

FRAGMENTATION – DORSET HEATHLAND

The main causes of fragmentation are agricultural conversion, afforestation, road building and urban development. What has happened to the Dorset Heathlands over the last 200 years has been well documented and typifies what has happened elsewhere. The series of maps clearly demonstrate the break up of large tracts of heathland into many small areas.

Today, the Dorset Heathlands are remnant patches of heathery vegetation set in much larger areas of farmland, forestry plantations and urban land. Comparison of the vegetation topography and land use in 1978 and 1987 reveals a reduction of 425 ha (5%) in the intervening years due almost equally to conversion to farmland and urban development, the latter including the building of roads, houses and factories. There were small losses caused by mineral extraction, forestry and conversion to recreational grassland.

A significant change noted in the same period is the increase in scrub and young trees as a result of a reduction in once traditional grazing, in the use of controlled burning as a management practice and in accidental fires. Fragmentation creates a proportionally large edge to the heathland areas, increasing the scope for scrub invasion and colonisation by non-heathland species from surrounding land. Sites close to urban development are particularly subject to human pressure such as motor bike and mountain bike scrambling, frequent fires, dumping and the disturbance of sensitive species.

A clear picture of fragmentation and a consequential decline in the quality of the habitat thus emerges. The future of the Dorset Heathlands will depend on tight planning control and the availability of appropriate incentives from Countryside Management Schemes to encourage the grazing of such agriculturally unproductive areas. With judicious management the decline in the quality of the surviving areas can be reversed. The reduction of the invasion and succession of woody vegetation by cutting and clearance, or the re-introduction of grazing is essential if open heathland is to remain but in many counties this now depends on the activities of Heathland Management Projects and these must continue to be supported. Controlled burning may be considered providing there is no significant threat to other components of the community,

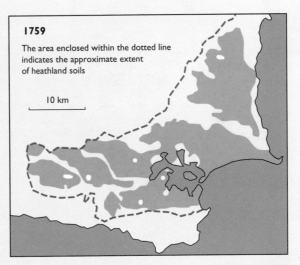

1759

The area enclosed within the dotted line indicates the approximate extent of heathland soils

10 km

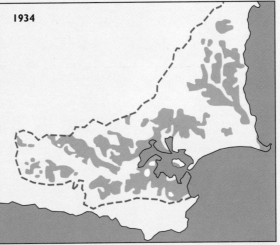

1934

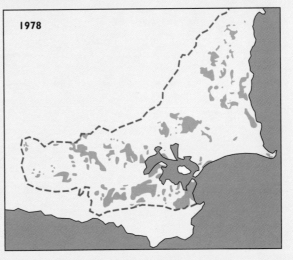

1978

Dorset heathland.

especially invertebrates. English Nature has recently launched a National Lowland Heathland Programme to address the management issues. Initiatives such as the Forest and Heathland Project which involves clearing 150 ha of plantation to link and extend SSSI heathlands lying close to Forestry Commission plantations should be encouraged.

Opportunities for reversing the effects of fragmentation in other habitats are fewer. New woods can be created to link up existing sites but the full suite of communities and features associated with ancient woodland can never be replicated. Given time, perhaps centuries, new woods may be able to achieve the same level of biodiversity as ancient woodland.

4.46 In the case of geological sites the aim is to identify and conserve the minimum number of nationally important sites needed to demonstrate current understanding of the diversity and range of geological features.

4.47 By the end of November 1993 the following area and number of SSSIs or ASSIs had been designated:

Number and area of SSSIs and ASSIs			
	Number	**Area (hectares)**	**% of territory**
England	3,759	885,742	6.8
Scotland	1,364	845,609	10.7
Wales	876	205,714	9.9
Northern Ireland	46	48,083	3.4
TOTAL	6,045	1,985,148	8.1

National Nature Reserves

4.48 National Nature Reserves (NNR) are areas of national and sometimes international importance which are owned or leased by the appropriate statutory conservation body, or bodies approved by them, or are managed in accordance with Nature Reserve Agreements with landowners and occupiers. NNRs serve a variety of purposes, notably the conservation of the special interest of sites, the provision of sites for research and study, the provision of advice on and the demonstration of conservation management, the furtherance of education, and providing facilities for amenity use and access for the quiet enjoyment of nature. NNRs are also classified as SSSIs and attract similar protection.

4.49 At the end of March 1993 there were 45 NNRs in Northern Ireland with an area of 4322 ha. In Scotland the

equivalent figures were 70 (114,486 ha), in Wales 49 (13,397 ha) and in England 140 (57,335 ha).

Nature Conservation Review

4.50 A major review of the best examples of various habitat types in the UK was published in 1977. The SSSIs identified in this work are referred to as Nature Conservation Review sites (NCR). Although this designation has no statutory basis it can be taken into account when development proposals are being considered. A Geological Conservation Review (GCR) performs a similar function for geological SSSIs.

4.51 Marine areas where additional management measures are required to conserve nature conservation interest have been provisionally identified by the nature conservation agencies and are called Marine Consultation Areas in Scotland and Sensitive Marine Areas in England.

Beinn Eighe, Britain's first National Nature Reserve.

EC Birds Directive: Special Protection Areas (SPAs)

4.52 The Directive requires the designation of Special Protection Areas for breeding and migratory species and measures to prevent damage or disturbance to the Areas. 74 SPAs had been designated in the UK by November 1993 covering over 245,000 ha.

EC Habitats Directive – Natura 2000: Special Areas of Conservation (SACs)

4.53 The Habitats and Species Directive sets out requirements for the creation of Special Areas of Conservation. These SACs will, with SPAs classified under the Birds Directive, form a European Community series of sites to be known as Natura 2000. This coherent European ecological network is designed to maintain habitats and species of community interest at favourable conservation status, a status defined in terms of the natural range being stable or increasing and of the existence of structures and functions necessary for the long term maintenance of that status.

4.54 The Annexes of the Directive list habitats and species of Community interest. They are listed because within the Community they are endangered, vulnerable, rare or endemic, have a small natural range, or are outstanding examples of characteristics typical of the community's biogeographical regions. Annexes I and II of the Directive list those habitats and species the conservation of which requires the designation of the Special Areas of Conservation which will contribute to the Natura 2000 network. Of these, some 75 habitat types and 40 taxa of animals and plants occur within the UK. Some are classed as priority habitats and species for which stronger protection within SACs is required.

4.55 In the UK, the protection of SPAs and SACs will be based on the habitat conservation measures established by the Wildlife and Countryside Act 1981 through the notification of SSSIs. Additional measures necessary to ensure that the requirements of the Directive can be delivered will be enacted by Regulations under Section 2 of the European Communities Act 1972. This will ensure, inter alia, that damage or deterioration to Natura 2000 sites is only permitted, if there is no alternative, for reasons of overriding public interest.

4.56 The Directive requires Member States to bring the necessary legislative and administrative provisions into force by June 1994. National lists of candidate SACs should be submitted to the Commission by June 1995. The Commission then must agree the Community list with Member States by June 1998. Designation of SACs to secure the Natura 2000 network must be secured by 2004. The UK intends to meet these deadlines.

Implementing protected areas legislation

4.57 The conservation of protected areas is provided in two main ways. In the first place there is legislative protection. In the main this derives from the Wildlife and Countryside Act 1981 and the Nature Conservation and Amenity Lands (Northern Ireland) Order 1985. Under these provisions operations likely to damage the nature conservation interest of SSSIs are subject to control. The Town and Country Planning Acts are also very important and come into play where there are cases which involve development proposals or uses which can be regulated by the planning system to be determined (see section on land use planning).

4.58 Operations likely to damage the conservation interest of SSSIs, and which are proposed to be undertaken by the owners and occupiers are subject to a statutory notice period. Owners and occupiers may not carry out such operations unless they have given up to four months written notice to the nature conservation body. The agency can seek to persuade owners or occupiers to modify or refrain from their proposals and can make payments in the form of management agreements to retain the special interest. Where agreement cannot be reached between an owner or occupier and the nature conservation agency within four months, the relevant Minister may make a Nature Conservation Order to prevent damage to nature conservation features of national importance, or on which the UK has international obligations. The Order extends the period of notice to allow for further negotiations. However the agency cannot ultimately prevent damaging operations in the absence of agreement save by compulsory acquisition of the land which can be authorised by the relevant Minister. The operations of bodies who are not 'owners' or 'occupiers', for example suppliers of energy and telecommunications are not subject to the common statutory notice period. A variety of consultation procedures are available to ensure that any damage to nature conservation interests from such operations is minimal.

4.59 The second source of protection is from the arrangements for positive management on the site. Whilst the Wildlife and Countryside Act and Northern Ireland Order make provision for identifying activities which might damage the interest of an area and for the negotiation of arrangements for the management of the site, they do not require the preparation of a management plan.

STRANGFORD LOUGH PROPOSED MARINE NATURE RESERVE

Strangford Lough, on the east coast of Northern Ireland, is one of the most important sites in the UK for marine life. It supports large numbers of ducks, geese and wading birds in winter and has a wide variety of underwater and shore-line habitats.

The Department of the Environment for Northern Ireland published in 1991 a consultation paper on Strangford Lough which included amongst its proposals the establishment of a management structure for the Lough and the declaration of the whole marine area of the Lough and a triangle of open sea beyond its mouth as a Marine Nature Reserve (MNR). There was strong support voiced by local interests for a local management structure and DOE(NI) responded by setting up the Strangford Lough Management Committee (SLMC).

The SLMC is comprised of representatives of the community around the Lough, Lough users and those with specialist knowledge of the Lough. It is serviced and assisted by a Liaison Officer funded by DOE(NI) and the two District Councils whose territories adjoin Strangford Lough.

One of the primary goals of SLMC is to work with DOE(NI) towards the establishment of the MNR including the preparation of an accompanying management plan. To date the focus has been on preparing a document concentrating on the management objectives of the proposed MNR and setting out the issues and principles behind them. Agreement with SLMC has now been reached and this document will be published early in 1994 along with the formal proposal from the Secretary of State for the declaration of the MNR.

The establishment of SLMC encompassing such a diverse range of interests is greatly assisting in what otherwise would have been a very lengthy and complex consultation procedure.

4.60 Since the ownership of the sites is unchanged by designation, and since there is frequently scope to improve the nature conservation value of the sites, there is usually merit in the preparation of a simple plan setting out the guidelines for existing management practices as well as activities which would produce enhancements. Financial incentives for such positive management are now available through the Wildlife Enhancement Scheme in England.

Marine Nature Reserves

4.61 The ability to create Marine Nature Reserves (MNR) out to the limits of UK territorial waters and including both the sea and the sea bed was provided in The Wildlife and Countryside Act and Article 20 of the Nature Conservation and Amenity Lands Order 1985 in Northern Ireland. The complicated consultation process and the need to reach consensus has meant that only two have been designated, the islands of Lundy and Skomer. Two further Reserves are under active consideration. The legislation provides for MNRs to be managed by the Countryside Agencies for the purpose of:

- conserving marine flora or fauna or geological or physiographical features of special interest in the area; or
- providing, under suitable conditions and control, special

opportunities for the study of, and research into, matters relating to marine flora and fauna and the physical conditions in which they live, or for the study of geological and physiographical features of special interest in the area.

4.62 The requirement to designate appropriate marine areas in the Habitats Directive is likely to provide stronger protection of marine conservation resources. Effort will focus on this approach in the immediate future, but not to the exclusion of Marine Nature Reserves.

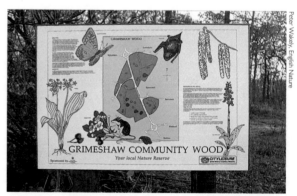

Many LNRs are close to centres of population and provide visitor facilities and nature trails.

Local Nature Reserves (LNR)

4.63 These are designated by local authorities under National Parks and Access to the Countryside Act 1949. The LNR designation is made in consultation with the conservation agencies who provide advice on the suitability of the site. Many LNRs are close to centres of population and provide visitor facilities and nature trails. Most LNRs are owned by local authorities, but some are managed on their behalf by other bodies such as local wildlife trusts. At the end of March 1993 there were 12 LNRs in Scotland totalling 3,165 ha, 19 in Wales totalling 3,423 ha, 3 in Northern Ireland totalling 51 ha, and 337 in England with an area of 13,977 ha.

Action planned for Protected Sites

4.64 The Government and the conservation agencies plan to:
- ensure that summary management plans are prepared and where possible implemented for each biological SSSI by the year 2004.
- continue to designate additional protected areas to deal with acknowledged gaps in the existing coverage.
- complete the designation of all identified Special Protection Areas and Ramsar sites. Comply with the timetable for the designation of Special Areas of Conservation set down in the Habitats Directive by the year 2004.
- create mechanisms for effective protection and management of key wildlife areas in the marine environment.

THE WIDER COUNTRYSIDE

Other designations and schemes:
Nature reserves owned by non-statutory bodies and individuals

4.65 In addition to the land protected by these official designations there is a further tranche of land protected by a wide range of voluntary organisations. This includes non SSSI land held as reserves or identified by a voluntary body and notified to the local planning authority. The RIGS (Regionally Important Geological/geomorphological Site) movement now extends to most counties and is essentially based on groups of volunteers identifying and protecting important local sites. Indeed these organisations are sometimes owners or lessees of NNR or SSSI land and frequently work in partnership with the appropriate government agency. They have often been able to bring a considerable degree of professionalism to the management of the land involved. The designations described in the preceding paragraphs all have the conservation of nature and hence the conservation of biodiversity as a raison d'être. There are a number of other designations in use which, whilst they may not have

biodiversity as a major consideration, can nonetheless provide important opportunities for work in that direction under the action plan.

National Parks

4.66 The UK National Park system has been created on the basis of sites in England and Wales only. Whereas there is legislative provision for National Parks in Northern Ireland, this does not exist in Scotland. None of the UK National Parks meet the IUCN definition of national park but they all meet the definition of 'protected landscape'. Concern over the lack of emphasis on the conservation of nature in the original remit of National Parks was expressed

Snowdonia National Park, Gwynedd.

in *Fit for the future*, a review of the National Parks conducted for the Countryside Commission in 1991. The National Parks authorities are taking a number of positive initiatives to improve nature conservation. The Government intends that there should be legislation to make nature conservation a primary National Park purpose.

National Scenic Area (NSA)

4.67 In 1980 special development control measures were introduced by the Scottish Development Department (SDD Circular 20/1980) for 40 designated National Scenic Areas. NSAs are chosen as the best examples of Scotland's landscapes and part of the natural heritage of Scotland. This designation replaces two earlier categories of importance for scenic interest which served to fulfil some of the approaches embodied in the National Park and AONB designations in England and Wales. The first covered the five National Park Direction Areas and the second a variety of local authority-inspired regional landscape designations such as Areas of Great Landscape Value and Areas of Scenic Value.

The Forestry Commission and the Department of Agriculture for Northern Ireland (DANI)

4.68 The Forestry Commission and DANI have, since their inception, had a vision of the use of their landholding for purposes other than forestry. As well as providing for recreation, the Forestry Commission and DANI regard state owned forests as an important ecological resource. Management aims to enhance the nature conservation

OTHER DESIGNATIONS DIRECTLY OR INDIRECTLY RELEVANT TO WILDLIFE

Biogenetic Reserve

The European network of Biogenetic Reserves set up by the Council of Europe aims to conserve representative examples of Europe's fauna, flora and natural areas. There are 19 Biogenetic Reserves in the United Kingdom.

Biosphere Reserve

An area of land or coast that has been designated by IUCN and UNESCO (as part of the Man and the Biosphere programme) as being of international importance for conservation, study and sustainable development. The aim is a worldwide network of BRs each qualifying under at least one of the following categories:

- representative examples of natural biomes;
- unique communities or areas with unusual natural features of exceptional interest such as a population of a globally rare species;
- examples of harmonious landscapes resulting from traditional patterns of land-use;
- examples of modified or degraded ecosystems capable of being restored to more natural conditions.

There are 13 Biosphere Reserves in the United Kingdom.

Ramsar Site

These sites are designated under the Ramsar Convention, which is concerned with protecting the internationally important wetlands, especially the chain of habitats used by migratory water birds. 68 sites have been designated in the UK, more than by any other contracting party, by November 1993.

World Heritage Site (WHS)

Areas designated by the IUCN and UNESCO as being of global importance for conservation and study. The World Heritage Convention concerning the protection of the world cultural and natural heritage came into force in December 1975. Its aim is the protection of cultural and natural heritage of outstanding value. Natural Heritage is defined as: 'natural features consisting of physical and biological formations, or groups of such formations, which are of outstanding universal value from an aesthetic or scientific point of view' and, 'geological and physiographical formations and precisely delineated areas which constitute the habitat of threatened species of animals and plants of outstanding universal value from the point of view of science or conservation', and 'natural sites or precisely delineated areas of outstanding universal value from the point of view of science, conservation or natural beauty'.

value of these forests as a whole as well as safeguarding special habitats. The Forestry Commission and DANI have designated certain forests (17 in Great Britain and 9 in Northern Ireland) as national Forest Parks. In addition to SSSIs and ASSIs, special habitats include Forest Nature Reserves and other conservation areas identified in forest conservation plans which have been drawn up for all national forests. There is considerable scope for the enhancement of biodiversity as the new forests created this century are re-structured and re-designed for their second and third rotations.

Agricultural departments

4.69 The agricultural departments in consultation with other organisations have been developing a package of programmes to encourage farming practices that protect and enhance wildlife habitats, valued landscapes and natural resources as well as promoting new opportunities for public access to the countryside.

4.70 A designation which is of great importance for wildlife habitats is that of Environmentally Sensitive Area (ESAs). ESAs are areas of high landscape and conservation value in which farmers and crofters may benefit from payments for managing their land in ways which conserve and enhance the landscape and wildlife habitats. Participants in the scheme enter 10 year management agreements which are reviewed after 5 years. Each designated area has its own distinctive character and the payments offered relate to specific requirements supporting and promoting local diversity.

4.71 By December 1993 there were 16 ESAs in England, totalling 831,000 ha, and 6 more were planned covering

Buttermere Fells ESA, Cumbria.

318,000 ha. There were 4 in Wales totalling 358,700 ha, and 2 more were planned covering 143,000 ha. In Scotland there were 10, totalling 1.4 million ha. In Northern Ireland there were 3, totalling 131,000 ha, and 2 more were planned covering 116,700 ha. In all some 15% of the total agricultural area of the UK will have been designated as ESAs by the end of 1994. The scheme's flexibility means that it can match incentives to specific local requirements and can therefore support and promote local diversity.

4.72 There are a number of other incentive schemes planned to be launched by the agricultural departments in 1994. These include a Moorland Scheme to protect and improve heather and other shrubby moorland; a Habitat Scheme to recreate a range of specific habitats such as water fringes, upland scrub and salt marshes, an organic farming scheme to encourage conversion to organic production and new Nitrate Sensitive Areas. These initiatives have been developed in response to the European Community Agri Environment Regulation, an important element in the Common Agricultural Policy reform package agreed in 1992. The Agricultural Departments also operate a Farm Woodland Premium Scheme which encourages farmers to plant new woodlands, especially broad-leaved, on land taken out of productive agriculture. These schemes offer considerable potential for enhancing biodiversity.

The National Trust

4.73 The National Trust for England, Wales and Northern Ireland, and The National Trust for Scotland all have significant land holdings which include semi-natural habitats. They have sought to ensure that their land continues to make a significant contribution to the conservation of biodiversity in the UK.

Land use planning

4.74 The town and country planning system regulates the development and use of land in the public interest, reconciling the needs of conservation and development, and securing economy, efficiency and amenity in the use of land. It guides development to the right place, ensures that it is carried out in an environmentally sensitive manner, and prevents unacceptable development. The planning system contributes to the objective of ensuring that development is sustainable.

4.75 Planning permission is required to carry out development. Applications are normally considered by the local planning authority. They must be decided in accordance with local authorities' development plans, unless material considerations indicate otherwise. Authorities must take Government planning guidance into account in preparing their development plans. It may also be material to decisions on individual applications and appeals.

4.76 The Government is about to publish a Planning Policy Guidance note (PPG) on Nature Conservation, updating and expanding earlier advice. This will reaffirm its objective of conserving the abundance and diversity of British wildlife and its habitats, or minimising the adverse effects on wildlife where conflict of interest is unavoidable, and meeting its international responsibilities and obligations for nature conservation. The PPG will provide guidance on how to reflect these objectives in land use planning, including paying proper regard to nature conservation outside designated sites. The Scottish Office will shortly issue draft guidance for local authorities and others on the natural heritage in Scotland.

4.77 The key importance of SSSIs means that development proposals in or likely to affect them are subject to special scrutiny. Planning authorities must consult English Nature or the Countryside Council for Wales before granting permission for such development. The Secretary of State will normally call-in for his own decision planning applications with a significant effect on NNRs and NCR sites, and may also call-in other applications affecting SSSIs if they raise issues of more than local importance.

4.78 The Government expects shortly to lay before Parliament draft Regulations to implement the planning aspects of the EC Habitats Directive, requiring decisions taken under planning and related legislation to accord with the relevant requirements of the Directive. The Nature Conservation PPG will advise on the Regulations.

4.79 Planning policies preventing unnecessary urbanisation of the countryside also help to protect biodiversity.

GOVERNMENT INITIATIVE TO CONSERVE PEATLAND IN NORTHERN IRELAND

Government in Northern Ireland published in June 1993 a Policy Statement on Peatland Conservation. Peatland covers about 12% of the land area of Northern Ireland and the protection of raised and blanket bogs is regarded as one of the top priorities for nature conservation there. Although Northern Ireland accounts for as much as a quarter of the total UK area for lowland raised bog, the surface of no more than 9% is intact, in that it is neither cut nor drained.

The Policy Statement also addresses the extraction of peat and its uses in horticulture. Government recognises that extraction of peat for horticulture is a well established industry in Northern Ireland providing employment in rural areas. It is, however, not indefinitely sustainable and results in loss of peatland with ensuing environmental consequences. Extraction from areas with existing bog vegetation causes loss of important wildlife habitat, even if sensitive rehabilitation occurs.

The horticultural industry in Northern Ireland uses in the region of 40,000 cubic metres of peat each year. A major user of peat, and probably the most exacting in its requirements, is the mushroom growing sector. In the open ground peat has been used both as a mulch and as a soil conditioner. The use of peat to assist the establishment of trees and shrubs in gardens and landscaping schemes is declining and may be both wasteful and unnecessary.

The Department of the Environment (NI) has been leading the way in tackling the issue of peatland awareness through its creation of Peatlands Park, near Dungannon. The purpose of the 250 ha Park is to combine education with enjoyment of the bogs, their unique flora and fauna, their traditional exploitation and their value as wilderness in an increasingly developed and managed countryside. The Department is committed to improving its facilities at the park to widen its interest amongst the public and to enable visiting schoolchildren and students to further their studies in peatland ecology.

Main Action Points:

- All remaining areas of intact lowland raised bog will be declared ASSI where they meet the minimum scientific criteria.
- Four extensive areas of blanket bog will be declared ASSI.
- Peat extraction will be opposed from sites which have been declared ASSI, or which are likely to be ASSI on the basis of current knowledge.
- Away from ASSIs permission for the extraction of peat will only be granted where there is little nature conservation value and where the amenity of the area is not prejudiced by the operations.
- Government reaffirms its commitment away from further afforestation on deep peat.
- Government will cease to use peat in open ground situations in the management of its estate and will exclude such use of peat in contracts.
- Construction of a classroom for environmental studies at Peatlands Park will begin this year.
- A video and accompanying education pack on peatland conservation will be produced and made available to all secondary level schools.

4.80 Local authorities are encouraged to undertake an environmental appraisal of the policies contained in development plans. Advice is currently being prepared on techniques and good practice. The Government is committed to ensuring that development proposals which are likely to have significant effects on the environment are thoroughly assessed. It will be publishing guidance to developers on good practice in the preparation of environmental statements (see box).

4.81 A separate Government initiative relates to strategies for the location of new forestry planting. For the approach taken in Scotland (see box).

4.82 In developing these strategies local authorities had regard to, among other considerations, the needs of local plants and animals. This was especially important for moorland bird assemblages since their habitat was most at risk. Another initiative has been developed in the major conurbations.

INDICATIVE FORESTRY STRATEGIES IN SCOTLAND

During the 1980s it was recognised that there was a need to find some means to help guide the location of new afforestation so that it could be integrated harmoniously with other land use interests and contribute to, rather than hinder, the landscape and nature conservation. In 1986 the Countryside Commission for Scotland proposed that local authorities should undertake the preparation of Indicative Forestry Strategies. The idea was widely supported. In 1987 the Convention of Scottish Local Authorities recommended that all Regional Councils should prepare such strategies: the Government responded by publishing guidance. In essence, the local authorities draw up maps indicating a presumption for or against forestry. Areas where insufficient information is available are also identified. These broad brush zonations are then used to help steer applications into the parts of the local authority area where they were unlikely to be the subject of controversy and hence delay. While many other factors are considered, all of the studies give due regard to the conservation of biodiversity. All existing information relating to biodiversity is utilised, including the location of SSSI and rare species localities. One of the most important indicators is the presence of breeding birds. Maps of high, medium and low ornithological interest have been produced for feeding into the process of identifying areas where there should be presumption for or against afforestation. This ornithological evaluation has now been carried out for all 9 Regional Councils in Scotland, largely through the efforts of the Joint Nature Conservation Committee working with Scottish Natural Heritage.

Several local authorities have developed strategies which have given priority to conserving any remaining semi-natural habitats, encouraged the enhancement of any existing 'green corridors' such as river valleys, and provided incentives for the rehabilitation of waste ground in such a way as to encourage increased species richness. Other bodies have also taken a strategic look at their responsibilities for the wildlife occurring on their landholding. In addition to their work relating to access provision, the Forestry Commission have created a responsibility at the local forest level within their estate, to identify and conserve features of significance. This can include recognition of small stands of native species or individual badger setts. They have also issued a series of guidelines for use by the private sector, which provide useful advice on practices which are beneficial to the maintenance and enhancement of biodiversity. In a comparable fashion, the Ministry of Defence has sought to establish a Conservation Group for each of its major landholdings. These Groups seek to identify the key nature conservation interests on the land and to devise ways and means of preventing it from being affected in the course of routine activities on the site.

Initiatives for extensively distributed species and habitats

4.83 The conservation organisations have started to develop new initiatives to find a more effective way of dealing with the conservation of species and habitats that occur over extensive areas of countryside. These included attempts to improve knowledge of the resource through surveys such as Coastwatch, launched by the Nature Conservancy Council, which motivated a considerable number of volunteers to report on both the habitats present and the use being made of them. In contrast, Operation Brightwater, launched in 1990 by Scottish Conservation Projects, was a scheme designed to encourage people to enhance the quality of local freshwater and marine resources through practical work. The Pond Conservation Group is a consortium of environmental organisations whose aim is to counter the threats to ponds of pollution, drainage, infilling and neglect by a six point agenda for action which includes the maintenance and promotion of buffer zones around ponds, and the introduction of pond protection orders.

The conservation agencies

4.84 The nature conservation agencies are trying to persuade all interested parties to play their part. Thus the Campaign for a Living Coast initiated by English Nature aims amongst other things to coordinate its work in coastal, estuarine and marine habitats and to encourage

The Pond Conservation Group in action.

the management of England's coastline and inshore waters in a way which will sustain their amenity and wildlife value. A part of the campaign seeks to promote the development of estuary management plans which would seek to integrate conservation and development and hence would require to have been fully discussed with all the interested parties.

4.85 Statements of intent are also being developed between statutory agencies, industry and voluntary organisations as a way of forging closer links and a better understanding of each others needs, aims and objectives.

4.86 The Countryside Stewardship Scheme is an initiative involving the Countryside Commission, English Heritage and English Nature. Under the scheme, financial incentives are available to farmers and landowners in respect of certain types of land throughout the country. Chalk and limestone grassland, lowland heaths, waterside landscapes, the coast, uplands are among the landscapes and habitats where payments are made for farming practices which will enhance wildlife, scenery and, where appropriate, public access. A similar scheme is operated under the name of TIR CYMEN by the Countryside Council for Wales in two parts of Wales. The Countryside Council for Wales are also partners, along with the Forestry Commission, local authorities and others in a special initiative for woodlands called Coed Cymru which aims to rehabilitate existing broadleaved woodlands and secure their management. Another initiative entitled Rural Action is jointly sponsored by the Countryside Commission, English Nature and the Rural Development Commission in England and has the backing of five major national voluntary bodies. The scheme is designed to empower people to take environmental action in rural areas by making available the technical advice and skills needed for a project. This can include pond restoration and nature reserves.

4.87 English Nature, together with Countryside Commission, Countryside Council for Wales and the National Park Officers, have recently signed a joint statement on nature conservation in National Parks. This will be implemented by an action plan which seeks to cover topics such as strategies, environmental audit and collaboration on survey and data collection, as well as developing joint codes of conduct and good practice. Within individual National Parks in England and Wales there have been localised schemes to encourage enhanced species richness for example in meadowland. Such schemes have been based on financial rewards based on physical evidence such as the presence of selected plant species. The RSPB, SNH and the Scottish Crofters Union have come together to run a scheme under which crofters are rewarded for adopting management practices favourable to the survival of corncrakes (see box).

The need for a framework to coordinate initiatives

4.88 If we are to maintain and enrich the characteristic biological diversity and natural features of the UK across their traditional ranges, the countryside as a whole must be managed in a way which will support and complement our best areas. The Government intend to support the nature conservation agencies in establishing agreed objectives for the conservation of wildlife and natural features so that efforts can be targeted to achieve the best return for maintaining and enriching biodiversity. There is a need to reverse fragmentation of the wildlife resource and to benefit wide ranging species which have suffered particularly by isolation of sites within a hostile landscape. A series of local groups would enable the conservation agencies and other statutory and voluntary bodies to work together with local communities. They could develop agreed targets and a shared vision in order to concentrate their wildlife enrichment efforts into those areas where there is scope for significant conservation gain. One approach developed by English Nature to provide a framework for such initiatives is described in the box on Natural Areas in England. A vital ingredient is the opportunity for local involvement within a national framework to develop shared goals.

Action planned for the wider countryside

4.89 The Government will make clear in the Planning Policy Guidance Note on Nature Conservation that biodiversity objectives should be taken into account in the land use planning system. The Government and the nature conservation agencies plan to:

- improve the databases of the Countryside Surveys of Great Britain and Northern Ireland, while further developing the Scottish Office Land Cover of Scotland survey;
- utilise existing knowledge to identify prime biodiversity areas in the UK based on best available levels of data recorded, and agree a strategy to protect and enhance them involving all interested parties;
- complete and implement action plans for the key UK habitat resources;

Urban Areas

Urban greenspaces

4.90 The greenspaces in urban areas comprise remnants of ancient natural systems (primary woodlands, lakes, rivers, bogs); pre-industrial rural landscapes with arable land, meadows and villages; managed green spaces including town

CORNCRAKE INITIATIVE 1993

Corncrake.

The craking song of the corncrake was once a common sound throughout Britain. Now numbers of corncrakes have declined severely and the range has contracted alarmingly. Today, corncrakes are common only in the Inner and Outer Hebrides, and even here numbers are now starting to decline. In 1992 140 singing corncrakes were recorded in the Inner Hebrides. The main causes of the decline have been earlier cutting of the grass harvest which has inadvertently lead to the destruction of eggs, young and adults, and the loss of meadows to other land uses, especially sheep. Similar problems have occurred throughout Western Europe.

In view of the serious plight of this species, and the urgent need to protect nesting birds, the Royal Society for the Protection of Birds (RSPB), Scottish Natural Heritage (SNH) and the Scottish Crofter's Union (SCU) have devised a Corncrake Initiative, which was initiated in 1992. It closely resembles a smaller scale scheme introduced by the Department of the Environment for Northern Ireland and the RSPB which has operated in Co Fermanagh since 1990.

Under the Initiative crofters and farmers are invited to delay mowing of grass until after 1 August 1993. In return, a management payment of £50 per hectare for the delayed cutting of hay or grass silage is being offered to crofters and farmers who have breeding corncrakes and are prepared to enter the Corncrake Initiative. A payment of £10 per hectare is available to crofters and farmers to adopt a corncrake friendly mowing technique (ie in strips, small blocks of circular mowing from the centre of a field outwards) in order to reduce numbers of breeding corncrakes killed or injured. This payment is available either in addition to, or separate from, payments for delaying cutting. An accompanying leaflet explains the detail of mowing techniques.

This Corncrake Initiative is being operated from funds raised by RSPB supporters throughout the UK and an equal amount contributed by SNH. The scheme covers the islands of Coll, Tiree, Colonsay, Oronsay, Iona, Mull and Islay, and other areas at the discretion of the RSPB or SNH officers.

---

parks and private gardens; and finally naturally seeded sites, (demolition sites, disused railway lands, spare and derelict industrial land). Remnant habitats are modified by urban pressures and the altered climate but often hold relic populations of uncommon species. Increased public interest in wildlife is contributing to the increased presence and abundance of some species through feeding, pond creation and the availability of waste.

The types of species

4.91 The more characteristic urban habitats may hold warmth-loving species which can extend their range northwards in cities. Species associated with unstable habitats – screes, landslips, river banks and coastal areas – find similarities in urban disused land. Urban areas hold major populations of early colonisers of bare ground and ruderal species which have become less common in rural areas due to changes in management there. Gardens, parks and disused land hold significant populations of specialised invertebrates (eg stem breeding parasitic wasps) and nationally scarce species may occur anywhere in urban areas.

Important habitats for people in urban areas

4.92 Contact with the natural world is important for many people. For the bulk of the population gardens, parks and their associated ponds and streams provide the main day-to-day contact points between themselves and wildlife. For the majority of schools they are a valuable resource for stimulating interest in and understanding of environmental

Urban ecologists studying plant colonisation on a demolition site.

NATURAL AREAS IN ENGLAND – THEIR IDENTIFICATION AND PURPOSE

Dividing England into natural areas based on ecologically distinct divisions provides a framework for integrating planning and management of the countryside. A study carried out by English Nature identified 76 terrestrial divisions. These are related to land use and the biological and physical characteristics of the land and based on agricultural information, landscape accounts and county floras. Botanists recognised ecologically distinct divisions within counties and included maps of such divisions in country floras. The ideal natural area should be a discrete geographical area encapsulating unique features, be easily recognised and acceptable by the relevant organisations and parts of the community for whom it should generate a feeling of identity.

The 23 maritime areas were based on the major sediment cells and taking into account the occurrence of major estuaries and local factors such as changes in geology or geomorphology.

Natural Areas can provide an effective way to integrate local and national objectives for enriching biodiversity.

They are based on a sense of place and are not constrained by administrative boundaries. The Greater Cotswolds, for example, stretch through eight English counties.

In each Natural Area, a partnership between the statutory agency for nature conservation and local organisation and individuals can lead to agreement on key objectives for all to pursue within their own remits and capabilities. English Nature intends to publish these objectives alongside key biodiversity facts for each area by 1996.

Prime biodiversity areas within natural areas

Much can be achieved by initially concentrating effort in a few locations where there are local concentrations of special sites and other areas of high biological interest. Where there is potential to manage clusters of the best areas and the land between them in away which sustains or enhances the contained biodiversity, large areas of good habitat can be created. Prime biodiversity areas are places within Natural Areas where the current state of the nature conservation resource reflects the overall character best and offers the greatest potential for full restoration of the character of that natural area. The characteristic wildlife of the natural area within which they fall will set the standard of biological diversity expected. Natural or semi-natural ecosystems with inherently low species richness still make an important contribution to the UK's total biodiversity as they may contain species not found elsewhere.

Such areas can be identified as part of the characterisation of the current state of the wildlife resource within Natural Areas. They are not a designation and precise boundaries are not necessary; in any case, opportunities for expansion may present themselves later.

There are a number of large areas which would qualify, for example the North Norfolk Coast, the Suffolk coast from Southwold to Felixstowe areas, the New Forest. Dorset Heaths and significant parts of the various ESAs in existence, to mention just a few. Others are less obvious and may occupy as little as one 10 km square or less. To locate these areas a variety of methods can be used and the results compared or superimposed.

issues. The values people place on the more natural features of the urban landscape and the uses they put them to have led local authorities to accept the need to ensure their continued availability. Since most such areas have been designed for a purpose other than nature conservation there can be problems in conserving key sites or in providing new facilities. In the case of existing parks and playing fields management often needs adjustment if public needs for contact with nature are to be met. Grants schemes such as the School Grants, with a budget of £100,000, or Community Action for Wildlife, with a budget of £250,000, run by English Nature enable local people to carry out improvements such as pond creation, tree planting, rubbish clearing, building hides, purchase of tools, production of leaflets and interpretation boards etc.

Future needs

4.93 Certain plant communities are associated with neglect and public authorities may regard them as undesirable. There is pressure in favour of features clearly designed and

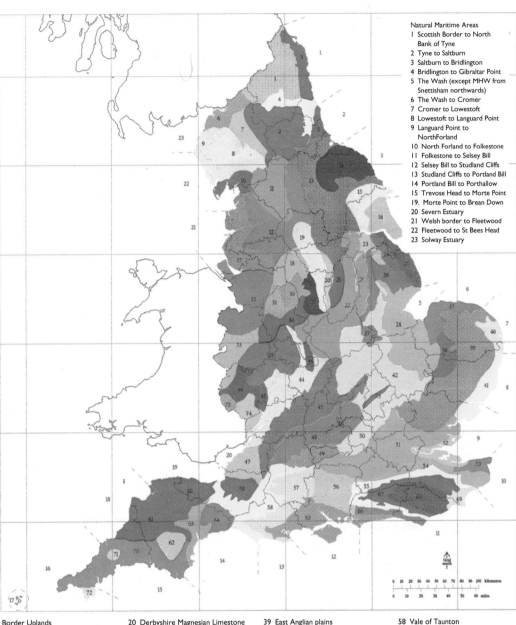

Natural Maritime Areas
1 Scottish Border to North
  Bank of Tyne
2 Tyne to Saltburn
3 Saltburn to Bridlington
4 Bridlington to Gibraltar Point
5 The Wash (except MHW from
  Snettisham northwards)
6 The Wash to Cromer
7 Cromer to Lowestoft
8 Lowestoft to Languard Point
9 Languard Point to
  NorthForland
10 North Forland to Folkestone
11 Folkestone to Selsey Bill
12 Selsey Bill to Studland Cliffs
13 Studland Cliffs to Portland Bill
14 Portland Bill to Porthallow
15 Trevose Head to Morte Point
19. Morte Point to Brean Down
20 Severn Estuary
21 Welsh border to Fleetwood
22 Fleetwood to St Bees Head
23 Solway Estuary

1 Border Uplands	20 Derbyshire Magnesian Limestone	39 East Anglian plains	58 Vale of Taunton
2 Northern Pennines	21 Sherwood Forest	40 Broadland	59 Somerset Levels
3 Northumberland Coastal Plain	22 Trent Valley and Levels	41 Sandlings	60 Exmoor and Quantocks
4 Tyne Vale	23 Cover Sands	42 East Midlands Lowlands	61 Culm Measures
5 Durham Magnesian Limestone	24 Lincolnshire Wolds	43 Greater Cotswolds	62 Dartmoor
6 Solway Basin	25 Lincolnshire Coastal Plain	44 Severn Valley	63 Devon Sandstone
7 Eden Vale	26 Lincolnshire Clay Vales	45 Malvern Hills	64 Blackdowns
8 Lake District	27 Lincolnshire Limestone	46 Hereford Plain	65 Hampshire Basin
9 Cumbrian Coastal Plain	28 Fenland	47 Mendips	66 South Downs
10 Morecambe Bay Limestones	29 Lower Derwent Valley	48 Oxford Clay Vales	67 Low Weald
11 Yorkshire Dales	30 The White Peak	49 Wessex Downs	68 High Weald
12 Southern Pennines	31 Staffordshire Northern Upland	50 Chilterns	69 Romney Marsh
13 Vale of York	32 Mosses and Meres	51 London Basin	70 South West Plain
14 North of York Moors	33 Shropshire Uplands	52 Thames Marshes	71 Bodmin
15 Yorkshire Wold	34 Upper Trent Valley	53 North Kent Plain	72 The Lizard
16 Plain of Holderness	35 Birmingham Plateau	54 North Downs	73 Black Mountains
17 Lancashire Plain	36 Wark Sandstone Plateau	55 Greensand	74 Severn/Wye Plateau
18 The Dark Peak	37 North Norfolk	56 Hampshire Chalk	75 Beds Greensand
19 Coal Measures	38 Breckland	57 Salisbury Plain and Dorset Downs	76 Oxford Heights
			————————— County boundary

MARINE NATURE CONSERVATION REVIEW

The Marine Nature Conservation Review (MNCR) is a major research programme being undertaken within the support unit of the Joint Nature Conservation Committee and the nature conservation agencies.

This programme was initiated in 1987 to consolidate and complete the information already collected on British marine ecosystems including the extensive data collected from marine survey projects commissioned by NCC since 1974. The principle objectives of the MNCR are to:

- extend our knowledge of British marine ecosystems, particularly the distribution and extent of habitats, communities and species;
- assess the nature conservation importance of habitats, communites and species;
- provide the information required to promote marine nature conservation principles and counter the adverse effects of developments and pollution in the marine environment.

The MNCR is based on descriptions of habitats and the recorded abundance of conspicuous species for the whole of the coastal waters of England, Scotland and Wales from the high water mark out to the limits of British territorial seas, extending into estuaries to the limits of maritime influence. In practice, most of the survey work is logistically limited to the littoral and sublittoral within the 50 m depth contour.

The MNCR Report Series is intended for the rapid dissemination of topics other than field survey reports, such as information reviews and accounts of methodology. As such, these reports will be of limited circulation, they are open to comment and update as necessary and will provide the source material for the wider circulation 'theme report' series which will constitute the published Marine Nature Conservation Review of Great Britain.

John England, Countryside Commission

Local people clearing a pond in Pulborough pocket park in west Sussex.

maintained such as ornamental landscapes around offices, park flower beds and close-mown grass. These perceptions may be accommodated or changed by encouraging both types of landscape blending with one another. As the cycle of urban renewal proceeds consideration should be given to a variety of manicured and more natural urban greenspaces. Urban tree and forestry initiatives should encompass wildlife as well as recreational and ornamental objectives.

Action planned for urban areas

4.94 The Government and the agencies working with local authorities will:

- encourage public bodies to review the management plans for all land owned by them to ensure that provisions for wildlife and natural features and the enjoyment of these by the public is made, where appropriate;
- encourage the designation of more Local Nature Reserves;
- deliver these policies through environmental charters.

The marine and coastal environment

The marine environment

4.95 The marine environment is extensive in area, diverse in nature and rich in wildlife. Like the atmosphere, it is a resource that we share with other nations. Since it is a continuum covering about two-thirds of the earth's surface, conservation must operate throughout the resource as well as at local level in order to be effective. The oceans are far richer in species than terrestrial or freshwater environments but are much less studied. Agreements at World and European levels therefore have special significance for conservation of the seas. Unlike terrestrial ecosystems, and with few exceptions such as fish farming, our exploitation of the sea for food has not involved noticeable habitat management. Some fishing methods have resulted in major habitat modification and major changes in population sizes of individual species. In

MARINE MAMMALS

The UK has no endemic marine mammal species but large numbers of grey seals and common seals breed around our coasts. In fact, the UK holds 40-45% of the world's grey seal population, and following the 1988 phocine distemper virus epizootic, which caused wide scale mortality among common seals in mainland Europe but which had a lesser effect on UK populations, the UK also holds nearly 40% of the European population of common seals. At least nine species of cetacean are regularly recorded in UK waters, although no species occurs in large numbers. However, there are only a small number of resident populations of bottlenose dolphin in Europe; at least two of these are in the UK.

Grey seals and common seals are protected by the Conservation of Seals Act 1970 and all cetaceans by the Wildlife and Countryside Act 1981. All the major grey seal colonies are surveyed annually by the Natural Environment Research Council's Sea Mammal Research Unit (SMRU). Some local populations of common seals are also surveyed annually, others are surveyed on a five-year cycle. Grey seal numbers have increased annually by 10% in recent years. The resident population of bottlenosed dolphins in the Moray Firth is monitored by Aberdeen University and SMRU, sightings of cetaceans from land stations are collated by the Seawatch Foundation, and the Seabirds and Cetaceans Branch of the Joint Nature Conservation Committee collects information on the distribution of cetaceans at sea from ships of opportunity. Information on stranded cetaceans is collated by the British Museum (Natural History), and pathological examinations of stranded animals are conducted by the Institute of Zoology (in England and Wales) and by the Scottish Agricultural College Veterinary Investigation Service in Scotland. These latter studies are funded by the Department of the Environment. Information from monitoring is compiled and published in the UK Digital Marine Atlas which is maintained by the NERC's Proudman Oceanographic Laboratory. The SMRU is co-ordinating a major international survey of small cetaceans abundance and distribution in the North Sea which will be conducted in 1994. This survey also aims to identify important habitats areas and potential threats to the different species.

Potential threats to marine mammals include entanglement in fishing gear, the high contaminant levels recorded in certain individuals, disturbance, and their perceived competition with commercial fisheries. The UK has recently ratified the Agreement on the Conservation of Small Cetaceans of the Baltic and North Seas, which requires signatories to take specific action to reduce threats to these species. The interim secretariat for this agreement is provided by the UK and is housed at the SMRU.

the sea there is a reliance on natural systems to provide sources of food. Intense and extractive uses affect such systems and the species dependent on them. Sustainable use is, therefore, critical to the long term survival of traditional uses such as fisheries. Good resource management is, in addition, beneficial to other uses such as tourism, angling, sailing and other water sports including scuba diving.

Our state of knowledge of the marine ecosystem

4.96 Knowledge of the distribution and extent of marine wildlife and natural features is substantially less than it is for terrestrial ecosystems, doubtless because the marine environment is difficult to study. Consequently there is only an imperfect picture of the distribution and extent of marine habitats and species. Our understanding of the biology of many species is also limited. Likewise we have a poor knowledge of the factors which govern biodiversity. Progress with improving our information base is currently disappointingly slow. Marine conservation is at a point

Keith Hiscock, English Nature

Fishing, a traditional use of the marine environment.

Knowledge of marine wildlife and natural features is substantially less than it is for terrestrial systems – doubtless because the marine environment is difficult to study.

similar to that for terrestrial ecology in the 1950s where we can describe outstanding marine wildlife areas around our coasts and provide generalised descriptions of the distribution and extent of individual habitats and species. The Marine Nature Conservation Review (MNCR) is the major basis for this. It has collated existing information and obtained new data through survey programmes.

4.97 For birds good information exists through the work of the Seabirds and Cetaceans branch of JNCC. Information on the nature conservation implications of man's activities in the marine environment has been compiled but marine habitat and species dynamics and how habitats and species respond to man-induced changes are imperfectly understood. Rapid progress needs to be made in these areas to supply information to underpin environmental appraisals or audit and the development of management plans as well as to contribute to the development of sustainability principles for the marine environment.

The Coastal Zone

4.98 In contrast to the marine environment, coasts and estuaries have a long history of management, modification and development through intensive exploitation. However the coastal zone is naturally very dynamic, eroding and accreting in response to powerful natural forces. We now know that the creation of fixed lines of defence on the coast has caused loss or damage to significant areas of coastal habitats and when associated with rising relative sea levels, it can result in the loss of inter-tidal habitats. There are instances, however, where the building of defences has led to the creation of areas which are now considered to be of high conservation value. Maintaining fixed defences will, in some circumstances, particularly areas of long term potential erosion, have a significant impact on habitats and the environment. The defences will

also become increasingly difficult and expensive to maintain. While recognising the need to safeguard lives and to protect important natural and man-made assets, it is also necessary to apply the principle of sustainability to the management of the coast.

4.99 The need to take account of natural coastal processes is an important feature of the strategy for coastal and flood defence in England and Wales published in October, following widespread consultation, by the Ministry of Agriculture, Fisheries and Food and the Welsh Office. The strategy makes clear that in assessing applications for grant aid for such works, the two Departments will start from the presumption that coastal processes should not be disrupted except where life or important manmade or natural assets are at risk. Grant will only be offered for schemes which the Ministry or Welsh Office judge are environmentally acceptable; the potential impact on habitats and the environment generally should be a key consideration, based on an understanding of natural processes, and, as far as possible, working with those processes.

4.100 Wider management of the coast and coastal zone is also important to achieve a balance between the range of potentially competing demands on this finite resource. Sectoral controls already ensure that many uses and

Coastal zone erodes in response to powerful natural forces.

activities are subject to systems of appraisal and regulation which take full account of environmental considerations: for example, harbour construction, dredging, disposal at sea, oil and gas exploration and production, and submarine pipelines and cables. Details of these arrangements were set out in a comprehensive discussion paper – 'Development Below Low Water Mark' – issued in October by the Department of the Environment and the Welsh Office. The paper concludes that, with some improvements, the present structure of sectoral controls can meet its objectives for the control of development in the coastal and marine environment.

4.101 In September 1992 the two Departments issued advice on the location of built development on the coast – Planning Policy Guidance Note No 20 – 'Coastal Planning' – which emphasised the need for local planning authorities to recognise that on-shore development can often have an impact off-shore; that few developments require a coastal location; and that new development should not generally be permitted in areas which would need expensive engineering works to protect land from erosion or inundation.

4.102 Separate consideration is being given to coastal policy in Scotland, and a consultation paper covering coastal issues will be issued by the Scottish Office in due course.

Integrating local interests

4.103 Lessons from overseas indicate that local action and stewardship are also essential elements to the overall success of habitat protection programmes. Coasts, estuaries and the sea are vital to the nation as a source of food, for transport and other commercial uses, and for recreation and leisure. In the past fifty years, however, the pressures on marine and coastal environments have increased significantly. Careful consideration needs to be given to where the balance lies between our use of coasts and seas and their importance for biodiversity, especially in situations where use threatens not just biodiversity conservation but also man's long-term interests. There is a growing realisation that some activities may cause long-term and at times significant alterations to the marine and coastal environment and wildlife (see box). These concerns have to be balanced against national and local economic needs and social requirements.

4.104 Where the coast is of great conservation or recreation value or where there are substantial conflicting uses – for example, in estuaries or individual stretches of open coast – more broadly based approaches may be needed. In such cases integrated management may be required to promote the sustainable use of these vulnerable areas. To this end it may be appropriate for local authorities, acting in close consultation and liaison with all

MAJOR HARMFUL INFLUENCES ON THE COASTAL AND MARINE ENVIRONMENT

- the disposal of wastes in rivers, estuaries and the seas, although reduced in extent by licensing, still affects the environmental quality of the seas;
- some fisheries operations are now so intense that it may be necessary to consider whether they may be damaging the habitats upon which the commercially important species themselves depend whilst others may be adversely affecting non-target species;
- requirements for large modern ships have resulted in land claim for ports and dredging of channels. Government research is to be carried out into the introduction of non-native species on hulls and in ballast water (which is also the subject of controls under the International Convention for the Prevention of Pollution from Ships [MARPOL]);
- the expansion of resource extraction, such as aggregates, gas and oil;
- water-based sports continue to grow, with increasing demands for onshore facilities and increasing user pressure. This leads to conflicts between different users and between users and wildlife.
- extensive land claim and development around the coasts of the United Kingdom over the centuries have led to widespread coast protection and flood defence works. These have fixed naturally dynamic coasts, reducing sediment supplies, disrupting coastal processed and preventing coastlines from maintaining a natural equilibrium. In many places continual investment will be necessary to maintain defences in order to safeguard life and the important natural and man-made assets which the existing defences protect;
- where long term marine erosion has combined with widespread fixation of this shoreline the phenomenon of 'coastal squeeze' has been produced.

interested parties, to take the lead in preparing management plans for such areas.

4.105 Such plans would form the basis of a broader strategy for evaluating priorities in those areas, and provide those concerned with a guide for implementing these. Management plans cannot replace the statutory powers and rights of existing bodies, but must build on and complement relevant existing structures. The scope and format of such plans was considered in detail in a DOE-Welsh Office discussion paper – 'Managing the Coast' – issued in October 1993.

4.106 Publication of this paper and its companion on development below low water mark fulfil a commitment made by the Government in its wide-ranging response to a report on coastal protection and planning issued in April last year by the House of Commons Environment Committee. In responding to the Committee's report, the Government stressed that it was firmly committed to the effective protection and planning of the coast, and set out in detail the extent of existing and proposed measures already in hand to safeguard this 'unique, varied and valuable asset'. The response also accepted the need for a 'national overview' of coastal issues, and in this context drew attention to the

work of a standing Inter-Departmental Group on coastal policy which acts to provide a mechanism for discussion of key policy issues involving different interests.

Planned action on the marine and coastal area

4.107 The Government and the nature conservation agencies plan to:

- Complete the Marine Nature Conservation Review.
- Continue to implement new approaches to coastal flood defence and coast protection which manipulate and work with natural processes.
- Continue to devise arrangements to prevent uncontrolled introductions of non-native marine species.
- Promote active management of bay marine wildlife areas including management plans to secure the integrated management of vulnerable areas.
- Review the intertidal SSSI network to ensure it covers the important marine wildlife habitats and species.
- Utilise voluntary and statutory marine reserves and other relevant initiatives as mechanisms to involve individuals and communities in practical marine conservation work.
- Designate sufficient marine SACs and SPAs and ensure that mechanisms are in place for their effective conservation under the Habitats and Birds Directive.

CHAPTER 5

CONSERVATION OUTSIDE NATURAL HABITATS

INTRODUCTION

5.1 The preceding Chapter has described how biodiversity in the UK is maintained through the conservation of habitats and ecosystems, often using groups of species of plants or animals as indicators. Such *in situ* conservation is insufficient to maintain genetic stocks of some species, either because:

- of their natural rarity;
- they are directly at risk as a result of human activities or exploitation;
- they or their natural habitats are in some way threatened, or because
- they are difficult to obtain from the wild.

5.2 In these cases conservation of species away from their natural habitats, so called *ex situ* conservation, can play a critical role in supporting species through crisis periods. *Ex situ* populations can provide valuable resources for research into basic aspects of species biology which may be critical in devising appropriate and effective *in situ* programmes. For successful conservation the establishment of *ex situ* populations should precede any crisis period and should be implemented when wild populations are still quite numerous.

5.3 In reality *in situ* and *ex situ* conservation are opposite ends of a spectrum with no absolute distinction between them. They are not alternatives, rather complementary approaches, *ex-situ* conservation being particularly well suited to maintaining variety within a plant species. A seamless blend of both in an integrated programme is therefore appropriate to conserve biodiversity. In the UK, as elsewhere, *ex situ* methods are used:

- to complement in situ conservation, for example when populations are severely threatened and reduced in numbers;
- to provide material for industry, education and research;
- to provide reservoir populations or stocks which can be used to support the survival of species in the wild, particularly by reintroduction and restocking, to support habitat restoration and rehabilitation, or for screening programmes;
- to maintain existing genetic stocks and develop new crop cultivars and domesticated strains through breeding programmes;
- as an insurance policy through holding stocks in long-term storage (germplasm banks), for future needs;
- for use in general and environmental education;
- to maintain patent and industrial strains of micro-organisms.

5.4 The UK has historically played a leading role in the development of *ex situ* techniques for a wide range of organisms, and a number of institutions are internationally recognised as among the world leaders in this field. The techniques of *ex situ* conservation include: collection, translocation, storage, propagation, characterisation and evaluation, management at individual and population level, introduction to wild habitats or reintroduction to historical ranges, and support for wild populations. Problems of conserving genetic material vary considerably for different organisms and the three main groups, plants, animals, and microorganisms, are considered separately in the sections below.

PLANT CONSERVATION

Conservation techniques

5.5 Many plants are conserved in 'field gene banks' in botanical gardens, arboreta, and agricultural and horticultural institutions. These collections of growing plants are carefully maintained and looked after either out in the open or under glass. Clones, varieties and cultivars of particular species are kept to maintain stocks of genetic diversity.

5.6 For sexually reproducing plants seed banks are the most efficient and effective method of long-term storage provided the seeds are 'orthodox'. The Royal Botanic Gardens, Kew, for example, holds seeds for some 40% of native British seed-producing plants. Cold storage (-10°C to -20°C) of seeds for some species increases long-term viability for at least 100 years, but for other species seed stores need to be replenished more regularly. Pollen can be stored in a similar way to seed, but there are virtually no such conservation collections in the UK.

5.7 *In vitro* (literally 'in glass') preservation of parts of plants, such as meristem tips, buds or stem tips, is used

An example of a field gene bank; the national collection of thyme at Hexham Herbs in Northumberland.

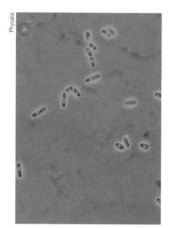

Many microorganisms are conserved in culture collections.

The monkey orchid; one of the orchids from the Sainsbury Conservation Project.

infrequently in the UK with more than 1,000 taxa being maintained in this way. Cryo-preservation is used to slow down growth rates of this material and enhance long-term conservation.

5.8 Many microorganisms, including viruses, bacteria, protozoa, and most algae and fungi are conserved in culture collections and these are discussed more fully in the section on microbial conservation.

UK institutions for plant germplasm

5.9 There are more than 50 botanic gardens and arboreta in the UK which hold a vast and rich resource of living germplasm. The UK ranks third in the world for the number of accessions in cultivation with over 200,000 cultivars and species of mostly exotic plants. Some of these collections are extremely important for the preservation and cultivation of rare and endangered native and exotic species. For example, the Royal Botanic Gardens at Kew and Edinburgh and Glasgow Botanic Garden between them have living collections of more than 4,000 species of orchid, many of which are threatened in the wild. Collectively the UK botanic gardens hold over 2,300 accessions of threatened trees including some that are now extinct in the wild.

5.10 Many government funded and commercial agricultural and horticultural research stations/collections have important holdings of native and exotic agricultural

The national apple collection at Brogdale.

or horticultural crop cultivars such as cereals, vegetables, fruit trees, and crop relatives. The UK Government funds a number of plant genetic resource collections in this area including the Vegetable Gene Bank (Wellesbourne), the National Fruit Collection (Brogdale), the Pea Gene Bank (Norwich), the collection of wild species at the Royal Botanic Gardens (Kew and Wakehurst Place), and the Commonwealth Potato Collection, Barley Collection and Soft Fruit Collection (Invergowrie).

5.11 There are also a number of important private organisations which maintain specialist collections of plants. The Henry Doubleday Association, for example, which has large collections of old cultivars of garden plant and vegetables, has a 'Heritage Seed' programme. Other major collections are held by members of British National Societies for ornamental plants such as Fuchsias, Pelargonium and Geranium, Chrysanthemum, Rose and Iris. The UK also has numerous specialist societies for bulbs and alpines.

5.12 Some 60,000 taxa of ornamental plants, mainly cultivars or species of exotic plants, are available through commercial nurseries in the UK. These and over 600 National Collections of garden plants are cultivated in the numerous UK public and private gardens and arboreta, under a scheme organised by the National Council for the Conservation of Plants and Gardens (NCCPG). Many UK universities have small specialized collections of wild and cultivated plants of both native and exotic species which are used for research and teaching.

5.13 The Tree Register of the British Isles (TROBI) provides an index of significant specimen trees in major UK private and public gardens. The Woody Plant Catalogue held by the National Trust is the largest catalogue of woody wild collected plants in the world and contains over 35,000 accessions. Numerous forestry institutions/organisations also play a role in ex situ conservation specifically of trees. For example, Westonbirt Arboretum, Castlewellan Arboretum in Northern Ireland and Bedgebury Pinetum include collections of 3,500, 1,200 and 900 taxa, respectively. The Forestry Commission and the Department for Agriculture for Northern Ireland maintain clone banks and provenance trials of 16 species of commercial importance in the UK with 13–120 seed origins for each species.

5.14 In 1992 the Government carried out a review of UK policy for the *ex situ* conservation of plant genetic resources, this is being implemented by MAFF and SOAFD. The main proposals were to:

● produce a strategy document for *ex situ* conservation of

- plant genetic resources;
- consider long-term funding commitments to 'designated collections';
- look to users to fund work outside the core activities associated with the upkeep of gene banks;
- issue a booklet to publicise the existence/details of current UK collections;
- establish a small interdepartmental group to, inter alia, review funding priorities at 3–5 yearly intervals, and
- continue to participate fully in international efforts to establish comprehensive networks of *ex situ* plant genetic resource collections.

The holdings of UK culture collections with those for the European Culture Collection Organisation (ECCO) member organisations shown for comparison				
Organism	ECCO	UK National Collections	Other collections in UK	Total in UK
Algae	2890	1870	154	2024
Animal cells	6540	6000	-	6000
Animal viruses	545	-	*	*
Bacteria	103620	16800	28015	44815
Filamentous fungi	97575	18530	29550	48080
Phages	1110	100	-	100
Plasmids	12805	10400	-	10400
Protozoa	405	385	2134	2519
Plant cells	720	10	-	10
Plant viruses	545	-	760	760
Yeasts	27010	3700	2238	5938
Total	**253765**	**57795**	**62851**	**120646**

Note: * Numbers not available

ANIMAL CONSERVATION

5.15 There are over 70 major zoos and aquaria in the UK with collective experience of the maintenance and management of a wide array of species. These house over 64,000 vertebrates (mammals – 14,200, birds – 25,779, reptiles – 4,014, amphibians – 1507, fishes 19,036). Historically, most collections have focussed on the larger vertebrates but there is an increasing emphasis on smaller vertebrates, such as reptiles and fish, and on aquatic and terrestrial invertebrates such as insects and molluscs. There is also some evidence that more scientifically based management is taking place in private collections, particularly with birds and reptiles.

5.16 The 52 collections which form The Federation of Zoological Gardens of Great Britain and Ireland hold many exotic and native species of animals, the majority of which are captive bred. Details of individuals are recorded on various databases such as Federation inventories, annual censuses of the International Zoo Yearbook, and the on-going inventories of the International Species Information System (ISIS).

5.17 The Federation, via its Joint Management of Species Committee (JMSC) and its Conservation and Animal Management Committee (CAM), organises and co-ordinates all species conservation programmes in UK zoos and similar collections. Individual animals are seen as part of a whole population and this population is kept genetically and demographically healthy. Priorities for species are based on their status and management in captivity and in the wild and are the responsibility of the Taxon Advisory Groups (TAGS) overseen by JMSC. TAGs set the priorities for each species and are responsible for the development and maintenance of breeding programmes and studbooks.

5.18 Many of these programmes are part of the larger European programmes maintained by the European Association of Zoos and Aquaria (EAZA). Some species (mainly exotic threatened species) are part of international programmes which are recognised and endorsed by IUCN and the specialist groups of the Species Survival Commission (SSC).

5.19 The problems of maintaining viable populations of animals are very different from those for plants and microorganisms and are generally much more costly. The capacity of many zoos to maintain diverse collections is therefore limited by financial constraints. The Institute of Zoology (which with London and Whipsnade Zoos is part of the Zoological Society of London) in particular, plays a prominent role in the development of techniques for the preservation of gametes (eggs and sperm) and embryos of vertebrates and is one of the leading institutions in Europe in this field. Other mainly agricultural and medical institutions also play a role in developing these techniques.

5.20 In spite of their immense richness in species terms, there is very little ex situ conservation of UK invertebrates. A few zoos and most aquaria have living exhibits of invertebrates but these are mainly of common and non-native species.

5.21 The Rare Breeds Survival Trust plays an important role in ensuring that strains of domesticated animals which in the past have been important or may in the future be important, are maintained. Such well known varieties as the Soay and Loghtan sheep, Tamworth Pig and Shire horses add considerably to the UK's cultural heritage. Other UK organisations, such as the Otter Trust, play an important role in helping to maintain stocks of native UK species in the wild.

In 1969 there were only 18 white eared pheasants in captivity and the wild population was unknown. Since then Jersey Wildlife Preservation Trust has ensured the survival of this species in captivity by rearing over 200 birds and sending them to zoos all over the world.

MICROBIAL CONSERVATION

5.22 Ex-situ collections of preserved microorganisms are the microbiologist's equivalent of botanic gardens, seed banks, zoos and aquaria. Cultures are required for identification purposes, particularly with bacteria, yeasts and some filamentous fungi where the living 'types', that fix the application of names, must be maintained. Many isolates held would be very difficult to find again in their natural habitat, and ex-situ collections provide the only practical option for making them available for identification, research and screening. These collections have a research and applied value, particularly in industry (eg National Collection of Industrial and Marine Bacteria (NCIMB) for industrially significant bacteria), and also act as depositories for patent and British Standard testing strains.

5.23 Since 1947 the UK has had a network of 10 'national' culture collections for microorganisms, each collection being housed with parent institutions offering relevant expertise, and with a remit to provide cultures and related services to the scientific community. These institutions hold approximately 68,000 strains of algae, animal cells, bacteria, fungi, phages, plasmids, plant cells, and protozoa. They, and 32 other UK member organisations of the European Culture Collections Organization (ECCO), had total holdings of 253,765 strains in 1992. Only the USA and Japan hold equal or greater numbers of ex-situ conserved microorganisms and cell cultures. About 30–45% of the isolates maintained originate from the UK, but these represent only 10–25% of the known British species.

5.24 The 1978 UK Directory of Culture Collections lists 64 collections of microorganisms. However, not listed are an increasing number of biotechnological companies, as well as many established pharmaceutical and microbiological companies and university departments which hold strains of microorganisms for their own use. Many of these organisations are not suitably equipped or prepared to supply documented and authenticated cultures or to ensure long-term preservation.

5.25 In order to improve the availability of these strains, and to ensure their long-term security, there is a need to consider a network of UK 'national' collections. The Government response to the House of Lords Select Committee on Systematic Biology Research recognised that there was a need for a coherent national policy on the UK's microbial culture collections and is to arrange a review to determine national needs and develop an appropriate future strategy.

Collections of Preserved Plants, Fungi and Animals

5.26 The UK has some of the finest collections in the world of preserved plants, fungi and animals, such as those in The Natural History Museum, Royal Botanic Gardens of Kew and Edinburgh and the International Institute of Mycology. The collections in these and other national and local museums and herbaria provide a systematic, geographical and historical perspective for present day activities in *ex situ* conservation. Identifications of living material as part of *ex situ* programmes usually can not be made without reference to these well-maintained collections of preserved organisms. Some of these museums and herbaria also hold living collections. For example, The Natural History Museum holds living collections of microscopic algae and diatoms, and vectors and parasites causing certain human diseases.

5.27 There are over 200 UK museums with natural history collections and over 50 of these hold 'type' specimens for species. Although we know, for example, that three of the largest collections, those of The Natural History Museum and the Royal Botanic Gardens of Kew and Edinburgh, hold over 75 million specimens, the full extent of UK resources in preserved specimens is not clear. The vital next step in capitalising on the world resource that these collections represent is, therefore, to conduct a comprehensive survey of the nature, extent and location in the UK of preserved reference specimens and the associated staff expertise. The Government response to the First Report of the House of Lords Select Committee on Systematic Biology Research (1993) endorsed the proposal that there should be a new forum for systematics collections. The forum will be involved primarily in the dissemination of information and good practice.

Research in Ex-Situ Conservation

5.28 The immensely rich UK collections of preserved (dead) and conserved (living) organisms, be they plant, animal or microorganisms, are an unequalled resource for research into ex situ conservation and many UK institutions are leaders in their fields. For many studies it is useful, if not essential, to have diverse collections of living and dead plants and animals so that species can be observed more easily than in the wild and they can be compared with other related indigenous and exotic species, particularly in terms of taxonomy, ecology and behaviour. These vast collections

The type specimen of Gentiana sino-ornata held at RBG Edinburgh.

are also an unequalled resource for systematic research and the UK continues to be in the forefront in this field.

5.29 World-class research into horticultural, propagation, and plant conservation techniques, involving population genetics, breeding biology, cryo-preservation, micro-propogation, re-introduction and recovery planning, is undertaken in many UK research institutes, botanic gardens and universities. Research on seed germination and storage is undertaken at Universities (eg Reading) and botanic gardens (eg Royal Botanic Gardens Kew at Wakehurst Place).

5.30 Ex situ collections in zoos and related institutions provide the opportunity to study a range of biological subjects, particularly biotechnics, population biology, behaviour and diseases. The following are a few examples of research areas at the Institute of Zoology in London:

- genetic techniques for identifying biological populations, sub-species and species for elucidating family structures, long-term storage of viable embryos and gametes, especially of mammals,
- artificial breeding techniques,
- monitoring and management of the reproductive cycle,
- genetic and demographic management of small and closed populations for conservation, including captive breeding programmes.

5.31 At UK microbiological institutes research is carried out to enhance preparation techniques, and long-term storage methods – especially with liquid nitrogen. New protocols for preservation are being developed using cryogenic stage microscopy enabling some species to be preserved satisfactorily for the first time.

RE-ESTABLISHMENT PROGRAMMES

5.32 The re-establishment and re-stocking of rare and endangered native species are being undertaken by the UK nature conservation agencies. Many zoos and botanical gardens are involved in collaborative conservation programmes for UK species. Inter alia they provide material for reintroductions or

Counting germinating seeds in a viability assessment at RBG, Wakehurst Place.

restocking, some from their existing collections. Some plants are propagated clonally from surviving wild populations (eg Plymouth pear by RBG Kew). Other recovery plans for plants and animals are coordinated by groups such as Plantlife, local naturalist trusts and botanic gardens (eg RBGs Kew and Edinburgh, Cambridge University BG, The Herpetological Conservation Trust, The British Herpetological Society, and the Federation of Zoos).

5.33 Several UK botanic gardens play an important international role in reintroduction programmes overseas for non-native plants, in collaboration with in-country institutions and UK research institutions (eg *Trochetiopsis* spp in St Helena – RBG Kew, ODA, University of Oxford). Collaborative programmes exist with botanic gardens in countries such as Mauritius, India, Republic of South Africa, South Korea, St Helena, Mexico and Spain.

RGB Kew have propagated clones of the Plymouth pear from the surviving wild population.

5.34 Plant exchanges (seed, micropropagated plantlets, spores) between botanic gardens internationally are also being used for in-country reintroduction programmes using material maintained in the UK.

5.35 Similarly, in recent years the focus of attention for many zoos in the UK has shifted to captive breeding programmes for the reintroduction of rare and endangered species. Many zoos play a vital role in reintroduction programmes for species of international importance, such as the Arabian Oryx, Scimitar-horned Oryx, Arabian Gazelles, Mauritius Kestrel and Pink Pigeon. Some have a wider role providing management plans for areas and species of conservation interest (eg for Round Island, Mauritius, and the Una Biological Reserve, Brazil – Jersey Wildlife Preservation Trust). London Zoo, for example, is involved in 52 nationally and internationally coordinated captive breeding programmes for exotic species and manages 29 such programmes.

COLLABORATIVE CONSERVATION PROGRAMMES FOR UK SPECIES INVOLVING EX-SITU CONSERVATION IN ZOOS

There are many examples of collaborative conservation programmes for UK species involving ex situ conservation in zoos. This involvement ranges in scale from on-going managed programmes in which there may be a reintroduction or restocking element to a smaller number of projects where captive breeding is one facet of a multidisciplinary approach. Some examples of these are given below.

Species		Zoos Involved
Invertebrates:		
Moths	Barberry Carpet	Dudley Zoo
	Reddish Buff	Paignton Zoo
		Marwell Zoo
		Penscynor Wildlife Park
Crickets	Field Cricket	London Zoo
	British Wart-biter	London Zoo
Vertebrates:		
Amphibians	Natterjack Toad	Marwell Zoo
Reptiles	Sand Lizard	Marwell Zoo
Birds	UK Waterfowl	Wildfowl & Wetlands Trust
	Red Kite	London (Veterinary Dept)
	Great Bustard	Whipsnade Wild Animal Park
	Capercaillie	Highland Wildlife Park
Mammals	Otter	Chestnut Centre
	Wild Cat	Highland Wildlife Park
	Red Squirrel	London Zoo
		Highland Wildlife Park

EDUCATION IN EX-SITU CONSERVATION

5.36 UK botanic gardens and arboreta, zoos, aquaria and wildlife parks receive well over 18 million visitors a year. These, along with the national and local natural history museums, provide an important and unparalleled educational resource for the role of ex situ conservation in the UK and elsewhere.

5.37 The potential for conservation education is immense and the living animals and plants in ex situ conservation organisations are an outstanding conservation education resource. For many visitors, and in particular for children from urban areas, a zoo or botanic garden can be the stepping-stone to the countryside. An appreciation of the need to conserve and to retain biodiversity both within the UK and elsewhere can be initiated and fostered by the direct and indirect educational resources of these institutions.

5.38 A recent survey showed that half a million people used the education services of Federation zoos, with at least 350,000 receiving professional tuition on-site. There are many examples of innovative and imaginative schemes being used, often in collaboration with education authorities, colleges and universities. Formal educational services range from pre-school to post-graduate. Informal

Mauritius pink pigeon. Since 1984 a programme of reintroductions of birds bred in captivity in Jersey and Mauritius has substantially increased the wild population.

educational services include people coming to zoos to enjoy and staying to learn from good labelling, audio-visual displays, talks and controlled close contact with selected animals.

5.39 Many UK ex situ institutions are important centres for public environmental education, and their extensive world-wide collections help to teach the public about biodiversity and the global threats it faces, the importance of all kinds of life forms and the work of botanic gardens and zoos in maintaining biodiversity. Most receive regular and frequent visits from parties of school children and have developed programmes specifically geared to the UK national curriculum in subjects such as biology, geography, and history. Some institutions are active in teacher training in these and other subjects.

5.40 The extensive and well documented ex situ collections of many UK botanic gardens, zoos, museums, universities, and research institutes are a vital resource for many UK and overseas visitors and researchers. The availability of such extensive collections greatly facilitates a wide range of biological research and in particular studies of the systematics of plants, animals and microorganisms. Many visit the UK to access the valuable information they hold. These institutions also play an important role in the education of undergraduate and graduate students, and training of other wildlife specialists from the UK and elsewhere. The courses cover a wide range of fields from taxonomy, plant physiology, biochemistry to crop production.

5.41 Training in horticultural and other botanical subjects of relevance to ex situ conservation of plants is provided mainly by botanic gardens and universities for national and international students (eg Kew and Edinburgh Diploma Courses, UNEP-sponsored and other MSc and MPhil courses at Universities of Reading and Birmingham University). The MSc training course at Birmingham entitled *Conservation and Utilization of Plant Genetic Resources* is of national and international importance, and since its inception in 1969 has trained over 400 students, mostly from Third World countries, to MSc level. Short courses on Plant Conservation Techniques are run by the RBG Kew and Birmingham University and environmental education courses for international students are run by such organizations as the International Centre for Conservative Education, Gloucestershire. Some of the 'national' microbial centres also hold international and national courses in preservation

techniques for research workers, those involved in industry and others.

5.42 Some zoological institutes are deeply involved in training courses for ex situ conservation. For example, since 1978 330 people from 70 countries have attended the International Training Programme in Conservation and the Captive Breeding of Endangered Species run by the Jersey Wildlife Preservation Trust. This course is designed to help top decision-makers from wildlife departments and organisations understand the role of zoos and captive breeding programmes. Similar courses are run by the Durrell Institute for Conservation and Ecology, Kent.

SUMMARY

5.43 This Plan has provided an opportunity for all ex-situ conservation to be reviewed. It allows, for the first time, an overview of the UK's resources in marine and terrestrial invertebrates, as well as the more widely known resources in plants, micro-organisms and vertebrates.

5.44 The UK is one of the world leaders for *ex-situ* conservation, and in this field is probably catering as much or more for its own fauna and flora as any other nation. The UK is also very much at the forefront in terms of care and development of collections of preserved and conserved plants and animals, and research and education.

Jersey Wildlife Preservation Trust International Training Programme. A trainee from St Lucia receives advice from the Senior Curator.

ACTION

The Government will review microbial (and possibly botanical and animal) genetic resources, and then consider whether to develop a formalised strategy for future ex-situ conservation across all genetic resources taking account of international obligations and developments in this field.

CHAPTER 6

SUSTAINABLE USE

INTRODUCTION

6.1 The conservation of biodiversity cannot be achieved solely through collections, nature reserves and other protected areas. We need to influence what happens in the wider environment. Most uses of land and water have some impact on biodiversity. In addition, man makes direct use of some species for food, wood products, clothing, sport, and other functions. Patterns of resource consumption, energy use and transport also have an impact on biodiversity.

6.2 This chapter is concerned with the use of those natural resources which contribute to biodiversity, and ensuring that through their wise use biodiversity is not only protected but is conserved and enhanced for current and future generations. For all uses and activities, it should be an aim of policy to minimise further losses of biodiversity due to human activity and, where possible, to increase biodiversity. The context for the chapter is provided by Article 10 of the UN Convention on Biological Diversity.

6.3 In the following paragraphs, a number of general principles and approaches which will help to ensure sustainable use of biological resources and conserve biodiversity are outlined. Land uses and activities which have a particular significance for biodiversity are then examined in turn under the headings: Farming; Woodlands and Forests; Built Development and the Urban Environment; the Coastal Zone; Harvesting from the Sea; Exploiting Wildlife for Sport; Recreation and Tourism; and Other Activities.

PRINCIPLES AND APPROACHES

6.4 To ensure that biodiversity objectives are incorporated into all levels of decision making, the Action Plans for achieving sustainable use within each sector draw upon a number of key principles and approaches. Many of these will have general application in relation to sustainability. This chapter should, therefore, be read in the context of the UK Strategy for Sustainable Development. Appropriate mechanisms will be put in place to ensure integration in the implementation of the two plans.

Long term policy integration

6.5 Objectives for biodiversity should reflect the contribution each activity can make to the achievement of biodiversity goals. Very often, biodiversity goals can be achieved alongside other uses of land or water, with little need to compromise primary objectives. In forestry, for example, woodland is managed increasingly for conservation and amenity alongside the purpose of timber production; and water supply reservoirs can provide valuable freshwater habitats and are attractive to wildfowl.

6.6 Integration of environmental objectives across all sectors requires close cooperation between Government departments. Government departments and agencies ensure that biodiversity objectives are taken into account when developing policies and programmes. Progress is reported in the annual Environment White Paper.

Article 10 of the Convention on Biological Diversity says:

'Each Contracting Party shall, as far as possible and as appropriate:
a) Integrate consideration of the conservatrion and sustainable use of biological resources into national decision making;

b) Adopt measures relating to the use of biological resources to avoid or minimise adverse impacts on biological diversity;

c) Protect and encourage customary use of biological resources in accordance with traditional cultural practices that are compatible with conservation or sustainable use requirements;

d) Support local populations to develop and implement remedial action in degraded areas where biological diversity has been reduced; and

e) Encourage co-operation between its governmental authorities and its private sector in developing methods of sustainable use of biological resources.'

6.7 When considering the levels of use a given area or resource system is able to sustain, an understanding of its environmental capacity or carrying capacity is important. This represents the amount of use the area or resource is able to sustain without damage to its important environmental features, based on its natural or physical properties. Very often, this capacity cannot be readily defined in absolute terms, and may be dynamic in the sense that it can be increased through sound resource management or decreased through poor management. Once the capacity of an area or resource has been established, appropriate forms of management can be introduced to ensure that use is kept within sustainable limits, and remedial measures can be agreed and implemented should these limits be exceeded. This principle can be applied to many aspects of resource management; for example, the volume of recreational use an area can withstand without unacceptable physical damage or the sustainable quantity of water that can be abstracted from rivers or aquifers.

6.8 In order to define environmental capacity, it is necessary to have a sound understanding of how robust populations and ecosystems are to land use changes and other impacts. However, in many cases the interactions are complex and our knowledge of natural systems is incomplete. In line with the precautionary principle (see glossary) the interactions are complex and where the available evidence suggests that there is a significant chance of damage to our biodiversity heritage occurring, conservation measures are appropriate even in the absence of conclusive scientific evidence that the damage will occur.

Demand management

6.9 Managing the demand for natural resources is one of the fundamental measures through which society can move towards a more sustainable way of life. When considering developments affecting biodiversity, an important option for central and local government and its regulatory agencies is to consider whether the demand for the activity or product should be limited through pricing or regulatory measures. A coherent framework of incentives, charges and fiscal measures can help to influence consumer behaviour together with public information and awareness campaigns.

Reflecting environmental costs and the polluter pays principle

6.10 Environmental consequences need to be incorporated fully into decision making processes, and particularly into the cost-benefit analysis of major new projects, to enable fully informed decisions to be taken. Those who impose environmental costs on society through environmental damage, or their use of important environmental resources, should strive to minimise such costs and/or compensate for them, either through environmental enhancement or through direct financial payments. This is known as the polluter pays principle.

MAJOR ACTIVITIES WHICH IMPACT UPON BIODIVERSITY

6.11 Society in considering many industrial and commercial processes essential to modern living may fail to place a sufficiently high value on conserving biodiversity, particularly for those processes which consume scarce natural resources, cause pollution or involve the direct loss of wildlife habitats. Examples include the use of water resources, the generation and use of energy, and transport systems, particularly roads and their associated traffic. The main impacts on biodiversity arising from these three key sectors are discussed briefly below. The UK Strategy for Sustainable Development considers these and other related issues in greater detail.

Water

6.12 The use of water for domestic, agricultural and industrial processes can affect biodiversity in a variety of ways. During prolonged periods of low rainfall many rivers naturally dry out from their headwaters especially during late summer and autumn. This was apparent in the recent drought affecting eastern and southern England that lasted intermittently over a wide area between November 1988 and February 1992. In many rivers the problems were compounded by excessive river and groundwater abstractions for domestic supplies and agriculture, leaving stretches of depleted and even dried up rivers, lakes and wetlands. This had a serious and added impact on freshwater ecosystems and other wetland habitats such as marshes and water meadows already stressed by drought.

6.13 The National Rivers Authority is charged under the Water Resources Act 1991 with promoting 'the conservation of flora and fauna which are dependent upon the aquatic environment'. As a consequence it identified 40 rivers in England and Wales with low flows excessively depleted by abstractions. In March 1993 it reported on progress achieved in restoring flows in these rivers.

6.14 There are a variety of options available for promoting new water resources. These include inter-regional transfers by river, canal or pipeline; new or enlarged reservoirs;

reducing leakage; river regulation by intermittent groundwater abstraction and additional groundwater development. In some areas a combination of these may be proposed. Water resource developments can have a positive or negative effect on biodiversity, and the National Rivers Authority, in providing a licence for such schemes in England and Wales, can select the most appropriate and take account of environmental considerations.

Survey of the impacts of a sewage discharge in a small stream.

6.15 Aquatic diversity is also affected by point or diffuse pollution arising from a number of sources such as effluent from sewage treatment works and industrial processes, runoff from agricultural chemicals or farm waste and chemical spills. When groundwater becomes polluted the contaminants may persist for some time, with the result that spring flows can be polluted for many months. Problems include low dissolved oxygen levels, high nitrate and pesticide concentrations, mine drainage and fuel spills.

6.16 Action to control individual forms of pollution remains essential. However the cumulative impact of these is what counts in the final analysis, in maintaining the ability of our freshwaters to support a natural diversity of life. The regulatory controls now in place and the investment programmes under way will help to sustain this. New monitoring techniques will also be used to make direct assessments of the biological quality of water. Data from the Countryside Survey 1990 indicate that 89% of the sites surveyed were of good or fair environmental quality (according to the classification system used for the purposes of this survey), as indicated by their macro-invertebrate assemblages.

6.17 Over the next twenty years a number of important factors will help to maintain and further improve overall freshwater quality and lead to further reductions in the levels of dangerous substances, nitrates and eutrophication. The establishment of independent environmental regulators,

in the form of the NRA, Scottish River Purification Authorities (SRPAs) and DWI, has already led to a tighter regulatory regime. Further progress will take place through the implementation of existing domestic legislation on pollution, the implementation of EC Directives and action to meet other international commitments.

Energy

6.18 Most systems for producing, transmitting and using energy have a direct or indirect impact on biodiversity, particularly those associated with electricity generation and transport. The combustion of fossil fuels to produce energy releases Carbon Dioxide into the atmosphere – the main cause of the greenhouse effect. If it is established that climate change is likely to result from greenhouse gas emissions, there will be significant implications for biodiversity. Changes in the distribution and composition of plant communities are predicted.

The combustion of fossil fuels to produce energy releases carbon dioxide into the atmosphere – the main cause of the greenhouse effect.

New climatic conditions may favour colonisation by new species and the loss of others which are unable to adapt.

6.19 The burning of fossil fuels also results in acid deposition, which can damage some ecosystems, particularly in upland forests and lakes although improvements may be expected to result from the implementation of existing international agreements and the gradual impact of integrated pollution control.

6.20 Technologies employed in the generation and supply of electricity can have a direct impact on biodiversity through land use, particularly power stations and related infrastructure. Generally, new and renewable energy resources confer great environmental benefits by displacing fossil fuels and some, such as short rotation coppice, can have a beneficial effect on biodiversity.

6.21 The Government fully recognises the links between energy use and biodiversity and, as part of its commitment to sustainable development, will ensure that energy policy has proper regard to its environmental committments including those on biodiversity.

6.22 The Government will continue to promote strongly the efficient use of energy. Renewable energy will continue to be supported through the Non-Fossil Fuel Obligation and the Government will support research into cleaner forms of coal fired generation for electricity. Planning controls and other regulatory measures will continue to ensure that the planning and management of power stations and other energy-related installations is carried out in accordance with the Government's environmental commitments.

Transport

6.23 Growth in transport, especially road transport, has a significant impact on the environment. Road construction and the upgrading of existing roads can cause loss of, and damage to, wildlife habitats and wider landscape features. These impacts occur directly through the use of land and indirectly through increasing demand for construction aggregates and pressures generated for development alongside the roads.

6.24 Car travel in Great Britain has increased dramatically in the past 40 years. Between 1977 and 1987 alone, road traffic volumes increased by 41%. The Department of Transport forecasts that traffic will continue to increase by a further 84% to 142%, depending upon the rate of economic growth, by 2025. It is recognised that such a rate of growth cannot be accommodated entirely through new capacity. Large scale upgrading of the road network in the countryside could on the basis of these trends have a damaging impact on biodiversity, unless it were very carefully managed. The Government is pursuing a range of measures to reduce the environmental impact of transport and influence the rate of traffic growth.

Car travel in GB has increased dramatically in the past 40 years. Road construction can damage widlife habitats and landscape features.

6.25 The Government will take full account of the implications for biodiversity when formulating and reviewing its transport policies and will ensure that biodiversity objectives are fully incorporated into assessment and benefits of new transport infrastructure.

6.26 Traffic and tourism management schemes which aim to manage access to environmentally sensitive areas can only play a valuable role. These can also encourage forms of transport such as walking and cycling which have less widespread impacts on the environment.

6.27 Through its planning policy guidance to local authorities, the Government will ensure that the land use planning system takes account of the implications for travel demand when determining the location of new development. This will help to ensure that new housing, retailing and industrial developments will, where possible, be accessible by foot, bicycle or public transport, so minimising the need to travel by car.

BIODIVERSITY AND LAND USE

Farming

Significance for biodiversity

6.28 Almost 77% of the UK land surface is in farming use. Agriculture is, therefore, a key determinant of biodiversity, and farmers and landowners are key partners in implementing measures to further biodiversity. Today's countryside has been shaped and maintained largely by farming activities, and most semi-natural areas are managed with agricultural production as a prime motivation. However, changes in farming practices have reduced the value to wildlife of many farming areas, despite the fact that many farmers and landowners are very conscientious about conservation matters.

6.29 Within the relatively small area of the UK there is a great diversity of farming types. This reflects our varied climate, geology, soils and local traditions. Each farming type makes its own contribution to biodiversity, and many habitats and species depend upon traditional agricultural practices for their survival. Agricultural habitats may be highly diverse at the local level. Others may have relatively low local biodiversity, but nonetheless support unusual assemblages of species, which are nationally or internationally rare, and therefore contribute to global biodiversity.

6.30 Maintaining biodiversity can have commercial benefits for agriculture. For example, biological pest control – which has been developed through an

Biodiversity has played a vital role in enabling agriculture to develop to its current productive state.

understanding of ecosystems and predator/prey relationships – has in some cases allowed a reduction in the use of pesticides. An attractive countryside, rich in wildlife, is also a basis for farm diversification through the growth in farm tourism, and can bring benefits to the wider rural economy.

6.31 Biodiversity has played a vital role in enabling agriculture to develop to its current productive state. Genetic variation has allowed plant breeders to select desirable characteristics and manipulate plant character and productivity. Maintaining genetic diversity will be a significant factor in the stability and future development of agriculture, while modern biotechnology is likely to lead to the cultivation of new crops and crop strains for food and industrial use. On the other hand, a reduction in the variety of crops and livestock may result in greater vulnerability to disease and pest attack.

Threats and opportunities

6.32 There are three main concerns:
● the continuing loss and fragmentation of habitats such as chalk grassland, heather moorland, hay meadows and wetlands, as a result of such factors as intensified farming practices, land drainage and abstraction of water and road construction;
● the loss of habitats, linear features such as hedgerows, field margins and ditches, and individual species resulting from neglect or abandonment, and from the decline of traditional forms of management as they become increasingly uneconomic and difficult to sustain;
● damage to soils, water and ecosystems caused by inappropriate use of fertilisers and pesticides and atmospheric pollution.

Chalk grasslands depend upon traditional agricultural practices for their survival.

6.33 Biodiversity is enhanced by policies which encourage land management practices which produce benefits for wildlife. The aim of such policies are to:
● protect and maintain existing wildlife features and habitats which are important for biodiversity;
● enhance the wildlife value of farmland which is of low biodiversity at present;
● take advantage of opportunities to establish new, permanent areas of conservation value, especially when identifying alternative uses for agricultural land.

6.34 Opportunities for enhancing biodiversity include:
● recognising and strengthening those regional and local farming and land management practices that enhance the national diversity of flora and fauna, habitats, landscapes, historical features and character, and which will help to strengthen links between land use and local community identity;
● improving livestock management to minimise pollution from wastes and establishing stocking densities on moors, heaths and semi-natural grasslands which are related more closely to the environmental carrying capacity of the land;
● improving crop management to reduce the need for fertilisers and pesticides;
● encouraging the use of traditional, long established livestock breeds and crop varieties which are adapted to the climate and topography of each region;
● recognising the importance of those traditional skills and practices used by those who manage land, and upon which many valued habitats depend.
● introducing greater diversity on the farm, for example through the encouragement of reversion of arable land to pastoral use in appropriate areas and the wider use of rotations in arable farming;
● maintaining hedges, where possible and appropriate to the area concerned;

GOVERNMENT FARMING AND CONSERVATION PROGRAMMES

Environmentally Sensitive Areas (ESAs)

Run by the territorial agricultural departments, this scheme is targeted on areas of high conservation value. It provides incentives to farmers and crofters to protect and enhance environmental features of their land and to prevent damage to landscapes and wildlife which might result from some types of agricultural intensification.

Countryside Stewardship Scheme and Tir Cymen

Run by the Countryside Commission and the Countryside Council for Wales these schemes are pilot projects offering a flexible system of incentives to farmers and land managers to conserve, enhance and in some instances recreate, selected important landscapes and their wildlife habitats in England and Wales.

Wildlife Enhancement Scheme

The aim of the Wildlife Enhancement Scheme is to develop a new and more positive working relationship with owners and occupiers and to make full use of their land management skills and experience of local conditions. English Nature launched this three year pilot scheme in 1991. By the end of March 1993 the scheme had been extended to cover four areas.

An essential part of the scheme requires land managers to record what they have done on the land in a way that can be used by English Nature. This information is then used to fine tune management practices in the light of experience to achieve the best results for wildlife. Under the scheme a straightforward management agreement and management plan is agreed with English Nature in return for a fixed annual payment which reflects the additional costs of managing the SSSI for wildlife. Provision is also made for fixed cost works such as fencing which are needed to allow grazing for conservation purposes.

Farm and Conservation Grant Scheme

Run by the territorial agricultural departments this scheme allows grants to be paid to farmers for capital works which have an environmental value including traditional field boundaries and shelter belts, and heather management.

Farm Woodland Premium Scheme

Run by the territorial agricultural departments, this scheme offers incentives to farmers to plant and maintain primarily broad-leaved woodlands on farms, thereby contributing to biodiversity and providing other environmental benefits.

The Hedgerow Incentive Scheme

Run by the Countryside Commission, this scheme offers incentives to secure the long-term well-being and environmental value of threatened hedgerows, through the re-introduction of beneficial management.

In addition to these economic incentives, free technical advice is made available for farmers on pollution and conservation issues, in the form of on-farm visits and Codes of Practice, for example on Good Upland Management and on Good Agricultural Practice for the Protection of Water, Air and, shortly, Soil. Where necessary, regulations are also used to provide essential environmental safeguards, in connection with, for example, the approval of pesticides and the storage of slurry and agricultural fuelled oil. Underpinning all these initiatives is the Government's R&D programme, designed to improve our understanding of the complex interactions between UK agriculture and the environment (£67 million in 1992/3).

- withdrawing from productive agriculture altogether in selected areas and allowing natural succession to take its course.

Current policy and practice

6.35 The Government is working to integrate agricultural and environmental objectives and has introduced a range of programmes designed to conserve and enhance wildlife habitats in the farmed countryside (see box). They are targeted at selected areas and habitats and will help to secure biodiversity objectives.

6.36 The 1992 agreement reforming the Common Agricultural Policy includes new Community measures (EC 2078/92 Agri-Environment Regulations) for the promotion of environmentally friendly agriculture. The Government has announced programmes for England, Scotland, Wales and Northern Ireland. These include an expansion of the Environmentally Sensitive Areas Scheme, the existing Countryside Stewardship and Tir Cymen schemes, new Nitrate Sensitive Areas, and new schemes for the

Opportunities for enhancing biodiversity include encouraging the use of traditional, long established livestock breeds that are adapted to the climate and topography of each region.

improvement of heather moorland, the creation or improvement of selected wildlife habitats over a 20 year period, conversion to organic farming, and public access within ESAs and on set-aside land. The Government has also introduced a range of management options for non-rotational set-aside land designed to encourage the use of this land for specific conservation purposes, and has made revisions recently to Hill Livestock Compensatory Allowances to discourage environmentally damaging overstocking of upland areas.

Issues to be addressed

6.37 The Government initiatives described above have been widely welcomed and have had some success in reducing the loss of habitats and species and creating new wildlife areas. The measures proposed in the Agri-Environment Programme will help further. Even so, environmental incentives remain a relatively small part of agricultural support. The Government has therefore been seeking to integrate environmental considerations into agricultural support measures and has successfully done so in a number of areas. For example, in addition to changes already made to the Hill Livestock Compensatory Allowances, environmental considerations have been incorporated into the new EC set-aside arrangements. A change has been secured in the EC support arrangement for suckler cows to permit Member States to incorporate environmental conditions, and the Council of Ministers has asked the EC Commission to propose similar changes in the other livestock support payments. Further opportunities will be pursued as they arise.

Action

- The Government will continue to promote further 'greening' of the CAP. While recognising the need to work within the framework of the reformed CAP, the Government will press for closer linkage between agriculture and environmental policies and objectives.

LOSS OF HEDGEROWS

Between 1984 and 1990 there was a net loss of 23% of hedges (about 130,000 km) in Great Britain. The net loss of hedges was the result of a combination of hedge removal and hedge degradation, and it occurred despite the planting/regeneration of about 50,000 km of hedges. In addition to the reduction in the extent of this important linear habitat, there was also a lost of quality. Between 1978 and 1990, on average one plant species was lost from each 10 metres of hedge, an 8% loss of plant species diversity.

- Existing financial incentives to encourage environmentally sensitive forms of agriculture will continue to be monitored to ensure they are having positive effects on the habitats and landscapes targeted and are thus contributing to biodiversity objectives. The new incentive schemes planned under the agri-environment programme will be tailored to complement existing schemes and will similarly be kept under review.
- Regulations controlling the use and storage of environmentally damaging pesticides and fertilisers will continue to be strictly enforced, and, if necessary, new measures will be introduced.
- The Government will support organic farming and encourage more extensive livestock farming in selected areas.
- Government research on environmental management will be expanded and support and advice will continue to be available to farmers to help them to identify and adopt environmentally beneficial management practices which will conserve, and where practicable, enhance wildlife habitats on their land.
- The Government will continue to support measures for hedgerow management and restoration in England.

The importance of dead wood should not be overlooked. It supports many species of fungi, mosses, lichens, insects and other invertebrates.

Woodlands and Forests

The remnants of natural forest cover are the most valuable and diverse and cannot be replaced.

Significance for biodiversity

6.38 Woodlands once naturally covered about two thirds of the land area of the United Kingdom. Clearance by man over thousands of years reduced this figure to about 5% by the turn of the century, but new planting since the first world war, stimulated by the Forestry Commission and the Department of Agriculture for Northern Ireland, has seen the woodland area expand to about 10% of the land surface. Much of the new woodland area comprises non-native, coniferous species, but the planting of broadleaved species has expanded significantly in the last few years.

6.39 All woodlands and forests have some value for wildlife. However, the remnants of the 'natural' forest cover (the ancient semi-natural woodland – defined as having existed since 1600) are the most valuable and diverse, and are of special importance because they cannot be replaced. In contrast, recently planted woodlands are less diverse, immature ecosystems, though they can add greatly to the biodiversity of a previously unwooded environment, especially where they are planted on land of low wildlife value. New woodlands that are established close to existing ancient, semi-natural woodland, and woodlands that follow closely the natural processes of succession, have the greatest potential benefit. Single trees and hedgerow trees also make an important contribution to biodiversity.

6.40 The great variation in climate and soils in the UK has produced regional and local variation in the types of semi-natural woodland, and in the plants and animals which they support. This diversity must be maintained. Our native tree species generally have greater value for biodiversity than recently introduced species, as illustrated by the greater number of insect species they support.

6.41 The importance of dead wood should not be overlooked. It supports many species of fungi, mosses, lichens, insects and other invertebrates, provides valuable nesting and roosting sites for birds and bats, while well-

INSECT SPECIES ASSOCIATED WITH COMMON TREES AND SHRUBS IN BRITAIN

Tree or shrub	Number of Insect species	Tree or Shrub	Number of Insect Species
Oak (pedunculate and sessile)	284	Hornbeam	28
Willow	266	Rowan	28
Birch	229	Maple	26
Hawthorn	149	Juniper	20
Blackthorn	109	Larch*	17
Poplar species	97	Fir*	16
Crab apple	93	Sycamore*	15
Scots Pine	91	Holly	7
Alder	90	Sweet chestnut*	5
Elm	82	Horse chestnut*	4
Hazel	73	Yew	4
Beech	64	Walnut*	4
Ash	41	Holm Oak*	2
Spruce*	37	Plane*	1
Lime	31		

Introduced species*

rotted wood is a useful seed bed to allow many woodland herbs and trees to establish.

Threats and opportunities

6.42 There are three main concerns:
- any further reduction in the area of ancient and semi-natural woodland, which already amounts to 15% of the total woodland area and is greatly fragmented;
- loss of biodiversity through inappropriate woodland management, or lack of management. There are significant areas of woodland whose value for timber production as well as for wildlife is deteriorating;
- failure of woodland regeneration due to over-grazing by sheep, deer and cattle. This is of particular concern in the Highlands, where deer grazing is causing deterioration of woodland and a reduction in the diversity of woodland flora, but it is also a growing problem in the lowlands where deer populations are increasing.

6.43 Biodiversity may be enhanced by:
- the conservation, restoration and appropriate management of the remaining areas of ancient and semi-natural woodland;
- sensitive management of other existing forests and woodlands, including the restructuring of even-aged plantations to introduce a diversity of species and age classes, the use of silvicultural techniques that seek to mimic natural processes, the incorporation of open space, the retention of old trees and dead wood, improved management of rides and riparian zones, the creation of woodland edge habitats and the removal of invasive species;
- creating new woodlands, especially in areas of low wildlife value;
- encouraging the use of native species of local provenance and, where possible, establishment through natural regeneration;
- promoting the use of good quality, local genetic hardwood stock where native broadleaved tree species are being planted, especially where timber quality and productivity are not prime objectives. Careful selection of seed sources will help to ensure that local genotypes are preserved and that trees being planted are well suited to local environments.

Current policy and practice

6.44 Forests and woodlands in the UK are an important source of raw materials for industry, currently producing some 7 million cubic metres of wood each year. This represents 15% of UK wood consumption. It is UK policy to ensure that this component of biodiversity is harvested in a way which sustains the forest's capacity for renewal. Wood production is regulated by the Forestry Commission (Department of Agriculture in Northern Ireland). Conditions attached to felling licences (not required in Northern Ireland) ensure that forests are allowed to regenerate or are replanted following felling and that operations are conducted in a way that safeguards the environment.

6.45 In recent years, the value of trees in the landscape, for wildlife and for recreation has been recognised increasingly. In 1985, the Forestry Commission was given a statutory duty to balance the interests of forestry and the environment. The Department of Agriculture for Northern Ireland pursues a similar aim. Government forestry policy is now based firmly on multiple-purpose objectives. These include the protection, management and creation of woods and forests, landscape and wildlife conservation, the provision of recreation and access, and protection of water quality and soil fertility.

6.46 In the growing forest, opportunities to enhance wildlife and biodiversity are present in all stages of management. The Forestry Commission and Department of Agriculture for Northern Ireland provide training for forest managers to enable these opportunities to be realised and have published woodland management guidelines. They are conducting research into opportunities for enhancing biodiversity and will provide further guidance to forest managers.

Issues to be addressed

6.47 The UK Sustainable Forestry Programme, which pulls together the various strands of the Government's forestry policy, includes the aim of a steady expansion of tree cover. This also serves biodiversity objectives, provided that it is not at the expense of other threatened and valuable areas of natural and semi-natural vegetation. This includes encouraging the establishment of new woodlands close to areas of population in order to provide opportunities for recreational enjoyment and raise environmental qualtiy.

Urban forests can enhance the quality of urban living and raise awareness of the importance of trees in the environment.

6.48 Government policy is to encourage owners to rehabilitate neglected woodlands, for example by erecting fencing to prevent over-grazing and thus stimulate regeneration, and by reintroducing coppice management. Better marketing of traditional woodland produce, and hardwoods generally, is required.

Action

- Implement the biodiversity aspects of Sustainable UK Forestry Programme.
- Continue to protect ancient semi-natural woodlands and encourage forms of management which conserve their special characteristics.
- Continue to encourage the regeneration of woodland.
- Encourage the restructuring of even-aged plantations to create more varied forests with a mixture of types and ages of trees, including the implementation of forest design plans in state forests.
- Continue to encourage a steady expansion of woodland and forest cover.
- Encourage the extension and creation of native woodlands, including extending the area of Forestry Commission Caledonian Forest (native pine and broadleaves).
- Support the creation of community woodlands near population centres.
- Support the creation of a new National Forest in the English Midlands and the creation of multi-purpose woodlands in Scotland's central belt through the Central Scotland's Woodlands Initiative.
- Government will continue to encourage urban tree planting and care through research, support to voluntary organisations, and urban regeneration initiatives.

Built Development and the Urban Environment

Significance for biodiversity

6.49 About 10% of the land surface of the UK is in urban use. Development is by no means continuous and within urban areas there is much open land in parks, open spaces, road corridors, private gardens and other areas which contribute to biodiversity, and with appropriate management could enhance it.

6.50 Many urban areas contain relics of natural habitats which have survived development. They are also the home of many exotic species which make their own contribution to biodiversity. Parks and private gardens can be important for wildlife and are the main day to day contact points with wildlife for most of the population. Given the right conditions, wildlife can thrive in towns. This can help to raise awareness of the natural world and a concern for its conservation.

Parks and gardens can be important for wildlife and are the main day to day contact points with wildlife for most of the population.

Threats and opportunities

6.51 Development has a direct impact on biodiversity when it damages or destroys valuable wildlife habitats. Although protection of the environment can be a constraint to development in many cases, adequate provision must be made for essential development, such as new housing, work places and transport infrastructure. It is Government policy that effective use should be made of derelict and under-used land in urban areas. However, care must be taken with urban open spaces which have value as wildlife habitats. Development in rural areas will continue to be necessary and care must be taken to avoid the threats which this could pose to valuable wildlife interests and biodiversity.

6.52 Where new development takes place, much can be done to enhance biodiversity through landscaping and habitat creation. There are opportunities to create new urban 'wildspace' within existing built up areas through introducing more imaginative, conservation-based approaches to the management of parks, other public open spaces and road verges. Householders can also take action to enhance the biodiversity of their own gardens. The

An example of a good urban pond.

contribution of the land use planning system to meeting biodiversity objectives is considered in Chapter 4.

Current Policy and practice

6.53 The town and country planning system is designed to regulate the development and use of land in the public interest, guiding appropriate development to the right place, preventing unacceptable development, and ensuring that, where permitted, development takes place in an environmentally sensitive manner. By preventing unnecessary urbanisation of the countryside, the planning system has helped to protect biodiversity, and will continue to do so.

6.54 Local authorities are responsible for drawing up development plans, which establish the framework for development in their areas and set out the policies against which applications for planning permissions are judged. By amending the Town and Country Planning Acts, Parliament has emphasised the importance of development plans, by requiring development control decisions to accord with the development plan unless material considerations indicate otherwise. In its advice on the content of development plans, the Government has made clear its intention to work towards ensuring that development is sustainable. The Government also intends to ensure that biodiversity objectives are taken into account in the land use planning system, and that appropriate policies to protect biodiversity are incorporated into development plans. Local authorities are encouraged to undertake an environmental appraisal of the policies contained in development plans. Advice is currently being prepared on techniques and good practice.

Issues to be addressed

6.55 There are two key issues to address:
- How to ensure that development does not affect key environmental resources adversely, so that where new development has to take place loss of biodiversity is avoided or minimised;
- How to enhance biodiversity in existing open spaces.

Action

- The Government will encourage local authorities to make reasonable provision for Local Nature Reserves and natural green space in local plans and environmental charters.
- The Government will continue to support voluntary sector initiatives aimed at enhancing the conservation value of urban and urban fringe land, for example, further support will be given to the Groundwork Trust movement, enabling more urban trusts to be established,

ENVIRONMENTAL ASSESSMENT

The Government is committed to ensuring that all proposed developments likely to have significant effects on the environment are thoroughly assessed before being allowed to go ahead. Under regulations which implement the European Communities Directive on 'Environmental Impact Assessment', certain types of project must be subject to an Environment Assessment (EA) in every case. For certain other categories of project, EA is required where the particular proposal would be likely to have significant environmental effects. Approximately 300 developments are subject to EA each year in the UK.

The objective of EA is to take environmental considerations into account as early as possible in the planning and design of a project so that adverse effects can be avoided. Where such effects cannot be avoided, the aim is to minimise or offset them. When EA is required, the developer must prepare an Environmental Statement (ES) setting out his assessment of the environmental effects of the project and the measures proposed to avoid, minimise or mitigate any adverse effects. The public is given an opportunity to comment and environmental authorities such as English Nature, the Countryside Commission and Her Majesty's Inspectorate of Pollution (or their equivalents in Scotland, Wales and Northern Ireland) are consulted. Where, rarely, a project is likely to affect the environment of another member of the Community, that state is also invited to comment. Before reaching a decision, the authority responsible for deciding whether or not to grant development consent (usually the planning authority) must take into account the ES, and the comments of the environmental authorities, the public and, if applicable, any other EC state consulted.

The UK is committed to an effective and efficient system of EA. The Government has published guidance on criteria and thresholds to help local planning authorities decide whether or not a proposed development should be subject to EA. It plans to publish guidance to developers on good practice in the preparation of Environmental Statements, to help improve their standards. There will be further guidance to planning authorities on the evaluation of the environmental information (the ES and the comments of the statutory consultees and the public).

In 1991, a Convention on Environmental Impact Assessment in a Transboundary Context was adopted at Espoo in Finland. There are currently 29 signatories which include the European Community and all 12 Member States. The Convention will enter into force 90 days after ratification by 16 states. It is envisaged that the Community and its Member States will ratify simultaneously. The Convention applies to 17 categories of major development which may have transboundary environmental effects. Where such a development is proposed which is likely to have significant adverse effects on the environment of one country, the Convention will provide for the environmental authorities and public in the affected country to be involved in the EIA process (where both states are parties to the Convention).

and to the Royal Society for Nature Conservation to enable it to extend its 'Environment City' scheme in cooperation with local authorities.

The Coastal Zone

Significance for biodiversity

6.56 The UK has the most diverse coastline in Europe, ranging from the rocky coasts of the south west peninsula and south west Wales to the chalk coasts of south east England, the low lying soft coasts of East Anglia, the sea lochs of western Scotland and the basalt and limestone cliffs of Northern Ireland. It is also extensive. When all the tidal inlets and larger islands are included, it is approximately 15,000 km long, longer in relation to land area than most other countries.

6.57 The extent and variety of the UK coastline has resulted in rich assemblages of plant and animal species, and many habitats of international importance. Our estuaries are especially significant, since these form over a quarter of the estuarine resource of western Europe. Internationally, the UK has a particular responsibility for conserving its estuaries for their bird populations, though they are also important for their prolific marine plant and invertebrate life, as fish spawning and nursery grounds, and for populations of larger animals such as seals and otters. Rock and chalk coastlines, whilst not so diverse as soft coasts, also support many species rarely seen elsewhere in Europe.

Threats and opportunities

6.58 There are a number of threats to biodiversity within the coastal zone. These include:

- pressures on coastal habitats arising from built development (including coastal engineering projects such as sea defences and barrages), mineral extraction (oil, gas and aggregates), recreation and tourism.
- rising sea levels, which, taken together with coastal squeeze are contributing to a significant loss of coastal habitats;
- pollution, including organic enrichment from sewage and fertiliser run-off, chemicals, oils and antibiotics.

6.59 The adoption of soft engineering approaches to coastal defence, and in appropriate cases setting back the line of defences (through a policy of managed retreat) provides an opportunity to create new coastal habitats. These may go some way to replacing those lost through development, erosion or sea level rise.

COASTAL SQUEEZE

Recent research has shown that saltmarshes in Essex (which has more saltmarsh than any other county in England) have lost, on average, almost a quarter of their area in the past 15 years. Over the last 200 years, British estuaries have lost between 0.2% and 0.7% of their mud flats, sand flats and saltmarshes every year; an estimated 0.5% of the remaining area was under active land claim in 1989. A five-year survey found that more than half of our sand dune systems are moving landward, probably starved of sediment once supplied by eroding cliffs. Most of the remainder are stationary, instead of growing to seaward. The total picture is of a coastline where natural processes are being altered by man's use, and habitats and landforms are being eroded or fixed at one stage of their development. Everywhere, coastal features are being drowned, caught between man-made sea defences and rising sea levels in a process known as 'coastal squeeze'.

Saltmarsh at Chichester Harbour SSSI in West Sussex

Peter Wakely, English Nature

6.60 Conservation and enhancement of the coastal zone will be most effective if greater coordination can be achieved between those organisations responsible for managing inshore waters, the shoreline and the coastal fringe, and if there is closer integration in the management of the various coastal activities.

Current policy and practice

6.61 The Government is firmly committed to the effective planning and protection of the coastal zone. Recent planning policy guidance (PPG20 on Coastal Planning) makes it clear that the coast, particularly the undeveloped parts, will seldom be the most appropriate location for new major development, except where a coastal location is essential for that facility. Additional protection is afforded to coasts within National Parks and Areas of Outstanding Natural Beauty or which are defined as Heritage Coasts (in England and Wales).

6.62 Policies for coastal defence continue to confirm that protection of habitats will be central to the consideration of coastal defence schemes. There is a clear presumption that natural coastal processes should not be disrupted, except where life or important natural or man-made assets are at risk.

6.63 The Government intends to restrict the area licensed for marine aggregate extraction, in order to safeguard marine systems, sea fisheries and sediment movements.

Issues to be addressed

6.64 Responsibility for planning and managing activities within the coastal zone lies with many different organisations, each with different duties and responsibilities. This makes agreement on policies and priorities difficult to achieve. To address these issues, the Government has recently published two discussion papers, on regulating development below the low water mark and on the form and content of coastal zone management plans. These papers apply to England and Wales only, and form part of the Government's response to the House of Commons Select Committee report on Coastal Zone Protection and Planning.

Action

- The Government will consider responses to its recent discussion paper on the scope, where appropriate, for local authorites to prepare management plans to help reconcile competing activities in the coastal zone. Such plans should be drawn up in close consultation with all interested parties in the areas concerned, and should have full regard to the importance of conserving and enhancing biodiversity.

MILITARY USE

The Ministry of Defence owns some 240,000 Ha of land in the UK, with training rights over additional land, making it one of the largest land owners in the country. This estate contains examples of almost all the habitats found in the UK and hosts a wide diversity of flora and fauna. The fact that it contains some 220 SSIs is evidence of its importance for biodiversity.

An old tank now a target at the Ministry of Defence's training area on Salisbury Plain SSSI.

To fulfil training needs, the majority of military land is protected from many of the pressures experienced elsewhere in the countryside and is managed so as to maintain and create semi-natural habitats. The relative stability of most of the estate ensures that there is a national network of valuable wildlife sites. This makes an important contribution to maintaining biodiversity.

Changes in military priorities will mean changes in land use needs. For example, the withdrawal of troops from Germany will mean an increase in armoured tracked vehicles in the UK, with consequent increased pressures on training areas. In order to minimise the threat of damage to these areas, the MOD will be preparing long term management plans for its land holdings, in consultation with the statutory environment agencies.

- Conservation and enhancement of biodiversity is also an important consideration in the current Government review into the control of development below the low water mark.
- Further research will be undertaken to assess the scope for habitat creation through managed retreat. Finance is being made available to implement linked research projects around a full scale trial.
- In due course, the National Rivers Authority responsibilities for coastal water pollution control will be taken with them into the proposed new Environment Agency for England and Wales.

BIODIVERSITY AND SPECIES USE

Harvesting from the Sea

Significance for biodiversity

6.65 Some 75% of the Earth's surface is covered by oceans, which sustain a wider diversity of species than on land. The majority of these ecosystems are very isolated from man and his economic activities. The issue of sustainable use arises most particularly where marine biodiversity is exploited directly by commercial fishing.

6.66 The UK has a long history of harvesting the fish stocks found around its shores, and though the industry has declined

somewhat in recent years, it is still a large employer and is very important economically to local communities in certain coastal areas. The total catch by British vessels landed in the UK in 1992 was 567,000 tonnes, valued at about £400 million.

6.67 In recent years, fish farming has become increasingly important. In 1992 it registered a first sale value of £150 million.

6.68 Commercial exploitation of fish stocks interacts with the marine environment in many ways and has implications for other marine wildlife, habitats and ecosystems.

The UK has a long history of harvesting the fish stocks found around its shores.

Threats and opportunities

6.69 The current approach to fisheries management, as enshrined in the EC's Common Fisheries Policy (CFP), aims to conserve stocks in such a way as to ensure long-term sustainability. In doing so, the CFP requires the implications for the marine eco-system to be taken into account. The fisheries are managed through a mix of Total Allowable Catches and quotas, access arrangements and technical conservation arrangements involving controls on fishing gear and areas that can be fished. Despite this, many stocks remain under pressure.

6.70 The system of quotas and technical conservation measures has had a generally beneficial effect though some species are over-exploited and there is a problem of widespread discarding of undersized target species, non-target species and non-commercial species, which damages the fishery's long term prospects. These problems have been exacerbated by over-capacity within the EC fishing fleet. For some species, individual fish are not reaching maturity before being caught, and consequently are frequently small and below the age of maturity. Not only does this threaten the productive potential of the stock, in the longer term it may affect its genetic make up.

6.71 Despite the UK's good record in enforcing regulations, there are still problems with non-compliance. The deliberate catching of fish above quota levels and the landing of the resulting 'black fish' may also contribute to over exploitation.

6.72 Industrial fishing for small, pelagic species of fish, which are not generally used directly for human consumption, may also pose a threat to biodiversity. These species play an important role in the food chain and their decline might affect top predators and other fish. It has been suggested that there is a link between fishing for sand eels and the decline of many seabird species. The RSPB, together with the Scottish Office, are carrying out scientific work to see if there is any real link. However, the UK does not support the practice of industrial fishing, though there is no firm scientific basis to justify further restrictions than those already imposed by the CFP, either from the viewpoint of damage to human consumption fisheries or from disruption to the marine food chain though a precautionary TAC for sandeels may be a possible first step. The Government is continuing to press, within the EC, for further research to be undertaken in this area.

6.73 Certain fishing practices may cause physical damage to the sea bed and its communities. Such activity will tend to damage soft and brittle animals, and frequent fishing will favour the colonisation of the area by opportunistic feeders at the expense of larger long lived species. The Fisheries Departments in the UK are carrying out long term research in this area. Modern gears can be used in areas which hitherto could not be fished and may have acted as refuges. However, wrecks and, more recently, the exclusion zones around oil and gas installations continue to provide refuge areas for marine life.

6.74 Some vertebrates such as birds, seals and cetaceans may be caught in nets and drowned, although large ocean drift nets linked to cetacean mortalities are not used in Atlantic EC waters. In fact, most sea bird and seal populations have increased over the century and it is likely that the discarding of offal and unwanted fish from fishing vessels has contributed significantly to this increase.

6.75 Uncontrolled bait digging and shellfish collecting can have a direct impact upon biodiversity in some areas.

6.76 Threats from fish farming include organic enrichment of the surrounding environment, the transmission of diseases to wild fish populations, the introduction of toxic pesticides and antibiotics, genetic contamination of wild stocks arising from escaped farmed fish, and impacts upon predators, including entanglement in nets. At present, the degree of impact is uncertain, although insufficient research has been undertaken.

Current policies and practice

6.77 The Government's policy is to protect the marine environment and the fish in it from the effects of pollution and other adverse influences. The policy for managing and conserving exploitable sea fish stocks in the UK is guided by the CFP, the aim of which is to secure high catches from each stock while maintaining populations. The main means of achieving this is by setting annual weight quotas (Total Allowable Catch) for individual species and

The degree of impact of fish farms on the environment is uncertain.

particular areas. For each species, the UK is allocated a fixed proportion of the EC's total available catch. Fish are recorded on landing and no further fishing is permitted once the quota has been reached.

6.78 In addition, there are technical conservation rules which specify such things as mesh sizes and minimum landing sizes, and define areas where fishing is not permitted. The UK has pioneered the use of square mesh panels in fishing nets, which are particularly effective in allowing juvenile fish to escape, so that they can mature and breed. These have now been adopted by the EC and incorporated into Community wide regulations.

6.79 The UK has been in the forefront of international discussion on ways to minimise the capture of marine mammals in drift nets. As a result, there is now an EC regulation limiting the length of such nets. The UK Government is fully committed to its obligations to the International Whaling Commission and the North Sea and Baltic Agreement on small cetaceans.

6.80 In 1992, the Sea Fisheries (Wildlife Conservation) Act was passed. This requires the Government to take environmental aspects into account when regulating fisheries. Also in 1992, the CFP basic regulation was expanded to require account to be taken of implications for the marine eco-system.

Issues to be addressed

6.81 Marine fisheries are an important resource which needs to be managed sustainably so as to maintain fish stocks and avoid environmental damage. At present, fisheries policy is based primarily upon conserving fish stocks for commercial reasons. Less emphasis is given as yet to the impact on other species and the wider environment, and in many cases the full environmental impact of fisheries policies and practices is not fully understood. In view of this, the precautionary principle will be applied over both the level of exploitation and the methods used. Activities which could cause major damage to species' populations and ecosystems will be strictly controlled.

6.82 By its nature, harvesting of marine biological resources cannot be managed effectively by the UK Government alone. Fishermen from other EC countries will have an impact. Policies to conserve biodiversity must be integrated with those of other countries, particularly those within the EC.

6.83 Concerns about the impact of fishing on biodiversity cannot be restricted solely to commercial fish species, but must also consider other species within the marine environment which are affected directly and indirectly by commercial fishing.

6.84 The EC-wide enforcement of existing regulations needs to be improved. It is expected that the EC's new Control Regulation will be helpful in this respect.

6.85 Proposals to dredge for marine aggregates are controlled under the Government View procedure operated by DOE/Welsh Office/Scottish Office. This material makes an important contribution to the supply of aggregates. But the Government recognises that dredging may cause disturbance to fisheries and damage to the marine environment, particularly where there is a concentration of licences. In most cases an application for a production licence to dredge will need to be supported by an Environmental Statement which will cover the impact on the marine environment, sea fisheries and the potential effect on the coastline.

Action

- The Government will continue to promote development of the CFP and of national fisheries policies in ways which take proper account of the impact of fishing on, and preserves the biodiversity of, the marine environment.
- The Government will wish to help to reduce over-capacity in the UK fishing fleet through an effective, targeted decommissioning programme.
- The Government will ensure that fisheries research continues to provide, within available resources:
  - effective understanding of the natural processes that control the production and survival of fish and shellfish larvae;
  - the means of making accurate and timely assessments of fish stock numbers;
  - assessment of topical issues such as the interaction between towed gear and the sea bed.

Exploiting Wildlife for Sport

Significance for biodiversity

6.86 Field sports such as hunting, shooting, and certain forms of angling, which involve the killing of animals, have a direct impact on the populations of quarry species, and can have secondary impacts on other species. If exploitation is managed poorly, biodiversity may be affected adversely. Historically, there are many examples of species which have become extinct or endangered by over-hunting; particularly those whose populations have been reduced through habitat loss and other pressures.

6.87 Field sports have a long history in the UK and are enjoyed by a great many people. They also make an important contribution to maintaining rural employment and populations, particularly in Scotland.

6.88 Quarry species and the habitats upon which they and other species depend are important components of biodiversity. Managed sustainably, exploitation can bring conservation benefits, not just to the populations of quarry species but to other species which benefit from the creation and maintenance of wildlife habitats.

6.89 Hunting and shooting in particular influences the management of large areas of land. Many valuable wildlife habitats and landscape features are created or maintained through the actions of those managing sporting estates. For

Salmon fishing on the River Tay.

example, extensive upland areas are managed as heather moorland for grouse shooting or deer stalking, and providing game cover is a major reason for retaining and planting woods. Without field sports, it is arguable that many copses and spinneys would no longer exist.

6.90 This section is concerned with the ways in which field sports impinge upon biodiversity. The Government recognises that many people are concerned with moral and ethical arguments about the principle and practice of field sports; these, however, are primarily issues of animal welfare and animal rights rather than biodiversity, and do not fall within the scope of this Action Plan.

Threats and opportunities
6.91 Exploitation for sport gives rise to five main concerns for nature conservation:
- Without strict legal controls and sustainable forms of management, quarry species can become endangered. This may also have consequences for other dependent species.

- Hunting and shooting can impact upon non-quarry species. For example, wildfowling can disturb other birds.
- Poor management of quarry species can lead to the destruction and loss of habitat. For example, 'artificial' winter feeding and over-stocking has resulted in excessive populations of red deer in the Scottish highlands, causing damage to pine forests and preventing regeneration.
- The continuing use of lead shot for shooting releases lead into the environment, and this has particular implications for bird wildlife in wetlands.
- Artificial stocking of game species can affect populations of native species. For example, there is some concern that artificially stocked rainbow trout may be displacing native brown trout populations in parts of some rivers.

6.92 Legal predator control by game managers can assist the survival of rare and endangered species, particularly ground nesting birds such as the stone curlew, or the black tailed godwit. However illegal persecution, especially of raptors, remains a significant problem. It may be the principal factor limiting the distribution of threatened raptors (predatory birds).

Current policies and practice
6.93 Field sports are subject to a variety of statutory and voluntary controls. The killing or disturbance of certain protected species is prohibited; most shooting and fishing is confined to seasons; and for many species the method of exploitation is controlled. Several organisations representing field sports have issued Codes of Conduct to promote good practice among their members.

6.94 Responsibility for developing and managing salmon and freshwater fisheries rests with the National Rivers Authority in England and Wales, District Salmon Fishery Boards in Scotland and DANI in Northern Ireland. Populations of quarry fish species are managed in a variety

Extensive upland areas are managed as heather moorland for grouse shooting or deer stalking.

of ways, including controls over fishing methods, artificial breeding and stocking, anti-poaching measures and aquatic habitat management. River and lake anglers in England and Wales must obtain a rod licence.

6.95 The links between conservation and sport shooting have been recognised formally in a joint statement of common interest between the BASC and the former Nature Conservancy Council (NCC), issued in 1988. Work towards producing updated statements which will identify how shooting can increase its contribution to habitat management is progressing with the NCC's successor agencies.

6.96 The Government has set up a working party to develop strategies to phase out the use of lead shot over wetlands and introduce viable and effective non-toxic shot.

Issues to be addressed

6.97 Exploitation needs to be kept within sustainable limits and exploitation of non threatened species must be managed in their best interest. Population studies and regular monitoring are necessary to determine what levels of exploitation are sustainable, and should be a basis for any necessary controls. The Game Conservancy Trust has been involved in such monitoring since 1933.

6.98 Game management should, where possible, contribute to wider biodiversity objectives. Ways need to be found to channel more of the revenue generated from field sports into habitat and species conservation.

Action

- The Government will continue to give legal protection to threatened species and remains resolute in its determination to prohibit both the illegal persecution of protected species and the use of illegal means to control species which can be controlled.

Recreation and Tourism

Significance for biodiversity

6.99 This section is concerned with the enjoyment of biodiversity; its importance for recreation and tourism, the spiritual refreshment derived from it, and the contribution an understanding and appreciation of the natural world can make to protecting biodiversity.

6.100 Much of the countryside in the UK is of great beauty and is a focus for recreation and tourism. Our National Parks,

The information centre Yorkshire Dales National Park.

for example, receive over 100 million visits each year, while research for the British Tourist Authority indicates that overseas visitors are attracted as much by our varied landscapes as by our history and culture. The importance of the countryside near where people live, on the urban fringe for example, should also be recognised.

6.101 The geology and landforms of the UK countryside are remarkably diverse for its area, resulting in a great variety of habitats. Woodlands, moors, wetlands and coasts are particularly attractive to visitors, while other visitors to the countryside derive great pleasure from seeing wild flowers in profusion or unusual species. There is a strong interest in the UK in bird watching and wildlife photography, and new activities like butterfly watching are developing.

Threats and opportunities

6.102 The main threats to biodiversity lie elsewhere. Although excessive visitor pressures can be damaging, in practice this happens only at heavily used sites, as various studies into the effects of recreation on wildlife confirm. However, pressures can be significant locally. Examples of impact include wear and tear on some habitats from trampling, disturbance to moorland birds reducing breeding success at some sites, and disturbance to wildfowl in areas used for water sports. It is therefore important that noisy, disruptive and damaging activities are carefully managed.

6.103 Other threats arise from the fact that most recreational journeys are undertaken by car, which leads to increased traffic levels and road improvements, and from development pressures associated with tourism.

6.104 A concern for biodiversity should be a central theme in all countryside recreation and tourism initiatives. Recognition that natural areas are a recreational attraction

CULTURAL BENEFITS OF BIODIVERSITY

While the scientific and economic rationale for conserving biodiversity is important, the intrinsic value of plant and animal species should not be overlooked. The natural world enriches the quality of our lives in many ways and is an important cultural resource. For many people it has strong aesthetic and spiritual meanings, and can be a source of great enjoyment. People's knowledge that unspoilt, natural places exist, and their desire to conserve them even though they may have little direct contact with them themselves means the existence of the British countryside is important and valuable in itself.

Biodiversity is strongly linked to cultural diversity and identity. Human cultures are shaped to a large degree by the natural environment. Historically, biological resources have played an important part in local folklore and traditions. Plants form an integral part of many customs and rituals, and may be the source of superstitions. They have been celebrated in literature and in song, and are used frequently as a source of decoration for arts and crafts. Plants such as the field poppy, mistletoe and holly have strong symbolic associations, as do the English rose, the Welsh daffodil, the Scottish thistle and the Irish shamrock. Trees are often planted as memorials.

Preparing the May Queen's bower for Lustleigh's May Day ceremony, Lustleigh Community Orchard, Devon.

Plants and animals can contribute to the distinctiveness of a local area and help to instil a sense of place within local communities. Old trees often act as important landmarks or boundary markers. Areas may be characterised by particular plant species. Some species are so intimately associated with an area that they are reflected in place names. This cultural importance is also reflected in the variety of local names given to some wild plants.

If we wish to interest and involve the general public in conserving biodiversity, this cultural dimension is particularly important. Television and books can assist the appreciation of wildlife, but only direct experience can imbue a deeper understanding and appreciation of its richness, its intricacy and its vulnerability. Most importantly, direct contact with the natural world leads to support for policies to protect and enhance it.

can aid the case for their retention and proper management. Well managed recreation and tourism should be seen as a positive force; it brings economic benefits to rural areas and, potentially, to conservation. Through enjoying the countryside, visitors can learn about the richness of UK wildlife and the need for its conservation. This will help extend the constituency of individuals willing to support the conservation of biodiversity. An expression of this is the "conservation holiday", a growth market, where a week or more is spent undertaking conservation tasks.

Current policy and practice

6.105 The potential conflict between visitors to the countryside and the conservation of wildlife is recognised, and it is established policy, for National Parks, that where the two are in irreconcilable conflict conservation interests should prevail (the Sandford principle). Conflicts can normally be resolved through good management and the Government's recent Tourism and the Environment Task Force's Report 'Maintaining the Balance' illustrates examples of good practice. The location of appropriate tourism development will continue to be guided by the planning system. In PPG 21, the Government has provided guidance about the integration of tourism policies into development plans and the consideration of planning applications.

6.106 In rural areas the Government's aim is to promote small scale, sustainable forms of tourism, often known as green tourism. 'Principles for Tourism and the Countryside', published jointly by the Countryside Commission and the English Tourist Board, indicates the principles which should be followed.

Through enjoying the countryside, visitors can learn about the richness of UK wildlife and the need for its conservation.

Issues to be addressed

6.107 The tourism industry has a responsibility to ensure that people visiting areas which are environmentally sensitive do not destroy the things they have come to see. Indeed, those who benefit from tourism should contribute to the conservation of its greatest asset, the countryside itself, which is the foundation for much of the tourism in the UK. Approaches need to be found to encourage the tourism industry and visitors themselves to contribute to conservation efforts, either financially or in other ways.

6.108 More needs to be known about the impact of recreational activities upon biodiversity and ways in which damaging impacts can be reduced.

Action

- The Government will encourage the creation of more Tourism and Heritage Trusts, which have the potential to raise funds locally for conservation initiatives.
- Through its tourism agencies, the Government will continue to promote awareness and understanding of conservation issues within the tourism sector.
- The tourism industry will be encouraged to include more information about the need for environmental conservation in its promotional literature, and to develop the necessary skills to provide high quality information and interpretation, including information about local biodiversity.
- Research will continue to be undertaken through the Government's countryside agencies to increase understanding of the impact of disturbance on biodiversity and to develop visitor management techniques to reduce negative effects.

CHAPTER 7

PARTNERSHIP AND EDUCATION

INTRODUCTION

7.1 This chapter reviews the importance of environmental awareness and education, and how the general public can work in partnership with central and local government and its agencies. The themes of education, partnership and involvement are critical ones for a strategy which aims to conserve and enhance biodiversity. This chapter considers a range of proposals and highlights the need for a publicity campaign to support initiatives which promote local action to conserve and improve local biodiversity.

PARTNERSHIP

An agenda for supporting biodiversity

7.2 Building support for biodiversity calls for measures that range more widely than those which are directly concerned with nature conservation. These may include the values and attitudes that people apply to their everyday surroundings; the cultivated and constructed environment that they have created around themselves, and the practicalities of sustaining a lifestyle to which they feel entitled. These issues and the need to address them are discussed more fully in the Sustainable Development Strategy.

7.3 Public awareness and appreciation of biodiversity appears to be growing significantly as a result of a wide variety of initiatives. Government policy is seeking to strengthen and extend existing good practice, fill gaps, improve what is ineffective and give the participating bodies a sense of belonging to a national and international movement with well-defined aims and a common purpose.

7.4 Biodiversity is ultimately lost or conserved at the local level. Government policies create the incentives that facilitate or constrain local action. The agenda for action can be grouped, under the following headings:
- Action by communities;
- Action by supporting organisations;
- Action by informal education;
- Action by formal education;
- Action by Government.

Community action

7.5 As explained in Chapter 4 both protected areas, whether publicly or privately owned, and the wider countryside have a significant contribution to make to maintaining biodiversity. In addition to the role of public bodies and landowners the attitudes and actions of local communities have an important part to play in supporting these strategies. To exercise appropriate environmental care local people need motivation, education and training.

These qualities and the resources to sustain them have come to be known as capacity building. In this context it can be defined as the process through which people and organisations develop the skills necessary to manage their environment and development in a sustainable manner. It is as important in developed countries as in underdeveloped countries. Developed countries face a difficult task of re-examining and changing attitudes and values.

7.6 The word 'community' is used here for two kinds of association:
- a locality, the people who live there and the systems within which their lives are organised;
- groups of individuals who are associated through common responsibilities (such as landowners, parents), occupations (farmers, miners), cultures (ethnic, religious) or interests (bird-watchers, archaeologists, ramblers).

7.7 Communities of all kinds overlap, interact, sometimes cooperate and sometimes disagree. Resident communities have a fund of knowledge and understanding of their locality which may have been built up over generations. They may also have a strong commitment to maintain or improve its quality. Specialist communities have expert knowledge, experience, enthusiasm and links to specialised resources.

7.8 The starting point for promoting biodiversity is the resident community, calling on others for assistance

THE TREE WARDEN SCHEME

The Tree Council's Tree Warden Scheme is a good example of a local volunteer service. Tree wardens are volunteers whose task it is to encourage planting and other tree-related events at neighbourhood level. The philosophy is that action to protect our landscapes is most effective if taken by people on the spot, those who know their own localities intimately, and have most to gain from protecting and enhancing their immediate environment. To date about 4,500 wardens have been appointed, covering most parts of the country. Full training is given by the British Trust for Conservation Volunteers.

Tree wardens.

RURAL ACTION

Rural Action for the Environment is a scheme designed to help people to identify local environmental issues of concern to them, and to organise and carry out appropriate action themselves. It offers local project grants to local people and provides easy access to information and advice, supports training, helps in obtaining specialist professional and technical services and encourages the development of local support networks. The scheme is sponsored by the Countryside Commission, English Nature and the Rural Development Commission with the support of the DoE and five leading voluntary sector organisations.

according to the circumstances. Projects or schemes supporting biodiversity are likely to work best if they are divided into achievable stages and are seen to improve the local quality of life. They may be generated by members of the community or by local Government, residents' and tenants' associations, statutory environmental agencies, voluntary organisations and local volunteer services.

7.9 Community groups are well placed to:

- Compile and maintain inventories of local biodiversity;
- Prepare local databases incorporating not only species, ecosystems and distributions but also local names and traditional uses;
- Monitor changes, using local archives, old maps, old pictures, oral tradition and local memories, as well as a continuing programme of systematic observation;
- Make local improvements such as the reconstitution of local native vegetation and the development of community forests;
- Prepare and submit reports and evidence to bodies involved in local planning and conservation;
- Join networks that link local centres and groups with others elsewhere, and with other bodies concerned in fostering biodiversity.

Such activities may at some stage need the input of experts and resources from further afield.

Local distinctiveness

7.10 An aspect of biodiversity is the distinctive character of different localities across the country, brought about by differences in climate, geology, topography, vegetation,

SCHEMES THAT ENCOURAGE LOCAL DISTINCTIVENESS

There are already a number of initiatives that encourage local distinctiveness.

The voluntary organisation Common Ground has pioneered a community-based approach to a campaign for local distinctiveness based on all aspects of diversity whether natural or cultural.

English Nature also recognises these qualities, as they apply to natural features. English Nature is seeking local community involvement in identifying, within these Prime Biodiversity Areas which can become the focus for special management. Pilot schemes have been set up and strategies are being explored for ensuring community participation that will reflect local feelings and local experience.

The Countryside Council for Wales have sponsored Jigso in partnership with a number of other agencies. Its objectives are to encourage and facilitate community groups to carry out surveys in their area, to protect and enhance its character, describe its culture and traditions, identify deficiencies in services and inform planners and decision makers of local feelings. Guidance, technical assistance and support are offered for community appraisals and the compilation of local maps.

Dry stone walling, a traditional way of building field boundaries, contributes to the distinctive character of the Yorkshire Dales.

WHALEWATCHING

Many whale species are now recovering from centuries of depredation by commercial whalers. The UK is anxious to encourage sustainable use of cetaceans in a way which does not risk a return to the excesses of whaling. For that reason Government has strongly supported the development of whalewatching as a sustainable but non-lethal use of whales. Whalewatching is now a burgeoning global industry with an annual turnover of over £200 million. A UK led initiative succeeded in getting the industry recognised at the IWC Conference this year as an alternative use of whales.

husbandry, traditional building styles and cultural history. Over the years this diversity has been progressively diminished by changes in agriculture, forestry, road construction, standardised building styles and other forms of development. To help to reverse this trend local communities need to build pride in their own identity.

7.11 The celebration of local biodiversity can be promoted in many ways; through the media, tourism and through local Government policy. In the longer term it might also reflect the growing interest in building design in harmony with local landscape, materials and traditions. Cultivating a regard for diversity at community level, a consciousness of local identity and a realisation of the benefits that establishing a distinctive environmental identity may bring to the community, will help to re-emphasise the rôle of biodiversity in local culture. Common Ground's *Flora Britannica project, a people's cultural flora of Britain*, has collected local stories about Britain's wildflowers and is an excellent example of this perception.

Public desire to visit reserves is growing including the demand from schools and other institutions for learning facilities.

The rôle of the community in specific areas

Nature reserves

7.12 Nature conservation has traditionally been dominated by measures to protect rare species or habitats. Protected areas, in the form of nature reserves and SSSIs, continue to play a vital part in the conservation of biodiversity but they will be strengthened by the growing concern to prevent their isolation. The policies of both statutory and voluntary bodies responsible for reserves fully acknowledge the need for local cooperation. The recruitment of local help and advice in the management of reserves and in survey and monitoring work will help to develop a sense of local ownership for a valuable resource. This will be made easier, especially in the case of established reserves, if there is community interest in the importance of the site. Experience suggests that the most successful schemes are likely to be those for which the community feels a strong sense of ownership.

7.13 The value of an informed and sympathetic public should be an integral part of a nature reserve's management plan. The plan will need to take account of at least four possible sets of people – the area management, the local residents, visitors from outside attracted to the area and the wider society to which they all belong. Each of these learns inevitably from each of the others and the plan should aim to guide all learning pathways in support of good management.

7.14 Public desire to visit reserves is growing including the demand from schools and other institutions for learning facilities. Where increased visiting is incompatible with the management of a high quality site there is a need to develop other comparable sites for educational use to take the pressure off national reserves.

7.15 Due to a less good knowledge about the nature and life of our seas, the complexity of the habitats, their sensitivity to damage and the complexity of legislation relating to them, time and effort is needed to raise awareness and local understanding in support of marine biodiversity.

Urban areas

7.16 Biodiversity is a concern for the whole population, of whom 80% live in towns and cities. The promotion of biodiversity in urban communities requires a different kind of approach. Here there is considerable scope for biodiversity to be seen as an element of good quality in urban living.

7.17 There is already a growing understanding of the rôle of urban green space. Many urban local authorities now employ

Local people examining pavement lichens.

ecologists, the conservation agencies have become actively involved in urban ecology and there are many urban wildlife groups. This is now influencing local planning and development, for example, wildlife habitat is being encouraged on vacant sites and abandoned railway lines to which public have access, and more natural vegetation is being introduced into traditional parks and open spaces. Where these locations are close to city schools they provide an important educational opportunity for school groups and voluntary organisations to participate in their creation and management. The adoption of local environmental planning and its subjection to regular audit should raise public awareness of sites which require vigilance to protect them from damage or destruction.

7.18 Chapter 4 describes how the re-establishment of woodland and wetlands in and around urban areas is becoming a recognised strategy in urban planning. However, this is not the only way of developing urban biodiversity. A greater awareness is already growing of the value of urban gardens as wildlife habitat and much guidance is now available to householders on how to make their gardens more attractive to wildlife. Even where there are no gardens the use of walls and rooftops for growing a variety of plants is an approach now used in some continental cities, and good advice about how to do this wisely is now being prepared in this country. Recognition that an increase in urban vegetation will improve the health of the city as well as its beauty is another important educational message.

The rôle of local authorities

7.19 Local authorities provide the main framework within which environmental care is organised at local level and public attitudes to the environment cultivated. This is done through:
- strategic and local planning;
- community, youth and school education;
- environmental health;
- open space and recreation management;
- transport and other services;
- the deployment of staff and funding in support of public and voluntary sector activity;
- leadership and mobilisation of community views and action.

7.20 Local authority awareness of environmental concerns has been expressed in a growing number of ways including:

- environmental charters and policy statements;
- environmental committees;
- environmental forums;
- in Scotland, support of the Regional Environmental Education Forums (REEFs);
- appointing ecologists to their staff;
- initiating training programmes for employees;
- publishing strategies;
- undertaking environmental audits;
- adopting Local Agenda 21 initiatives.

The involvement of elected representatives and council employees in these activities is in itself an important learning process for those concerned, as are opportunities for the participation of local people in environmental planning and management.

7.21 The Local Agenda 21 initiative, promoted by the Local Government Management Board with Government support, is encouraging local consultation on the environment, dissemination of guidance on procedures and participation with other bodies. Local initiatives in support of biodiversity can be expected to result from this process. Local Authorities have a key role in developing public support for biodiversity, through provision of resources, facilities, services and cooperation, and encouraging a holistic approach to environmental care, including the historic environment.

A Citizens Environment Network

7.22 The Sustainable Development Strategy proposes a Citizens' Environment Network to help to mobilise the local community and individuals. Government will continue to work with voluntary bodies, Local Agenda 21, and business and will vigorously promote the schemes for which it is directly responsible. But in addition Government will aim to increase awareness of environmental issues, including conserving and enhancing biodiversity, and enlisting support and commitment.

7.23 These initiatives can take a variety of forms. They may be led in some instances by a local authority, in others by voluntary groups, the Chamber of Commerce, local churches and so on. The action taken could include roundtable discussions of local problems and opportunities, public awareness campaigns and practical projects.

7.24 In England the Department of the Environment will select a small number of voluntary groups, institutions, and consultancies and invite them to tender for a commission to act as a central secretariat to this process. The secretariat will build a register of the local initiatives and put people in touch with each other – creating an informal and varied Network. Similar arrangements will be made by the Scottish Office, the Welsh Office and the Northern Ireland Office in those countries.

The rôle of the nature conservation agencies

7.25 The principle that an informed and supportive public is necessary for the full achievement of good environmental management is accepted by the main nature and landscape conservation agencies.

7.26 In their policy statements these agencies make commitments to:
- Stimulate local action, strengthen local commitment and pride in the environment, involve local communities in setting conservation objectives and in managing protected sites;
- Build partnerships with local authorities, landowners, industry and other local concerns making an environmental impact;
- Encourage and support volunteer activities, and the work of voluntary and community organisations in the field;
- Provide training for their own staff and for members of partner organisations;

- Support environmental elements in school, community, further and higher education, and in business and professional training for environmental management;
- Provide demonstrations of exemplary environmental management in their own reserves;
- Provide interpretation facilities and activities to enhance public understanding of the needs and benefits of conservation;
- Produce clear, accurate materials for use in education, training and interpretation;
- Provide grants to support projects that enhance education concerning conservation and biodiversity.

All of these initiatives have an educational impact and will play an essential part in developing understanding of biodiversity. While the role of the above bodies is most directly related to biodiversity there are other agencies in the public sector with parts to play in its support. Biodiversity is a well established indicator of water quality and a concern of those responsible for the control of pollution. The support of an informed public is a valuable asset, and the National Rivers Authority (NRA) and some of the River Purification Boards (RPBs) in Scotland have also put a great deal of effort into mounting exhibitions, holding open days and maintaining links with schools, universities and voluntary organisations.

MUSEUMS

The Natural History Museum in London is visited by 1,700,000 people each year. Over the last 15 years the Museum has deliberately designed its exhibitions to make them an effective means of communication about the natural world for a lay audience. This shift of aim beyond display to communication is one that many museums are now following. It has meant that the public now has has access to information on critical issues of topical importance in museum galleries which are presented in an understandable and stimulating manner.

Exhibitions which touch on biodiversity show up in surveys to be consistently among the most popular. Thus in a recent survey at the Natural History Museum, 90% of visitors went to the Dinosaur gallery, 58% to arthropods, 48% to mammals and 47% to Ecology. Members of the public are coming to use museums as sources of information about the scientific background to topics of concern, such as conservation, to which they have been alerted by the media.

The rôle of collections and displays

7.27 Through their permanent displays and by special exhibitions museums present a worldwide picture of biodiversity to the public. They may also display local biodiversity on a scale suited to the nature of the museum. Their expertise in methods of presentation, and their understanding of the interface between science and the public makes them a particularly valuable resource. Along with art galleries they are also in a position to convey an inspirational message both through their exhibits and their ways of displaying them.

7.28 In addition to mounting exhibitions museums offer lecture and activity programmes and other educational services for the public and for schools, teacher training, and higher education. They also provide a focal point and resources for organisations and projects in the voluntary sector, including the recording of local natural history. To support the smaller museums the Scottish Museums Council has set up an environmental initiative.

7.29 The old Physick Gardens, which were forerunners of modern botanic gardens, are among the earliest public demonstrations of the importance of biodiversity to human

ZOOS

The Zoological Society of London attracts 69,000 school children a year to its two zoos, and uses nearly 200 volunteers to staff a range of programmes including an Outreach programme to local schools. The Federation of Zoological Gardens of Great Britain and Ireland, comprising 52 collections, with 14 million visitors a year including a million school pupils, of whom at least 350,000 receive professional on-site tuition, are one of the largest conservation education resources in the country.

Innovative approaches to education in zoos include the Royal Zoological Society of Scotland's scheme to develop a Darwin Centre. The centre aims to present the nature and evolution of biodiversity to the public with the help of a traditional yew tree maze and the zoo's collection of marmosets.

life, and the tradition has been maintained. The Royal Botanic Gardens at Kew and Edinburgh, along with some satellite gardens, draw some two million visitors a year, who are attracted by the great range of plant life, increasingly arranged to illustrate biogeographical aspects, including native plant associations. These and other distinguished gardens and arboreta around the country thus have an increased educational role. Like museums they have demonstrated their capacity to link with the arts. They also have an almost unique ability to develop education and interpretation of biodiversity at the genetic level. With its linkages to biotechnology this may be one of the most important services for the future.

7.30 To be in the presence of a living animal is an experience which cannot be replicated by television or other means. Zoos are now recognising that to promote understanding it is essential that animals be kept not just as spectacles but in breeding groups, in surroundings which will allow their behaviour to be as natural as possible. Most larger zoos have education staff and centres and run programmes for schools, teachers and the public extending to all aspects of conservation.

7.31 Zoos have traditionally given prominence to the higher vertebrates, but there is now a marked increase in public aquaria and butterfly farms. There is room for development also of joint projects between museums, botanic gardens, zoos and other facilities on the model of the Interlink programme which has run successfully in Edinburgh, for school children.

COUNTRYSIDE RANGERS

Where local communities, visitors and education or interpretation facilities come together the quality of the staff is vital. Countryside Rangers typify the qualities needed – a good knowledge of the local environment and its management, a personal knowledge of the local community, and communication and teaching skills adaptable to the varied groups with which they work. In many places they play a front line role in interpreting biodiversity for visitors while cushioning their effects on the locality. They pioneer innovative ways of involving school and community groups and in holiday play and adventure schemes. The appointment of rangers who belong to the region and are identifiable with the local community is to be encouraged.

7.32 More can be done to foster an interest in marine organisms; an example of public interest in a privately developed project is the opening of Deep Sea World at North Queensferry in spring 1993. Here visitors walk through a transparent tunnel to see thousands of fish in a natural environment created in a disused quarry.

The rôle of environmental centres and services

7.33 To gain first hand experience of biodiversity it is necessary to explore it in the field. A range of bodies offer facilities including the Forestry Commission and conservation agencies, local authorities, voluntary organisations and landowners. They cover residential and day field centres, interpretation centres often associated with national, regional and local parks and heritage sites, long-distance walkways, farms, urban study centres and city farms. All in their different ways combine education with an appreciation of biodiversity and its role in the environment. They are generally able to do so in a relaxed atmosphere where students are highly motivated.

7.34 Some, such as the Field Studies Council centres, are focal points for the study and recording of local biodiversity. Others may focus on historical or agricultural features or on outdoor recreation. Centres maintained by local authorities mainly for the use of schools often emphasise outdoor pursuits over environmental education. There is scope for more integration of these aspects which need not be in conflict. A project set up by English Nature in partnership with Wildlife Link Joint Education Group explored this.

The rôle of voluntary organisations and informal education

7.35 Many of the above facilities and services are provided by voluntary organisations who range from prestigious professional societies to small networks of specialists. To varying degrees they combine professionals and amateurs, and are an important source of specialised knowledge, enthusiasm and dedicated workers. Together they make up a large and influential section of the population with much to contribute to understanding biodiversity.

7.36 The first duty of voluntary organisations is generally to be a source of inspiration, information and structured experience to their own membership. In this way they raise the level of personal commitment to environmental stewardship. Some organisations promote this by an extensive use of volunteers. The strength of voluntary movements and their expertise in land management, conservation, community involvement and education, are considerable. A continuing increase in membership of voluntary organisations would in itself promote learning about biodiversity.

7.37 Some large bodies, such as the Royal Society for the Protection of Birds, the National Trust and the National Trust for Scotland, maintain their own reserves with interpretation and ranger facilities, and have their own education staff and programmes. Along with those of the Worldwide Fund for Nature their publications, audio-visual resources, action packs and other back-up materials are used by formal education, youth organisations and others. Some have their own sections for young people, such as the Young Ornithologists Club (RSPB) and Watch Clubs run in association with the Royal Society for Nature Conservation.

7.38 Some organisations (for example, the British Trust for Conservation Volunteers and Scottish Conservation Projects Trust) provide learning opportunities through work experience. Working holidays are becoming an increasingly popular combination of environmental learning and volunteer labour. They extend to work projects abroad – many of them directly related to biodiversity – through Earthwatch. They provide a valuable service to organisations who maintain properties on a limited budget and to community enterprises. They also provide opportunities for volunteers to experience wilderness conditions.

The rôle of industry and commerce

7.39 The business community is becoming increasingly aware of environmental issues; both the impact of their activities on the environment and the benefits derived from best practice. Many firms now have corporate environmental policies which include the need for staff training. In this they are supported by various industrial organisations including the International Chamber of Commerce, the CBI, the TUC and many others.

7.40 Environmental policies in the business community influence the environmental attitudes and understanding in the wider community. Business and industries do this by:
- setting an example by their own environmental sensitivity; this includes the siting and design of plant, their use of resources, transport policy, waste disposal, landscaping of the surrounding site, relations with the local community;
- presentation of goods and services to the public including packaging and marketing, meeting the changing expectations of green consumerism, and adopting a life-cycle view of products and processes.
- training all levels of staff in environmental management issues. This heightens environmental awareness within the community, and offers opportunities for collaboration with local environmental agencies and organisations;
- supplying materials to schools, colleges and other educational bodies is an important resource for education which is best provided in line with the CBI's guidelines on the production of such material.

THE BRITISH TRUST FOR ORNITHOLOGY

The British Trust for Ornithology enlists a high proportion of its 9,000 plus members to carry out survey and monitoring work, including some 2,000 volunteer bird-ringers each of whom is given extensive training before obtaining a ringing licence. Volunteers contribute half a million person/hours per year to the work and pay their own costs.

WYTCH FARM

Poole Harbour in Dorset and the heathlands that surround it are of national and international importance for wildlife. Both the heathlands and the Harbour are Sites of Special Scientific Interest and are situated in an Area of Outstanding Natural Beauty (AONB). The heaths are also a proposed SPA and the Harbour meets the criteria for designation as an SPA and Ramsar site.

Wytch Farm is the largest known onshore oilfield in western Europe. First developed by British Gas in the 1970s it was taken over by British Petroleum in the 1980s. Surveys carried out by BP in the late 1980s revealed that the main oil reserve, the Sherwood Reservoir, which extends under the sea under the western end of Poole Bay, contained about 100 million barrels of hydrocarbons. Exploitation of this part of the oil reservoir is the final phase of the Wytch Farm development.

Advances in technology in drilling techniques mean that wells can now be drilled horizontally for distances up to 6 kilometres. These advances will allow BP to recover the oil from an onshore wellsite more economically and with considerably less environmental impact than was possible before.

A group was set up in 1992 to advise on the onshore drilling options. The group included representatives from Dorset County Council, English Nature, the National Rivers Authority, the Countryside Commission, Purbeck District Council and Poole Harbour Commissioners. The group met regularly to ensure environmental considerations were accounted for throughout the design phase of the development and in its Environmental Statement supporting the planning application of a new wellsite.

Following environmental assessment of four possible locations BP selected a well-site within an area of dense conifers on Goathorn peninsula. A detailed study of the proposed well site on Goathorn looking at habitats, plants, lizards, birds invertebrates and badgers found that the area was of very limited ecological interest. In addition, noise and visibility issues were studied to ensure that there would be the minimum of disturbance to the local residents, tourists and the scenic quality of this region, Purbeck. Although the peninsula is within the SSSI and proposed SPA this option was judged to have the least environmental impact. BP have also agreed to manage 64 acres of the peninsula for nature conservation; felling the trees and where possible converting it back to heathland.

BP's planning application is currently awaiting a decision.

7.41 An increasing number of firms are undertaking these activities. We recognize, however, that businesses, especially small businesses, need assistance to understand how future environmental requirements and opportunities affect them and how they can best respond.

7.42 Collaboration between the business community and other sectors is increasing, for example with the conservation agencies, through partnerships with education (such as Groundwork's Esso Greenlink project), through training links with the voluntary sector and grant aid. These are important for bringing business concerns within the environmental community: the TECs, and in Scotland LECs, can be important agents in this process.

7.43 Environmental schemes such as the Environmentally Sensitive Areas advice and training are all helping to promote greater awareness of biodiversity in farming communities. The National Farmers Union, landowners organisations, countryside agencies, agricultural colleges and bodies such as the Farming and Wildlife Advisory Groups all have important roles to play in continuing to build a viable blend of biodiversity, local identity and sound management into the business of farming.

Cultural influences

7.44 For many people the most powerful cultural influences today are the press, radio and television. There is evidence that most people rate television as their main source of environmental information, with the press second and remaining sources insignificant. The superb natural history programmes which have done much to give meaning to biodiversity for the general public are not the only influence.

The way people behave on television can also constitute very influential models. The media also have a strong record of educational service beyond their own programmes, in the production, for example, of printed and audio-visual materials for schools. However television in particular tends to simplify issues, often focusing on a single species or impending disaster. It is an important role of education to develop people's critical faculties, and a cautious attitude to received information and opinions from whatever source – including their own.

7.45 Many people's behaviour may be determined by religious beliefs and associated cultural traditions and customs. The growing diversity of our own multicultural society makes generalisation difficult, but environmental issues have become the subject of interfaith and inter-church conferences and a considerable amount of agreement has been reached. The approach is positive and celebratory rather than problem-laden and concepts of the integrity of creation are particularly supportive of bio-diversity. The major faiths also have a degree of moral authority, commitment to a holistic model of humankind and its environment, as well as a more enlightened inter-pretation of stewardship. Useful publications and other materials are being produced to promote debate on environmental issues within church membership.

7.46 The support for learning reviewed so far falls into the category of informal or non-formal education. It offers the public a great amount of support for environmental action including the maintenance and enhancement of biodiversity. It carries a large and varied reserve of knowledge and experience, boundless enthusiasm, and commitment to action both individual and commercial. It is also somewhat fragmented, unevenly distributed and sometimes varying in its objectives. It would benefit from measures designed:

- to extend good practice to new places and groups;
- to develop closer partnerships, not just between like-minded organisations but also between different sectors, in environmental forums and round tables;
- to define common objectives for learning relating to the environment;
- to increase the number of facilitators, whether voluntary, as in voluntary warden schemes, or paid as in ranger services;
- to achieve better targeting of services to formal education;
- to give greater opportunity for local action and greater flexibility in the apportionment of resources to sustain it.

ACTION BY FORMAL EDUCATION

7.47 However important other influences may be on people's understanding of their environment, formal education has a crucial role to play. Formal education can help develop what society believes in and therefore rewards.

7.48 At the European level environmental education has been the subject of resolutions of the Council of the European Communities and Ministers of Education meeting within the Council (1988 and 1992), in the Ministerial Declaration on Sustainable Development made at the conference on "Action for a Common Future", at Bergen in 1990, and as part of Agenda 21 at the UN Conference on Environment and Development (UNCED) at Rio de Janeiro in 1992.

7.49 Formal education can promote environmental issues in three ways:
- by including issues which are concerned with the natural

In recent years environmental issues have become the subject of interfaith and interchurch conferences and events.

SCHOOL NATURE AREAS

Many schools are developing parts of their school grounds as nature areas and recording the plants, birds, butterflies and other wildlife associated with them: good ideas and much guidance is available to them from *Learning Through Landscapes* and in Scotland, *Grounds for Learning*. Visits to local parks and to ponds or streams extend the range of species brought into the classroom. Activities to improve the school grounds can develop into school and community projects, including tree planting and the management of wild areas in local parks and waste ground.

and built environment in teaching programmes;

- by setting an example of enlightened environmental management in its own institutions;
- by providing focal points and resources for local communities and for other organisations in the field.

Action through school education

School nature study includes observing and collecting things, giving children the opportunity to overcome fears of creepy-crawlies and can awaken interests that may develop in later life.

7.50 Biodiversity is often one of the first features of the environment to figure in school activities, although often not under that name. Even at nursery school nature study includes observing and collecting things, giving children the opportunity to overcome any fears of creepy-crawlies and to awaken interests that may develop in later life. In primary schools nature tables, wall displays, non-destructive collecting, for example of leaves, fruits and seeds, bark-rubbings and stones, are familiar ways of illustrating biodiversity. In secondary schools an understanding of how the buildings are made and the resources they consume can be extremely illustrative, eg use of non-sustainable resources, energy and water usage. These activities may also continue as informal education in nature clubs. In this way biodiversity can become as familiar a topic in schools as the water cycle or food chains. These activities can, however, be dependent on the presence of enthusiastic teachers, confident enough to approach situations where they do not have all the answers, and able to lead an investigative venture. They can be strongly supported by help from outside the school, for example by local rangers, but school commitment is essential.

7.51 In England and Wales the National Curriculum is the focus for teaching and learning in compulsory state education. Environmental education is therefore addressed through the individual subjects of the National Curriculum. The Government has specified for each subject the knowledge, skills and understanding which pupils of different abilities and ages are expected to achieve. Environmental education is one of the five non-statutory cross curriculum themes and as such

is part of the education of every school student. Opportunities to study a range of environmental issues arise in particular through the study of geography, science and technology. Other subjects including the arts can also provide a context for pupils to examine environmental issues. In Scotland the 5-14 programme provides many opportunities for environmental education through Environmental Studies and as a permeating element in other curriculum areas.

Concerns and opportunities

7.52 Factors which may limit the speed of progress on environmental and biodiversity matters include:

- conflicting curriculum pressures and problems in the definition of biodiversity as a concept within environmental education;
- the fact that biodiversity and environmental education are not generally a component of other examination subjects;
- the amount of preparation in Initial Teacher Training (ITT);
- the availability of suitable INSET programmes;
- the availability of suitable published material.

7.53 Opportunities for helping environmental education and biodiversity to achieve Government's objectives include:
a) For schools:

- consideration of an environmental policy for both

THE SECRETARY OF STATE FOR SCOTLAND'S WORKING GROUP ON ENVIRONMENTAL EDUCATION

In 1990 the Secretary of State for Scotland set up a Working Group to study and make recommendations on a national strategy for the development of environmental education in Scotland. It presented its report "Learning for Life" in April 1993. The Group divided its work between six contexts in which learning takes place – the home, the community, leisure and recreation, school, post-school education and the workplace. It also took note of the influence on learning exerted by national and local government policies and by others including the media, advertising and entertainment industries. Its recommendations were addressed to the Secretary of State, to local authorities and government agencies, to education, business and voluntary organisations and others associated with the learning contexts. The report was circulated for comment and is currently under consideration by the Secretary of State.

curriculum and institution;

- consideration of designating a member of staff to be responsible for coordinating environmental education;
- reviewing the relative priorities given to biodiversity and related environmental topics in their INSET programmes;

b) For teacher training institutions:

- consideration of the place of environmental education in the training of all teachers

7.54 As part of the Government's drive to raise standards of education in England, the National Curriculum is currently under review. Although the broad structure is not expected to change, the need to reduce the curricular load from 5-14, and to introduce additional flexibility for the 14-16 year olds, may well mean that the balance between different elements of a subject may change and that some will become discretionary rather than compulsory as now. Changes to the existing compulsory requirements for the national curriculum subjects will have to be considered in detail and new compulsory requirements are not expected to be introduced into schools until the autumn of 1995. While the review will not address environmental education directly, it will affect the context in which it is delivered.

THE TOYNE REPORT

The Toyne Report, sub-titled *Environmental responsibility; an agenda for further and higher education*, recommended that by the academic year 1994/95 every FHE institution should adopt and publicise:

- a comprehensive environmental policy statement;
- a policy and strategy for the development of environmental education;
- action plans for their implementation.

The funding councils have considered these recommendations and have decided how to reward environmental good practice in the institutions they fund. Assessment by the Further Education Funding Council of capital projects by FE colleges will include an assessment of the environment impact of energy saving in new buildings.

Many institutions have already progressed in these directions, for example the Universities of Edinburgh and Central Lancashire. The value of audits as a learning tool has been well demonstrated, for example at Glasgow Caledonian University.

7.55 Once environmental competence was a natural and basic objective of everyone's education. As technology advanced and as people became less in touch with their life support systems, it was allowed to decline. In modern times it has again become vital for our quality of life and therefore an essential component of school education. It is also worth remembering that when children, especially young children, return home they take back much of what they have learned to their parents.

Action by further and higher education

7.56 Further and higher education (FHE) covers a range of universities and colleges. These organisations are increasingly responsible for a network of off-site educational and training activities in addition to their main course programmes. These include community education, outreach and distance learning programmes and cooperation with in-house industrial training schemes. Research programmes are beginning to include studies of importance to environmental education, for example the Economic and Social Research Council is continuing to run a variety of programmes, including those on Global Environmental Change, and the effects of agriculture and transport practices on the environment. FHE institutions can contribute to public understanding of biodiversity through:

- teaching and research;
- exemplary environmental practice within the institution;
- their influence as focal points for community activities and resources;
- providing consultancy services to secure improvements in environmental practice;
- co-promoting with industry improvements to environmental practice.

7.57 Their role in environmental education was recently the subject of the Toyne Report and its recommendations are supportive of a better understanding of biodiversity within the environmental education framework; similar recommendations are made in the report of the Scottish Working Group *Learning for Life* set up by the Secretary of State for Scotland.

7.58 Environmental teaching in higher education can be divided roughly into three levels:

- the preparation of specialists in environmentally-related sciences;
- environmental modules in the courses of people whose work will entail environmental intervention;
- environmental teaching in the curriculum of all students as a part of their essential education.

KEW DIPLOMA

Students on Kew's conservation techniques course.

An additional Kew Diploma was established in 1987, in collaboration with the British Council, Commonwealth Science Council, and the International Board for Plant Breeding and Genetic Research, to train workers from many countries in herbarium curation and management. Following the Rio Summit, a Plant Conservation Techniques Course, the first of its kind, was introduced as a means of increasing awareness of the range of techniques now available for plant conservation, from protected-area management, through to botanic gardens, seed banks and cryopreservation. A third new 'capacity building' course on the management of botanic gardens also commenced in 1993.

The first and second levels are considered below. The third level is an extension from school of the permeation model of environmental education: its assessment is a main function of the audits associated with curricular greening.

Training specialists

7.59 The UK Government sees its role in higher education to be that of setting a framework and broad strategy; it is for the relevant institutions to decide what and how much should be taught according to student and employer demand. Support for training specialists in scientific areas relevant to biodiversity is provided by the Research Councils, universities and other agencies.

7.60 Over the past two decades classical taxonomy has come to be perceived as dull and unfashionable. Compared with other parts of biological research, funding, recruitment of young scientists, and provision of university courses have declined. In a White Paper of May 1993, the Government reaffirmed the importance of systematic biology, recognising that it was a fundamental tool for both

pure and applied research in the environmental, medical and agricultural sciences.

7.61 The Natural History Museum and the Royal Botanic Gardens at Kew and Edinburgh are the largest UK campuses for postgraduate training in taxonomy. In addition to the training given to their own systematatists and curators, staff from both institutions contribute to the undergraduate and MSc courses in universities. In their 1993 Corporate Plan the Royal Botanic Gardens identified three priorities in the field of education and training:
- to share knowledge effectively over as wide a front as possible;
- to establish Kew as a world leader in the interpretation and teaching of systematic botany, conservation,

STUDENT GRANTS

As part of the CEL scheme limited grants have been offered to students undertaking BSc and MSc project work on nature reserves. These grants enable students to carry out applied research into factors affecting the management of these sites. The terms and conditions of the grant give experience of project management, as well as providing the students with an introduction to English Nature and its strategies.

herbarium and botanic garden management, economic botany and horticulture;
- to collaborate closely with leading universities and other organisations in the development of relevant science education programmes.

7.62 The Royal Botanic Garden Edinburgh (RBGE), like Kew, has an important role in training. Its staff teach plant taxonomy and botany at Edinburgh University on a range of courses at under-graduate and post-graduate levels. In 1992-93, the RBGE jointly started with Edinburgh University a one year MSc course on plant taxonomy and biodiversity.

7.63 There is already a foretaste of how systematics might contribute to human well-being. Even at the present rudimentary state of understanding, taxonomists at Kew have been able to identify a better source of the anti-viral drug, castanospermine, from studying plant species closely related to the one in which it was first found. The newly-discovered animals and microbial communities living around hydrothermal vents in the deep ocean might have useful applications in biotechnology. The incorporation of genes of salt tolerance found in wild species closely related to barley might enable that crop to be irrigated with dilute sea water, as opposed to freshwater.

7.64 From such ventures, the rudiments of a triad are beginning to form in the biological sciences, embracing taxonomy, evolution and ecology. The conceptual framework for bringing the three subjects together is in place. A Natural Environment Research Council report, *Evolution and Biodiversity – The New Taxonomy* published in 1992, anticipated rapid advances in understanding the character and significance of biodiversity, both in an historical and contemporary context. In 1993 the NERC announced a major funding scheme to help revitalise taxonomic research, both directly and through attracting more young scientists into that area of the environmental sciences.

Training people whose work will affect the environment

7.65 For many students the basis for further training is established in qualifying courses prior to employment, the adequacy of which sometimes causes concern. One concern is that most prospective employees come from courses which are too research-orientated and there is a need for specialist environmental knowledge to be combined with practical skills such as survey work, project management and social and community relations. The recently instituted College-English Nature Link scheme may prove a helpful model for improvement.

7.66 In business management courses more attention needs to be given to the methods industry has developed to improve environmental management such as environmental audits, integrated pollution control and life-cycle analysis of products. The formal education of industrial managers, administrators and accountants needs to give more weight to recognising environmental mismanagement. These are matters for detailed curriculum audit.

7.67 Professional institutes have an important role in determining the content of vocational education in continuing professional development. Evidence collected for the Scottish report from 100 institutes in 1991 suggests that almost half had no reference to environmental matters in the courses required for membership and a further quarter considered these to be only peripheral, less than a third had an environmental policy and only a few included an environmental perspective in their codes of practice. On the other hand some had excellent policies and practice and a few had very progressive policies for education (for example, the Royal Town Planning Institute).

7.68 The Government believes that the following measures would strengthen the role of FHE in enhancing the understanding of biodiversity:

- extending good practice in environmental policy-making and implementation, and in institutional and curriculum audits throughout the sector;
- giving more importance to the environmental content of entry qualifications for courses;
- supporting cross-disciplinary units within institutions, to develop interdisciplinary teaching and research;
- funding councils encouraging and rewarding good environmental practice, the development of environmental education and the staff development to achieve these goals;
- establishing closer liaison on environmental issues with employers; giving more attention to the employment history of graduates and making greater use of work placements in environmentally related courses;
- establishing close links with the local community and associated organisations to strengthen the role of FHE institutions as a local resource for improved environmental care;
- professional institutes reviewing and where necessary re-defining their role to establish high standards of environmental competence within their profession and beyond it.

7.69 All of the above are included among the recommendations in the Toyne report and the report of the Scottish Working Group, *Learning for Life*. It is particularly important that biodiversity is both familiar and better understood in this sector. As such it needs to be given a higher profile in prospectuses, curricula, examinations and professional qualifications.

7.70 An important recent contribution to the inclusion of environmental issues in vocational education and training is the development of National and Scottish Vocational Qualifications (NVQs and SVQs) and their General equivalents (GNVQs and GSVQs). The Council on Standards and Qualifications in Environmental Conservation (COSQUEC) has become the industry lead body for a range of environmentally related occupations. It is important that other industry lead bodies should incorporate appropriate environmental standards into their qualifications and that biodiversity be seen to take its place as an indicator of quality in performance. Other useful guidance for training relevant to biodiversity is to be found in the work of the Countryside Staff Training Advisory Group, and, in an industrial context, in the CBI booklet on Environmental Education and Training.

Action by Government

7.71 The Government, in its White Paper on the Environment, has already committed itself to a broad-based policy of public awareness-raising and education, upon which it will build in order to provide as many people as possible with the opportunity to take an informed and active part in the care of the environment, its biodiversity and other vital qualities. In doing so the Government will also demonstrate its commitment to the relevant items in UNCED's Agenda 21, and to fulfil the objectives for an environmentally responsible citizenry.

7.72 A great deal is already going on to promote awareness and better understanding of biodiversity, albeit in a somewhat fragmented manner. Proposals are made that will support and enhance this activity and much can be done within existing resources by reassessing priorities and redefining roles. Many individuals, groups and organisations have parts to play, and all the main sectors of society have responsibilities for making progress. The role of central Government includes:

- giving a clear lead;
- promoting a collaborative approach between sectors;
- developing a sense of public ownership for biodiversity;
- improving access to accurate and understandable information;
- assessing and evaluating progress.

Commitment and leadership

7.73 Many Government departments influence biodiversity and environmental quality either directly or by guiding practice. The network of Green Ministers and their associated officials' network provide a structure reinforcing the commitment of departments to incorporate environmental requirements into the full range of their policies and programmes. Progress on this will be reported at appropriate intervals and will include references to biodiversity where relevant.

7.74 The concept of biodiversity and the reasons for its importance to human welfare may not be so fully understood by the public as some other topical environmental concerns. The Government will therefore consider a publicity strategy to make the concept clearer. This would explain the importance of biodiversity and the improvements which the Government hopes to achieve, for example by setting objectives for biodiversity policy. Such a strategy will need to embrace other agencies, local authorities, business, educational institutions and voluntary organisations. It could include practical guidance on ways

of protecting and enhancing biodiversity in a range of familiar, managed habitats, both rural and urban.

Strengthening inter-sectoral cooperation

7.75 In recognition of the provisions agreed in Agenda 21 and to encourage intersectoral cooperation at a local level the Government is facilitating local Agenda 21 round tables on sustainable development. The form and content of such initiatives will vary and be left to local discretion but biodiversity should feature significantly, recognising the dependence of biodiversity on sustainable development. In some cases these may lead to local sustainable development strategies which would include biodiversity plans. The Government and the nature conservation agencies will consider providing advice and assistance for such plans which should fit into the general framework provided by this plan.

Formal education support

7.76 In relation to Further and Higher Education the Government will consider the recommendations of the Toyne Report, and will stress the need for biodiversity to receive more explicit mention in the places where it is relevant.

7.77 Members of the public committed to action in support of biodiversity and of environmental quality need accessible,

MINISTRY OF DEFENCE EDUCATION AND AWARENESS

As one of the country's largest landowners the Ministry of Defence is putting a lot of effort into the appreciation and enhancement of biodiversity. The Ministry has a Conservation Officer and Conservation Groups attached to its Training Areas who undertake many survey and management tasks which have a very significant awareness-raising and educational role among service personnel. These activities extend to overseas bases, some of which exhibit a degree of biodiversity to which few people are fortunate enough to be exposed. Co-operation is developed with various other conservation bodies and the services have been responsible for many initiatives that have facilitated public access to areas of high biodiversity. These activities are regularly reported in the Ministry's conservation magazine *Sanctuary*.

reliable, accurate and understandable information, including detailed information about local conditions. Work on improving the accessibility and co-ordination of data on biodiversity, as set out in Chapter 9, will take account of this dimension.

ACTION

7.78 The Government and nature conservation agencies will:

- Consider a publicity strategy to explain the meaning and importance of biodiversity and to explain what needs to be done to conserve and enhance it. The campaign could:
  - support initiatives that enhance people's understanding of what is special about their local environment;
  - encourage the creation of a network of community wardens;
  - support initiatives that promote local action to conserve and improve local biodiversity.
- Incorporate environmental principles, including biodiversity, in their policies and programmes;
- Encourage where possible the adoption of agreed measures arising out of the Scottish Working Group report *Learning for Life*, and the adoption of measures proposed in the Toyne Report;
- Establish a Citizens' Environment Network which will encourage initiatives throughout local communities.

CHAPTER 8

UK SUPPORT TO BIODIVERSITY OVERSEAS

INTRODUCTION

8.1 The UK has a long and respected tradition of conserving its own biodiversity, and this has been explained earlier in the plan. But we also have a history of assisting others with the conservation of their biodiversity. This Chapter describes the Government's support for biodiversity conservation overseas, through the Darwin Initiative for the Survival of Species, through the Convention on International Trade in Endangered Species, and through the aid programme. It outlines proposals for future policy developments, particularly in the light of the provisions of the Biodiversity Convention, and reviews biodiversity conservation in Antarctica, the Crown Dependencies and the Dependent Territories.

THE BIODIVERSITY CONVENTION

8.2 Biodiversity as an issue of global importance was formally recognised last year with the agreement of the UN Convention on Biological Diversity. Within a few days of its opening for signature at the Earth Summit it had been signed by over 150 countries. Over 160 countries have now signed and over 30 of those have ratified. The Convention will therefore come into force before the end of 1993, only 18 months after the first country signed, an indication of the importance attached to this Convention by the nations of the world. The Prime Minister signed the Convention for the UK in Rio and, the UK intends to ratify the Biodiversity Convention given satisfactory progress towards securing safeguards regarding our concerns on the financial provisions of the Convention.

8.3 The Biodiversity Convention will pave the way for individual countries to set up a network of protected areas to safeguard habitats. It will assist countries to devise plans that meet their national circumstances. It will contribute to the global benefits of conserving biodiversity. It will facilitate the sharing of benefits, in the form of potentially valuable biological resources, between the countries providing them and those that develop them. The international support for the Convention is a recognition that no single country can preserve the world's biodiversity on its own; we must work together to find solutions to the problems which transcend national boundaries. Those countries which have the skills and experience should share those strengths with the countries who have not.

8.4 As a demonstration of the UK's commitment to the Convention, and our global reputation for basing conservation action on sound science, the Prime Minister announced in Rio the Darwin Initiative for the Survival of Species. The main aim of the Initiative is to build on the UK's scientific, educational and commercial strengths in the field of biodiversity to assist in the conservation of the world's biodiversity and natural habitats and the sustainable use of its components, particularly in those countries rich in biodiversity but poor in resources.

8.5 The UK has a long history of enterprising explorers and mariners, not least of course Darwin himself, who studied the diversity of the planet and gathered specimens from across the globe. Those specimens form some of the finest collections in the world and those collections, combined with the high standard of our gardens, museums, research institutes, universities, conservation agencies and voluntary organisations, have earned the UK her reputation in the biodiversity field. Following the announcement of the Darwin Initiative the Department of the Environment was involved in informal discussions and consultation with all these organisations to listen to ideas and to identify the biodiversity projects and research being undertaken in the UK and to avoid duplicating the excellent work already being carried out.

THE DARWIN INITIATIVE

The Darwin Initiative will fund projects which meet the objectives of the Initiative to the value of £9 million over the first four years of the Initiative. £1 million will be available this financial year, £2 million next year and £3 million in 1995/96 and in 1996/97. The Secretary of State established an Advisory Committee to advise him on priority areas to be targeted under the Darwin Initiative, the relative priority to be given to different programmes, and the financial support to be made available to projects. This Committee is comprised of experts drawn from a wide variety of organisations and institutions and with recognised experience in the field of biodiversity. Their collective knowledge and experience has been of great value in considering how to take forward the Initiative. The Chairman of the Committee is Sir Crispin Tickell. The other members are Janet Barber of WWF, Dr Brian Bayne of the Plymouth Marine Laboratory, Dr Eileen Buttle NERC, Mr Robin Herbert of the Royal Horticultural Society, Dr David Horrobin of Scotia Pharmaceuticals, Sir David Smith of Edinburgh University, and Professor Bob May of Oxford University. Mr Andrew Bennett of the Overseas Development Administration, and Mr Robin Sharp of the Department of the Environment are the Government assessors and Mrs Kate Mayes of the Department of the Environment is the Secretary.

8.6 The Government is anxious that the Initiative should not cut across any of the work already being carried out in our institutions or universities. The intention is to complement the extensive activity already being undertaken, including that supported by funds from the aid programme. The Initiative is designed to supplement existing activity; to be flexible enough to help fill gaps in that activity and innovative in providing funding for new and exciting projects.

8.7 The Advisory Committee's interim recommendations to the Secretary of State, which were published in July 1993, set out clear principles which form the framework for consideration of projects to receive funding under the Initiative. In brief, the Committee recommended that :

- funding under the Initiative should be clearly identifiable and used, where possible, as a catalyst;
- it should be used to raise awareness of the value of biodiversity and to fund projects which would make a real difference. Funding should be directed at areas not already receiving funding through the usual aid or research channels;
- it should be used to benefit the conservation and sustainable use of biodiversity in countries otherwise unable to afford it and rich in biodiversity; and should, where possible, fund projects engaging local people;
- it should be used to help such countries outside the UK fulfil their obligations under the Biodiversity Convention;
- it should be directed towards projects in a small number of countries and focused mainly on those countries where links with the UK already exist or where governments are likely to make particularly good use of it;
- projects funded under the Initiative should include those where a small amount of Darwin money could be used to generate additional amounts.

8.8 Based on these principles the Advisory Committee made the following recommendations on the projects areas which could be the main focus of the Initiative:

- the establishment of collaborative projects, including training based on established links between British institutions and institutions in developing countries;
- the provision of assistance to biodiversity institutions and to scientists working in the biodiversity field in need of support;
- support for short courses in the UK on conservation and sustainable use of resources within a scheme by which Darwin Scholars and Darwin Fellows would be brought to the UK;
- a study of issues relating to commercial activities associated with the sustainable use of genetic resources in order to inform the thinking of industry and others;
- a few research projects covering neglected or undervalued aspects of work on biodiversity particularly where carried out in cooperation with local people.

8.9 These recommendations were adopted by the Secretary of State and in early July applications were invited from British institutions and individuals to bid for funding under the Initiative for projects which were in line with the principles of the Initiative. Over one hundred applications were received and in November 1993 the Secretary of State announced the first 31 projects to receive funding under the Initiative. The total funding for these projects is £3.7 million over three years and projects come from all corners of the world: from the Russian Arctic to the mangroves of Malaysia. Projects to be funded include training programmes, a study of the commercial activities associated with biodiversity, the funding of Darwin Scholars and Fellows, support for botanic gardens and for conservation organisations, and studies on the effects of pollution and of invasive species of biodiversity.

THE CONVENTION ON INTERNATIONAL TRADE IN ENDANGERED SPECIES

8.10 In 1973, the UK was one of the original signatories of the Convention on International Trade in Endangered Species of Wild Fauna and Flora (CITES). With 120 parties, CITES is the most widely supported of the existing environmental conventions and the UK continues to play an active part.

8.11 The Convention prohibits commercial trade in wild-taken specimens of over 800 species, both animals and plants, and requires trade in more than 23,000 others to be controlled to avoid harm to wild populations. The Department of the Environment (DOE) acts as the UK CITES Management Authority, considering about 20,000 applications for import and export permits annually. It seeks advice from two Scientific Authorities: the Joint Nature Conservation Committee (JNCC) for animals and the Royal Botanic Gardens, Kew, for plants. With its long scientific tradition, the UK is able to make a major contribution to the operation of the Convention, participating in committees and collaborating with other countries in proposing species to be protected. The Government has also provided additional funds to CITES for enforcement globally, and in the context of CITES has responded positively to special requests for support for African elephants and rhino conservation.

8.12 The Convention allows parties to take stricter unilateral measures if they wish. The UK has always done so, where appropriate, and since 1984 has acted in concert with its EC partners. The Community currently bans commercial trade in over 700 more species than the Convention requires, while its scientists subject proposed imports of nearly 700 others to additional checks.

8.13 In 1991, DOE commissioned major reviews of the effects of the wildlife trade from its two scientific advisers, the JNCC and Kew. They concluded that the basic framework of controls was sound but could be better implemented. As a result, the Government pressed the European Commission to propose tighter EC controls and gave priority to discussion of the subsequent draft regulation during the UK's EC Presidency in 1992.

8.14 Twenty years ago, CITES accepted that the sustainable use of natural resources should be permitted and that international co-operation was essential. Since then, there has been growing recognition that trade may not just be tolerable but in some cases can be beneficial by giving wildlife a commercial value. The circumstances in which trade should be allowed have been the focus of lively and sometimes contentious debate at successive CITES Conferences, particularly in relation to the African elephant. In 1992, the EC called for dialogue to continue between conferences to increase understanding between the Parties. To this end the UK led an EC mission to Eastern and Southern Africa in late 1992 to explore the scope for a meeting on the elephant issue between the range states and others before the next Conference in late 1994. This quest is still being pursued.

8.15 The Government will ensure that the UK maintains its leading role in developing and implementing the Convention.

THE UNITED KINGDOM'S AID PROGRAMME

8.16 The primary role of the UK aid programme, which is administered by the Overseas Development Administration (ODA), is to promote sustainable economic and social development in order to reduce poverty and improve the quality of life of poor people.

8.17 Government's support to national efforts in sustainable use and conservation of biodiversity is part of our objective of assisting developing countries to tackle national environmental problems. However, as has been emphasised earlier in the plan, biodiversity and its conservation has a significant implication for economic growth. This is particularly the case in those countries that are highly dependent on the exploitation of renewable natural resources. As the international community has recognised in drawing up the Convention on Biological Diversity, biodiversity conservation is also an issue of global environmental significance, support for which is part of our contribution to the protection and conservation of the global commons. Its loss has potentially serious consequences for the international community. Through our external assistance programmes we are both assisting developing countries in the sustainable use and conservation of biodiversity as a natural resource, as well as assisting them with the additional, or incremental, costs of biodiversity conservation as a global asset.

8.18 Government's support to biodiversity conservation activities in developing countries is also closely linked to ODA's other programmes concerned with the exploitation and conservation of renewable natural resources. The most significant of these programmes is in forestry, but it is also supporting work in marine ecology and coastal conservation, including research into the conservation of threatened coral reefs.

OBJECTIVES WITHIN CITES WILL INCLUDE:

- to participate actively in the 1994 Conference, including contributing to the revision of the criteria determining species to be covered;
- to promote further dialogue on elephants and other contentious issues;
- to continue efforts to end illegal trade in and consumption of rhino horn products;
- to encourage the improved implementation of the Convention within the EC and globally.

THE PRIORITY OBJECTIVES OF THE AID PROGRAMME ARE:

- to promote economic reform and longer term economic growth;
- to enhance productive capacity;
- to promote good government;
- to help developing countries define and implement poverty reduction strategies;
- to promote human development, including better education and health, and family planning to allow choice in having children;
- to promote the social, economic, legal and political status of women in developing countries;
- to help developing countries tackle national environmental problems.

8.19 Tropical moist forests contain more species diversity than any other habitat. The benefits of sustainable forest management include the conservation of forest resources which provide food and medicines, and also includes the preservation of major reserves of carbon. Our objective is to assist developing countries to maximise the sustainable exploitation of the social and economic benefits of forests, while conserving them as major factors in the conservation of global biodiversity and as factors in climate change. In November 1989, the then Prime Minister, committed a further £100 million over three years to bilateral aid to forestry projects. This target was reached during the third quarter of 1992. Government has committed almost a further £110 million to 206 projects. Annual spending on bilateral forestry activities has increased from £7.4 million in 1988/89 to an estimated £28 million in 1992/93. We are also supporting multi-lateral forestry programmes, such as the Tropical Forest Action Programme, the International Tropical Timber Agreement and international forestry institutions.

8.20 In recognition of the growing sense of the importance of biodiversity resources and their conservation, the Prime Minister at the UNCED Conference in June 1992 identified biodiversity as one of five key areas of Agenda 21 on which the UK would concentrate activites and resources under the aid programme.

8.21 The UK's policies and programme of support for biodiversity conservation in developing countries were summarised in *Biological Diversity and Developing Countries: Issues and Options* published by ODA in June 1991.

8.22 As of July 1993 there were 78 projects either wholly or partly concerned with biodiversity and funded by Government, at a total cost to the aid programme of £37 million. Of these 61% were for Africa, 19.5% for Asia and 19.5% for Central/South America and the Caribbean. ODA has recently improved its project information system to enable better compilation of data on components of Government funded activities, including biodiversity.

ODA BIODIVERSITY STRATEGY

8.23 The main factor now influencing the policies and programmes of all countries in biodiversity conservation is, of course, the Convention. In recognition of its significance both at the national and global levels ODA have revised their biodiversity programme and strategy to reflect its provisions. The strategy encompasses both bilateral and multi-lateral aid, and takes into account bilateral country objectives and other natural resource strategies in existence or under development, particularly ODA's Forests Strategy.

8.24 Government support to this programme of activities will be directed through participation in the Global Environment Facility (GEF), and through continued efforts to influence its policies, programmes and the quality of its investments, as well as through targeted activity within the bilateral aid programme. Within targeted countries, and subject to agreement with the governments concerned in the context of agreeing overall country programmes, we shall aim for integrated programmes of support to biodiversity conservation including, support for capacity building and policy development, preparation of biodiversity inventories, drafting of legislation, support for conservation projects, training and education programmes, support for projects and programmes involving co-

---

BIOLOGICAL DIVERSITY AND DEVELOPING COUNTRIES: ISSUES AND OPTIONS

Actions taken within the programme include:

- the revision of ODA's Manual of Environmental Appraisal to give improved guidance for ODA project managers in addressing biodiversity issues in project development and project management;
- the establishment of an environmental research programme within which over £500,000 worth of biodiversity research activities are under consideration;
- expanded support to NGO activity in biodiversity conservation through the ODA's joint funding scheme. About £1.5 million is committed to such activities in 1993/94;
- increased provision of training for developing country nationals in environmental issues, including biodiversity;
- support for the drawing up of the Convention on Biological Diversity;
- support to and liaison with international agencies on biodiversity issues;
- funding of the Global Biodiversity Status Report published by the World Conservation Monitoring Centre in June 1992, and of a study of costs and benefits of biodiversity conservation in Kenya in the context of work led by the UN Environment Programme on assessing the costs of specific actions to conserve biological diversity in developing countries.

operation between national NGOs and communities and UK-based NGOs and joint ventures involving UK research institutions and companies.

8.25 Activities within the programme will be closely monitored and reviewed at regular intervals. Progress with the elements of the strategy will form part of the UK's report to the 1995 session of the Commission for Sustainable Development, which will review the actions taken by governments to implement the provisions of Agenda 21 in relation to biodiversity and its conservation.

CROWN DEPENDENCIES, ANTARCTICA AND THE DEPENDENT TERRITORIES

8.26 The UK Dependent Territories have a rich and varied biodiversity, with a wealth of endemic species; internationally important breeding populations of seabirds, marine turtles and marine mammals; and virtually undisturbed marine and terrestrial ecosystems. With the exception of British Antarctic Territory, the Dependent Territories are small land areas, mainly islands with low populations. Others are densely populated and subject to intense development pressures. All the Dependent Territories are worthy of enhanced biodiversity conservation attention in the implementation of the Rio Agenda. The development of Biodiversity Action Plans for the various Territories will help to protect internationally important areas of marine and terrestrial biodiversity.

8.27 Knowledge of the biodiversity of the Dependent Territories is incomplete, especially for the lower plants and invertebrates. There is still a need for baseline taxonomic research for use in assessing levels of endemism and relative biodiversity importance. Nevertheless, as the table shows there are 16 known endemic bird species in the Dependencies, nearly 200 endemic plant species, and probably around 500 endemic invertebrates. The Dependent Territories thus have an international responsibility to protect a considerable number of species which are found nowhere else in the world. In the past recorded losses of biodiversity have been considerable, for example at least 12 species of plants have become extinct in Bermuda, St Helena and the Falklands in the past 150 years.

8.28 Biodiversity conservation is primarily the responsibility of the Dependent Territory Governments who have developed their own legal and administrative measures for conservation. The fundamental importance of biodiversity as a source of ecological stability, income and well-being is increasingly recognised along with the need for sustainable utilisation of natural resources. The need for economic development is, however, more keenly felt and conservation measures in the Dependencies are

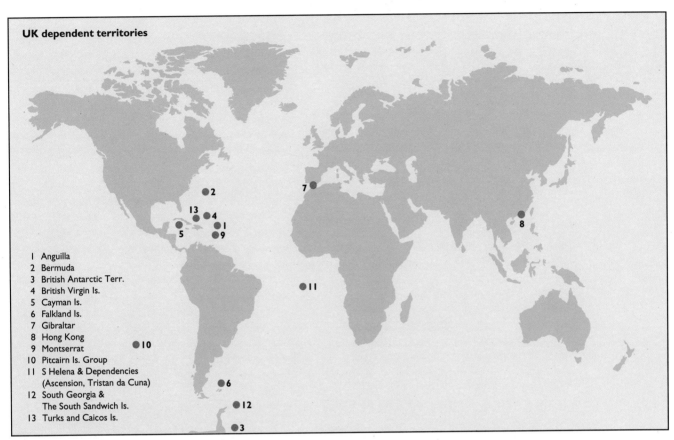

UK dependent territories

1 Anguilla
2 Bermuda
3 British Antarctic Terr.
4 British Virgin Is.
5 Cayman Is.
6 Falkland Is.
7 Gibraltar
8 Hong Kong
9 Montserrat
10 Pitcairn Is. Group
11 S Helena & Dependencies
   (Ascension, Tristan da Cuna)
12 South Georgia &
   The South Sandwich Is.
13 Turks and Caicos Is.

generally in need of strengthening and updating to prevent the further loss of biodiversity. Biodiversity conservation measures should be fully integrated into national development plans and developed locally in full consultation with all interested parties.

8.29 NGOs in the Dependencies play an important role in providing conservation expertise, maintaining links with the wider biodiversity conservation community, raising public awareness, and providing an additional source of funding for conservation initiatives. In some of the Dependencies they provide the only national capacity to address environmental issues. Other Dependencies have no local environmental NGOs, and are particularly reliant on external assistance.

8.30 Responsibility for the implementation of international agreements is retained by the UK Government. The major international and regional conservation conventions have all been ratified by the UK Government on behalf of overseas territories as appropriate. Inclusion in these agreements already provides a framework for biodiversity conservation in the Dependencies and should lead to the development of common standards. Ratification of the SPAW Protocol of the Cartagena Convention will be particularly important for biodiversity conservation in the

Caribbean Dependencies. Local implementation of international conservation obligations within the Dependencies remains relatively onerous, however, and the provision of external technical, legal and financial support will sometimes be needed.

8.31 The UK Government supports the conservation of biodiversity in some lower and middle income Dependent Territories through the provision of overseas aid. At the request of Dependent Territory Governments, the development of protected area systems, species and habitat inventories, and development of environmental management plans are all being undertaken with UK Government funding. The Biodiversity Convention calls on parties to take into consideration the special conditions resulting from the dependence on, distribution and location of, biological diversity within developing country Parties, in particular small island states (Article 20.6). The provision of financial and technical aid for biodiversity conservation in the Dependent Territories provides one of the main mechanisms by which the UK Government is implementing this.

8.32 Institutions and organisations in the UK play a key role in the study and conservation of biodiversity in the

Dependencies, and voluntary organisations such as WWF-UK provide a significant level of funding. Support provided by the voluntary sector in the UK to conservation initiatives in the Dependencies is becoming increasingly important and, in some cases, may be essential to ensure the implementation of the Biodiversity Convention. A liaison group, the NGO Forum for Nature Conservation in the UK Dependent Territories, was established in 1987 to help coordinate support for biodiversity conservation in the Dependencies.

GENERAL STRATEGY

The general strategy for biodiversity activities in the Dependent Territories is to encourage individual DTs to:

- develop a strategy for biodiversity conservation, including updating existing legislation and developing new legislation to protect species and habitats,, as appropriate;
- consider ways to develop their institutional capacity for the implementation of the Convention;
- identify priority areas for biodiversity conservation, as appropriate;
- co-operate in exchanging information about existing biodata for development of wider biodiversity databases.

Coastal and marine biodiversity are the most important natural assets of Anguilla.

ANGUILLA

8.33 Anguilla is the most northerly of the Leeward Islands, in the eastern Caribbean. It is a low coralline island with an area of 91 sq km. The dry tropical climate and thin soils support dry evergreen woodland and scrub vegetation, with some cacti. The island's population is estimated at 8500. Anguilla's economy depends on tourism with fishing also of economic importance. Shifting cultivation is still practised on a limited scale along with some permanent production of vegetables and livestock grazing.

8.34 Anguilla has regionally important breeding seabird and marine turtle populations. Coastal and marine biodiversity are the most important natural assets of the island. At present tourism development, in the absence of physical planning legislation or effective conservation legislation, is the main threat to the island's biodiversity. The Anguillan Government is therefore developing a comprehensive Marine Parks Programme to ensure the long term conservation and wise use of the coastal and marine environment. Partial funding has been provided by the British Government and World Wide Fund for Nature UK.

8.35 Responsibility for environmental matters is held by the Parliamentary Secretary for Environment and Education in the Office of the Chief Minister. The Department of Fisheries and Marine Resources has responsibility for the establishment and control of National Parks. No terrestrial or marine national parks have yet been created, but selection of wetland sites for listing as internationally important wetlands under the Ramsar Convention has been undertaken.

8.36 The Anguilla Archaeological and Historical Society is the main conservation NGO. Enabling legislation for the establishment of a National Trust for Anguilla, was passed in 1988, but further legislation is required to enable it to operate. The Trust will ultimately be responsible for protected area management.

ASCENSION

8.37 Ascension, a Dependency of St Helena, is a volcanic island situated in the central equatorial Atlantic Ocean, midway between Brazil and Africa. The island has an area of 97 sq km. The highest point is the Peak on Green Mountain Ridge at 860m. The climate is tropical but dry. The vegetation of Ascension has been substantially modified, mainly through the effects of introduced plant and animal species, and lower altitudes are largely barren.

CROWN DEPENDENCIES ANTARCTICA AND THE DEPENDENT TERRITORIES AND THEIR ENDEMIC BIODIVERSITY

DEPENDENCY	LOCATION	SIZE (sq. km.)	Vasc. plants	Terrestrial inverts	reptiles & amphib	birds*
Anguilla	Caribbean	91	1	0	0	0
Ascension	Equatorial Atlantic	97	10	13	–	1
Bermuda	West Atlantic	53	14	1	0	1
British Antarctic Territory	Antarctica	1.7 million	0	a few	0	0
British Virgin Is.	Caribbean	153	not known	1	5	0
Cayman Is.	Caribbean	259	24	insects >38	19	(16)
Falkland Is.	South Atlantic	12173	12	insects 70%	0	1(16)
Gibraltar	Mediterranean	6	5	3	0	0
Bailiwick of Guernsey	Gulf of St Malo	78	0	0	0	0
Hong Kong	South China	1076	<20	>20	3	0
Isle of Man	Irish Sea	588	0	0	0	0
Jersey	Gulf of St Malo	116	0	0	0	0
Montserrat	Caribbean	104	2	>6	5	1
Pitcairn Is.	South Pacific	54	19	Henderson c. 170	?1	4
St Helena	South Atlantic	121	46	about 300	–	1
South Georgia	Sub-Antarctic	3755	1	Insects Approx. 1/3 of total	–	2
South Sandwich Is.	Sub-Antarctic	310	0	not known	–	0
Tristan da Cunha	South Atlantic	169	40	at least 60	–	5(4)
Turks and Caicos	Caribbean	500	9	at least 2	8	0

Notes:

Information is sparse for certain groups of taxa and the numbers given above are estimates based on recorded endemics only.

* subspecies are given in brackets

– signifies no indigenous species in this group in the Dependent Territory

8.38 The resident population of Ascension is currently 1,012, made up of contract workers from St Helena, the UK, USA and South Africa. The main use of the island has been as a communications centre, but this role is declining. The Ascension Exclusive Fishing Zone (EFZ) is exploited by licensed fleets, mainly from Japan.

8.39 The biodiversity importance of Ascension results from its endemic species and internationally important seabird and Green Turtle breeding populations. The flora consists of 25 native vascular plants, 10 of which are rare or endangered endemics, and a further endemic species is believed to be extinct. Over 100,000 seabirds nest on the island with four species of tern, three boobies, two tropic birds, one storm petrel and the globally threatened endemic Ascension frigate bird.

8.40 Introduced species continue to be the major threat to the island's biodiversity. The impact of feral cats on the seabird colonies is for example a cause of international conservation concern. The World Conference of the International Council for Bird Preservation (ICBP), passed a resolution in 1990 recommending that the UK Government designate Ascension a 'protected natural area',

Masked booby, Bo'sun Bird Island, Ascension.

prepare a management plan to include the eradication of introduced animals and implement it as soon as possible.

8.41 The resident Administrator has local responsibility for conservation matters and a warden is designated under the island's conservation legislation.

BERMUDA

8.42 Bermuda is situated in the western Atlantic Ocean approximately 917 km from the coast of North Carolina in the USA. Bermuda consists of around 150 coral limestone islands and islets extending along the edge of an extinct submarine volcano. The ten main islands are connected by bridges or causeways to form a chain about 35.4 km long. The land area is 53.35 sq. km. With a population of about 59,000 Bermuda is densely populated and only small areas of natural habitat survive. Tourism and international business are the main sectors of the economy.

8.43 Bermuda's remaining natural habitats are important for biodiversity conservation, harbouring endemic and threatened plant species. The biodiversity is generally well documented. There are 165 native vascular plant species, 14 of which are endemic. The conservation status of flowering plants and ferns has been studied and measures are being taken to propagate rare species in the Botanical Gardens and to enhance wild populations. The terrestrial invertebrate fauna is depauperate with few endemic taxa. The avifauna has also been comprehensively studied and all species except for four pest species are legally protected. The Bermuda Cahow breeds only on Bermuda. Information on shoreline and shallow water marine communities has recently been published. The coral reefs are subject to regular research and monitoring.

Gentoo penguins, Petermann Island, Antarctica.

8.44 The Department of Agriculture, Fisheries and Parks has responsibility for conservation, through its Conservation and Parks Divisions. Comprehensive measures to conserve the biodiversity of Bermuda are in place, supported by a development planning system and the activities of environmental NGOs. Long term monitoring of wildlife sites and habitat restoration remain important.

Southern Elephant seal, Anven Island, Antarctica.

BRITISH ANTARCTIC TERRITORY (BAT)

8.45 The British Antarctic Territory (BAT) covers the area of land and sea between 80°–20°W, extending from the South Pole to 60°S. BAT is administered by the South Atlantic and Antarctic Department of the Foreign and Commonwealth Office.

8.46 The biodiversity importance of BAT results mainly from its marine resources and seabird colonies. The marine invertebrate fauna of the Antarctic Continental shelves is rich and diverse in contrast with the terrestrial invertebrate fauna. The Weddell Sea is one of the major embayments of Antarctica which appears to have a geographically distinctive fauna.

8.47 The global importance of Antarctica to biodiversity conservation is immense in terms of its modulating effect upon many complex physical and biological systems of the planet.

8.48 Conservation policy relating to BAT is determined by the Antarctic Treaty System and Dependent Territory legislation on fauna and flora. The 'preservation and conservation of living resources in the Antarctic' was named as one of the matters of common interest about which parties to the Antarctic Treaty should consult. The Treaty provides a framework within which conservation agreements can be drawn up by the Consultative Parties. The first such agreement was the "Agreed Measures for the Conservation of Antarctic Fauna and Flora" drawn up in 1964 as a voluntary agreement and given legal force in 1982. Subsequent Conventions have been introduced for the Conservation of Seals and Marine Living Resources.

8.49 In October 1991 a new Protocol on Environmental Protection to the Antarctic Treaty, including annexes on flora and fauna and protected areas, was signed by the 26

Consultative Parties. This is not yet in force, pending ratification, but the UK is already implementing provisions of the Protocol through the activities of the British Antarctic Survey (BAS). BAS is undertaking a major programme of scientific research in the Antarctic.

8.50 Measures similar to those required under the Biodiversity Convention already exist within the Antarctic Treaty system. For example, Annex V of the Environment Protocol to the Antarctic Treaty provides for the setting up of an internationally recognised system of protected areas in Antarctica. In view of this, the British Antarctic Territory will not be included in the UK's ratification of the Biodiversity Convention.

BRITISH VIRGIN ISLANDS

8.51 The British Virgin Islands (BVI) form the western extremity of the Lesser Antilles in the eastern Caribbean Sea. There are approximately 36 islands in the group with a total land area of 153 sq km. The main islands are Tortola (54 sq km), Virgin Gorda (21 sq km), Anegada (38 sq km) and Jost van Dyke (9 sq km). Most of the islands were uplifted from submerged volcanos and are hilly with steep slopes. In contrast, Anegada is an emergent coral limestone platform. The island is flat with a maximum altitude of 8m.

8.52 The population of BVI in 1991 was 17,733. Over the past ten years there has been a 47% increase in population, mainly as a result of immigration. Tortola is the most developed island and has a population of over 13,500. The economy of BVI is largely based on tourism, especially yacht chartering, and the offshore financial services sector is also important. The agriculture and fisheries sectors are being revitalised.

Tortola, Sage Mountain National Park, British Virgin Isles.

8.53 The rich biodiversity of BVI includes endemic plants, reptiles, and insects and internationally important coral reef systems.

8.54 The Conservation and Fisheries Department of the Ministry of Natural Resources and Labour is responsible for biodiversity conservation in BVI. The National Parks Trust is responsible for the development and management of the protected area system.

8.55 Conservation has concentrated on site protection over recent years. The selection of sites for conservation purposes is relatively well advanced in BVI. A comprehensive protected area system is being developed under a National Parks System Plan accepted by the BVI Government in 1987. The BVI Government has recently stated the need to carry out a full taxonomic survey of the plants and animals of these areas, and of some other unique areas not included in the System Plan. Revision of conservation ordinances relating to threatened species is also required.

8.56 Important work has been carried out to inventory, protect and manage areas of mangroves and associated wetlands, under the BVI Government's Mangrove Management Programme. A Coastal Resources Inventory has recently been completed.

CAYMANS

8.57 The three Cayman Islands are situated at the western end of the Greater Antilles in the Caribbean. The total land area of the islands is 259 sq km. The largest of the islands is Grand Cayman with an area of 197 sq km. It is a low limestone and dolomite island with a large area of mangrove and fringing reefs around most of the coast. Most of the population of the Caymans live on Grand Cayman and rapid development has transformed the island's environment. Development pressures on the island, and on Cayman Brac, continue to be the main threat to biodiversity. Little Cayman with a population of less than 100, has until recently remained relatively little disturbed. The number of buildings has, however, doubled in the past year and a new hotel has recently opened. The economy of the Caymans is based on tourism and the offshore finance industry.

8.58 The rich biodiversity of the Caymans has been relatively well-documented. The Flora, published in 1984, includes a floristic description of the different vegetation types. Since publication, 53 additional species have been discovered in the Caymans, and the Flora is due for

The economy of the Caymans is based on tourism and the offshore fishing industry.

revision. The plant collection assembled during preparation of the Flora forms the basis for a Herbarium maintained by the National Trust for the Cayman Islands. A recent assessment of the conservation status of wild plants of the Caymans shows that out of the 24 endemic vascular plant taxa, eight are vulnerable or endangered and one is presumed extinct.

8.59 The avifauna of the Caymans consists of 181 bird taxa. The endemic parrots have recieved particular conservation attention as 'flagship species'. The recently formed Bird Club carries out assessment and monitoring of bird populations and study of the life cycles of indigenous species. Nineteen taxa of reptiles and amphibians are endemic to the Cayman Islands. The National Trust currently has a conservation programme for the Grand Cayman endemic Blue Iguana. The invertebrate biodiversity of the Caymans is less well known.

8.60 The Caymans Government agency with responsibility for biodiversity conservation is the Portfolio for Tourism, the Environment and Planning. The Government has placed considerable emphasis on marine conservation, and a successful marine parks programme is in operation. Conservation of terrestrial habitats is now urgently required and the National Trust for the Cayman Islands has published a strategy for the establishment of terrestrial reserves on Grand Cayman. The extensive primary stands of low elevation dry woodlands on all three islands of the Caymans are of regional importance for biodiversity conservation.

FALKLAND ISLANDS

8.61 The Falkland Islands are situated in the South Atlantic. They cover an area of 12,173 sq km, with two main islands, East and West Falklands, and hundreds of smaller offshore islands. The climate of the islands is cool temperate oceanic and supports a vegetation consisting of oceanic heath, fern and bog and feldmark communities. Tussock grass vegetation is now mainly confined to the offshore islands. The resident population is around 2,120, with approximately 2000 British armed services personnel in addition. The traditional economic activity of the Falklands is sheep ranching for the production of wool. Since 1987 the chief source of income has been the sale of fishing licences to foreign squid and finfish fleets operating within a unilateral offshore fisheries conservation zone.

8.62 A comprehensive vascular flora is available which describes all known species and the main vegetation associations. The vascular plant flora consists of 163 taxa, 12 of which are endemic. Inventory of lower plants is incomplete. A checklist of insects is also incomplete, but the collections so far available indicate a high level of endemism. The avifauna is well documented and an Atlas of Falkland Islands Breeding Birds is due for publication in 1994. There are 61 breeding bird taxa including sixteen which are endemic. The Falklands are the most important site for Southern Rockhopper Penguin and Black-browed Albatross Southern Elephant Seal, Southern Sea Lion, and Falkland Islands Fur Seal breed on the islands. Major gaps remain in knowledge of the Falklands biota and there is a need for further flora and fauna surveys and ecological research.

King penguins on the Falklands

8.63 There is no government agency responsible for conservation in the Falklands. Charitable NGOs such as Falklands Conservation and the New Island Conservation Trust play a major role in conducting conservation activities, including research, monitoring, environmental education and provision of advice to the Falkland Islands Government.

8.64 Conservation legislation in the Falklands is in need of updating. At present there is no legal provision for habitat protection on private land, which accounts for most of the islands. In 1988 the Falklands Islands Government commissioned a report from its Honorary Conservation Advisor to form the basis of a conservation policy and legislation review. The report is currently being considered by an advisory Conservation Committee.

GIBRALTAR

8.65 Gibraltar lies at the tip of southern Spain and covers an area of 5.86 sq km. The Rock of Gibraltar, formed of Jurassic limestone, rises in a sheer cliff on the eastern side, reaching 426 m. and slopes more gently to the west. It is joined to Spain by a low-lying sandy isthmus. The population of Gibraltar is 28,000.

8.66 The biodiversity of Gibraltar includes endemic plant and invertebrate species, a rich marine fauna due to the convergence of Atlantic and Mediterranean influences, and an internationally important avifauna. The flora and fauna of Gibraltar is well-documented, largely through the activities of the Gibraltar Ornithological and Natural History Society. This voluntary organisation has recently begun computerisation of species records.

8.67 Comprehensive species and habitat conservation legislation have recently been enacted. The Upper Rock has been designated a Nature Reserve but there is concern about the future of other important wildlife sites on land no longer required by the Ministry of Defence.

HONG KONG

8.68 Hong Kong is situated on the south-east coast of China, joining the Province of Guangdong. The total area of the territory is 1076 sq km. Much of Hong Kong is hilly, with steep infertile hillsides rising to nearly 1000 m, and cultivated valleys, some of which are now abandonned. Flat alluvial plains occur in the north. Hong Kong is one of the most densely populated areas of the world. The current population is about 5.9 million. Natural vegetation has been extensively modified throughout the territory but nevertheless Hong Kong retains a variety of habitats which are very important for biodiversity conservation. Mai Po Marshes are, for example, an internationally important wetland site.

8.69 The biodiversity of Hong Kong is in need of further study to assess fully the degree of endemism and the conservation status of many animal and plant species. Over 420 species of birds have been recorded in Hong Kong with more than 117 species breeding in the

Territory. Nearly 100 reptiles and amphibians occur in Hong Kong. There are a number of endemic species including Romer's Tree Frog. The vascular plant flora consists of around 2800 species of which nearly 2000 are native.

8.70 The main threat to biodiversity is habitat loss resulting from development pressures such as urbanisation and industrial growth; construction of the new airport and associated dredging, dumping and reclamation activities; and pollution.

8.71 All species of birds are legally protected within Hong Kong together with most of the indigenous mammals, amphibians and some threatened species of plants. The Forests and Countryside Ordinance, 1984 (Cap 96), the primary legislation protecting native plants in situ, was revised in June 1993.

8.72 Land is designated for conservation purposes by a variety of means in Hong Kong. The Country Parks system, established mainly for conservation, recreational and education purposes, covers some 40% of the land area. The 21 Country Parks, account for around 408 sq km of mostly upland terrain, and there are also 14 Special Areas, designated for their conservation interest. In addition to the designated areas covered by site protection legislation, SSSIs may be declared by the Director of Planning on the advice of the Director of Agriculture and Fisheries. At present there are 50 SSSIs. These have limited legal status, but are taken into account for planning purposes. Preparations are under way to establish and manage Marine Parks and Marine Reserves for the protection of important marine ecosystems.

8.73 The Agriculture and Fisheries Department is the principal government agency responsible for the conservation of Hong Kong's flora and fauna. The Conservation Division, implements and reviews the mechanisms for species and habitat conservation and the Country Parks Authority is responsible for the protection and management of lands designated as Country Parks and Special Areas. The Agriculture and Fisheries Department is the contact Department for international conservation conventions although these are handled through the Government Secretariat. There are a number of active conservation NGOs in Hong Kong including local offices of the World Wide Fund for Nature (WWF HK) and Friends of the Earth and the Conservancy Association. WWF HK has developed a GIS ecological database and is including distributional data for flora and fauna.

THE BAILIWICK OF GUERNSEY

8.74 The Bailiwick of Guernsey consists of the Islands of Guernsey, Alderney, Sark, Herm, Jethou and Brechou, together with numerous islets and offshore rocks, with a total population of 61,600. They are located in the English Channel, off the north-west coast of France. The largest island, Guernsey, has an area of 63 sq km and a population of 59,000.

8.75 In biodiversity terms, the Bailiwick of Guernsey is part of France. Habitats include cliffs, coastal heathland, sand dunes, reed beds and extensive inter-tidal areas. The islands are cultivated primarily with livestock farming. There is an internationally important colony of Gannets off the coast of Alderney, and the wintering population of Turnstones in the Bailiwick is also of international importance.

8.76 Guernsey and Alderney have separate legislation protecting wild birds. Revised planning legislation, including the protection of wildlife habitats on Guernsey, is in preparation. 35 Sites of Nature Conservation Importance have been identified for protection.

8.77 The States of Guernsey (island government) departments with direct responsibilities in relation to environmental matters are the Board of Administration (Environmental Services) and Island Development Committee. A number of nature reserves have been established, and are managed by the States of Guernsey, La Societe Guernesiaise, and the National Trust of Guernsey.

JERSEY

8.78 Jersey is the largest (116 sq km) and most southerly of the Channel Islands, lying about 20 km west of the Cherbourg Peninsula of France.

8.79 Jersey has a wide range of habitats including extensive intertidal sand and rocky areas, sand dunes of international importance, heathlands, wetlands, woodlands and arable land. It has a high level of biodiversity. Its local fauna and flora is enriched by the presence of many species at the northern limit of their distribution which are more usually found on the Continent mainland. Jersey supports a few unique species of its own and many British plant Red Data Book species. Birds of national importance in the British context include ringed plover, grey plover, sanderling and turnstone.

8.80 Conservation legislation in Jersey includes the Island Planning (Amendment No 3) (Jersey) Law 1983, which provides for the protection of ecologically important habitats (Sites of Special Interest) and the Wild Life

(Protection) (Jersey) Law 1947, which protects all indigenous reptiles and amphibians. A new Conservation of Wildlife (Jersey) Law, which will protect wild plants and animals, is in an advanced stage of drafting.

8.81 A draft Biodiversity Strategy has already been prepared. It is anticipated that it will be finalised before the end of the year. The Strategy is based on a two tier approach – targets and recommendations. Targets have been set only for priority biodiversity resources which are specific, measurable, achievable, realistic and timed and they have been selected at international, British Isles and Jersey scales of importance. Recommendations have been made regarding the key socio-political issues affecting the Island's biodiversity.

ISLE OF MAN

8.82 The Isle of Man is located in the northern section of the Irish Sea, halfway between England and Northern Island. It has an area of 588 sq km. The population of the Isle of Man is now 69,788.

8.83 Habitats on the island include rocky coastline, beaches, dunes, woodland, moorland, marshes, peatland and agricultural land. Agricultural habitats account for 86% of the island's area. A comprehensive habitat survey is currently being undertaken in the Isle of Man. Bird species of national importance in the British context include hen harrier, peregrine, little tern and chough. Information on the conservation status of vascular plants is included in the British Red Data Book.

8.84 The Wildlife Act, 1990, protects specified plant and animal species and also enables the creation of terrestrial and marine nature reserves and Areas of Special Scientific Interest. In addition Clause 24.4 of the Marine Museum and National Trust Act 1959–1986 states 'The Trust shall promote the permanent preservation for the benefit of the people of the Isle of Man of land and tenements (including buildings) of beauty or historic interest and, as regards lands, the preservation (so far as practicable) of their natural aspect, features and animal and plant life.'

MONTSERRAT

8.85 Montserrat is situated in the Leeward Islands of the eastern Caribbean. It is a small volcanic island, 104 sq km, with three main forest-covered hill ranges. Montserrat's population is around 12,000. The main economic activities are agriculture which is in decline, real estate, construction and tourism. The economy is currently reliant on overseas aid.

8.86 Preliminary assessments of the conservation status of the birds, reptiles and amphibians have been made and an environmental database is maintained by the Montserrat National Trust. There is a need for a comprehensive inventory of biodiversity to be carried out. Montserrat is included in the Eastern Caribbean Endemic Bird Area as defined by ICBP, and as well as having an endemic bird species, 12 internationally restricted birds occur there. A Tropical Forest Action Programme mission, funded by the British Government made recommendations on biodiversity, national parks, forestry, land use and watershed management. The mission reinforced the need for the development of a National Park in the Soufriere Hills and the development of revised conservation legislation.

8.87 The Montserrat Government Agency with responsibility for biodiversity conservation is the Ministry of Agriculture, Trade and the Environment. The Montserrat National Trust is an NGO actively involved in conservation, through management of the only Bird Sanctuary on the island, provision of advice to Government and educational activities. The Islands Resource Foundation, a regional NGO, has identified Fox's Bay Bird Sanctuary as one of its focal sites in a new programme to conserve the biodiversity of the Eastern Caribbean, and funding for rehabilitation of the site will be provided by WWF-UK.

PITCAIRN ISLANDS

8.88 The Pitcairn Islands comprise four islands located in the South Pacific Ocean, roughly equal distance (4,800km) from the continental land masses of South America and Australasia, and close to the Tropic of Capricorn. Pitcairn Island is a small, inhabited volcanic island of 450ha, with a population of 60. The other three coral islands Henderson (3700 ha), Oeno and Ducie are uninhabited.

8.89 Henderson Island is included in the World Heritage List of Natural Sites under the World Heritage Convention. A management plan for the island is being prepared to ensure the conservation of this unique raised coral atoll and its biodiversity. Henderson has four endemic land birds together with ten endemic plant species. About one-third of the insects and probably all the land snails are endemic. Oeno and Ducie are remarkably undisturbed coral atolls supporting large and internationally significant seabird populations. The Pitcairn Islands are categorised as a high priority Endemic Bird Area by ICBP. They are the main breeding station for Murphy's Petrel.

Montserrat is a small volcanic island with three main forest-covered hill ranges.

8.90 A major independent multidisciplinary expedition, based on Henderson Island from January 1991 to March 1992, gathered considerable information on the current and historical ecology of Henderson and on the other islands in the group. Results from this Pitcairn Islands Scientific Expedition provide a substantially improved basis for assessing the conservation value of the islands' biota. No thorough inventory of the terrestrial invertebrate fauna of the Pitcairn Islands has, however, yet been carried out.

ST HELENA

8.91 St Helena is a tropical island situated in the South Atlantic Ocean. It lies some 1,960 km from the nearest point on the southwest coast of Africa and 2,900 km east of South America. The island is volcanic, representing the deeply eroded summit of a composite volcano. It is approximately 16 km long and 10 km at its widest point. A high central ridge dominates the topography, and the highest point, Diana's Peak, lies on this ridge rising to 823m above sea level.

8.92 The population of St Helena was estimated at 5443 in 1990. Agriculture, livestock rearing and fishing are the island's main economic activities. The island is principally maintained by public revenue from the UK.

8.93 The original vegetation of St Helena has been almost completely destroyed through centuries of modification and many species of birds have been extirpated The biodiversity importance of St Helena lies chiefly in its endemic flora and fauna. St Helena's flora includes 46 endemic species which are of great biogeographical

Green turtle on Henderson Island.

interest. Most of these species are endangered or rare. Recovery work for St Helena's flora, carried out with support from ODA, RBG Kew, FFPS and WWF-UK has concentrated on field survey, development of local propagation facilities, and reintroduction to the wild. The fauna of St Helena, particularly the invertebrates, is less well known, but is likely to be in need of similar conservation attention. Around 300 endemic invertebrates have been described. Of the 256 beetles recorded on the island, 61.3% are endemic. The endemic St Helena Wirebird is considered to be globally threatened.

8.94 The British Government is currently funding the development of a sustainable environment and development strategy, and action plan for St Helena commissioned at the request of the St Helena Government. Biosphere Reserve status for the island may be considered under the UNESCO Man and Biosphere Programme.

SOUTH GEORGIA AND THE SOUTH SANDWICH ISLANDS

8.95 South Georgia is an isolated sub-Antarctic island lying about 1400 km from the Falkland Islands and 1550 km from the nearest point on the Antarctic Continent. It is the largest of the sub-Antarctic islands with a surface area of approximately 3,500 sq km. Around the main island are several small offshore islands together with many islets and rocks. South Georgia is mountainous and there are few extensive ice-free flat areas.

St Helena ebony, one of the endemic plants receiving attention from Kew's Conservation Unit.

8.96 The biodiversity of South Georgia includes 26 vascular plants of which one is endemic. Unpublished distribution maps for the vascular and moss floras of the island are available at BAS. Of the 148 insect species recorded, 37% are apparently endemic. The avifauna is particularly significant with 29 breeding bird taxa, including two endemics. A survey of the breeding birds of South Georgia has recently been carried out and distribution maps have been prepared for all species. Huge seabird breeding colonies occur on South Georgia, notably on rat-free offshore islands.

8.97 South Georgia also has very large populations of marine mammals. The Southern Fur-Seal has now recovered from the effects of sealing activities which brought the species to the brink of extinction during the last century. South Georgia also hosts the only stable population of Southern Elephant Seal.

8.98 Scientific research conducted by BAS over the past 25 years has included studies on vegetation, effects of introduced reindeer and rodents, terrestrial production, pollution, marine biology, bird and marine mammal ecology, and geology. The ecology of the fauna and flora is well known in comparison with most other subantarctic islands. At the BAS research station at Bird Island research into the population biology, ecology and behaviour of seabirds and seals is carried out. Research into terrestrial and freshwater biology is undertaken at the BAS summer field station at Husvikresearch.

8.99 Conservation measures for South Georgia are similar to those under the Antarctic Treaty. Legislation currently designates a Special Protection Area, Cooper Island, and two SSSIs, Bird Island and Annenkov Island. There is a need for revised legislation to reflect recent survey information. A management plan is also required for South Georgia, taking into account issues such as the significant vegetational changes caused by expansion of the uncontrolled reindeer herd.

8.100 The South Sandwich Islands lie 470 km south-east of South Georgia and 1300 km from the Antarctic Continent. The group consists of twelve volcanic islands. The larger islands are largely ice-covered whereas the smaller ones are virtually ice-free. The South Sandwich Islands have been scarcely modified by human activities.

8.101 BAS has carried out a limited amount of biological research in the South Sandwich Islands on terrestrial and fresh water biology and botany.

8.102 Conservation measures for the South Sandwich Islands are similar to those under the Antarctic Treaty. No protected areas have been designated as yet. Revision of conservation legislation is necessary.

TRISTAN DA CUNHA

8.103 Tristan da Cunha, a dependency of St Helena, consists of a group of islands in the South Atlantic, only one of which, Tristan da Cunha, is permanently inhabited. Tristan da Cunha, Inaccessible and Nightingale lie close together, separated from Gough by 350 km. The population of Tristan da Cunha is around 300. Inshore fishing is the main source of revenue.

8.104 The Tristan da Cunha islands are extremely important in terms of biodiversity conservation. They are internationally important as breeding seabird colonies and also harbour endemic landbirds, invertebrates and plants. Overall species richness for most groups is low but endemism is high. Twenty of the 29 beetle species are, for example, endemic, as are 23 out of 124 liverworts and 59 out of 126 mosses. The invertebrate fauna of Gough has been subject to very limited investigation.

The grey-headed albatross breeds on South Georgia.

8.105 At the request of the Tristan da Cunha Government, a management plan has been prepared for the Gough Island Wildlife Reserve. This has been accepted by the Tristan Government but awaits legal ratification and publication. The UK Government has comissioned a proposal to list Gough as a natural site under the World Heritage Convention. The mammals, birds and plants of the other islands are legally protected.

8.106 Responsibility for conservation matters rests with the resident Administrator, who is advised by the Island Council. Tristan police officers act as Conservation Officers and two scientists at the Percy FitzPatrick Institute of African Ornithology, University of Cape Town, South Africa, also act in this capacity.

TURKS AND CAICOS

8.107 The Turks and Caicos are a group of islands lying at the southeastern extremity of the Bahamas Archipelago. There are over forty islands in the group of which six main islands and two small ones are inhabited. The islands are limestone with outlying coral reefs. Over half the land area consists of wetlands. Tourism is the main economic activity in the Turks and Caicos and the off-shore finance industry is also of growing importance. Fishing is now of minor economic importance.

The biodiversity of the Turks and Caicos includes endemic species of plants and herpetofauna and virtually undisturbed wetland and reef habitats. Rapid development is increasing the need for comprehensive conservation measures for the island.

8.108 Conservation legislation has recently been updated in the Turks and Caicos with the National Parks Ordinance enacted in 1992. Legislation protecting bird species has also been revised, but there is as yet no specific legal protection for other threatened animals or plants. All species are protected within national parks and other protected areas. Now that the legal basis for conservation is established there is still a need to inventory the fauna and flora and assess the conservation status of species.

8.109 Conservation is the responsibility of the Ministry of Natural Resources. A National Parks Adviser is funded by ODA. The newly created National Trust will be involved in most aspects of conservation including management of national parks, increasing public awareness and fundraising. WWF-UK is currently providing funds for both development of the National Trust, and for the prepartion of management plans by the National Parks Office of the Ministry of Natural Resources.

St Helena, Ebony.

CHAPTER 9

INFORMATION AND DATA

INTRODUCTION

Background

9.1 This chapter describes the major UK sources of information and data on biodiversity. The increasing demands for environmental data and the development of refined analytical techniques mean that organisations handling such data are constantly adapting and augmenting their data collections and maintenance practices. As data networks spread throughout Europe it is particularly important that levels of data quality assurance and co-ordination of systems are developed. There is therefore both the need and opportunity to improve the collection, organisation and co-ordination of information and data relating to biodiversity.

9.2 Although we are fortunate in the UK that relatively large amounts of data are collected on biodiversity, much of this is not readily available in a form that assists decisions on the management of species populations or on the direction of land-use change. The work of Government Departments, research and conservation agencies, NGOs and others has yet to be co-ordinated so that it forms a common, effective and distributed system. This means that decisions are sometimes made without access to all existing information, and scarce resources are wasted by unnecessary repetition of work in differing organisations. One example of the type

of integrated approach to data handling needed to support policy decisions is the Countryside Information System (CIS) commissioned by the Department of the Environment.

9.3 The need for accurate and accessible data on biodiversity is indisputable. Where accurate data are not available the precautionary principle should be emphasised in order to assess national priorities and to deal with projects and proposals which may affect biodiversity. Insofar as specific proposals for development or use pose a significant threat to biodiversity the onus for assessing the environmental impact must rest on those making the proposals.

9.4 The sections of this chapter are designed to follow the requirements under the Convention and indicate actions at each stage.

9.5 The need for data collection and monitoring under the Convention provides a framework into which requirements from a number of EC Directives and other Conventions fit. Table 1 (at end of chapter) illustrates this point. Gathering data on biodiversity, maintaining and organising data, monitoring populations and habitats, collecting information on designated sites, quantifying threats to biodiversity and the sustainable use of biodiversity are requirements under these Directives and Conventions. The Biodiversity Convention broadens the scope

---

ARTICLE 7 OF THE CONVENTION ON BIOLOGICAL DIVERSITY

The starting point for an examination of current practices and future needs is the text of the Convention on Biological Diversity. Article 7 states that each contracting party shall, as far as possible and as appropriate, for the purposes of in situ conservation, ex situ conservation, and the sustainable use of components of Biological Diversity undertake the following:

- Identify the components of Biological Diversity important for conservation and sustainable use.
- Monitor through sampling and other techniques the components of Biological Diversity paying particular attention to those requiring urgent conservation measures and those offering the greatest potential for sustainable use.
- Identify processes and categories of activities which have or are likely to have a significant adverse impact on the conservation and sustainable use of biological diversity and monitor their effects through sampling and other techniques.
- Maintain and organise, by any mechanism, data derived from identification and monitoring activities relevant to the above measures.

In the identification of biological diversity regard should be given to:

- Ecosystems and habitats: containing high diversity, large numbers of endemic or threatened species, or wilderness; required by migratory species; of social, economic, cultural or scientific importance; or, that are representative, unique or associated with key evolutionary or other biological processes.
- Species and communities that are: threatened; wild relatives of domesticated or cultivated species; of medicinal, agricultural or other economic value; of social, scientific or cultural importance; or important for research into the conservation and sustainable use of biological diversity, such as indicator species.
- Described genomes and genes of social, scientific or economic importance.

of these requirements and encourages greater co-ordination of effort. However, at present, apart from the examples cited, no organisation is statutorily required to establish or maintain national or regional biodiversity information. Biodiversity information should be recognised as a distinct type of resource to be documented in a similar way to other heritage data e.g. architectural or archaeological.

Links from data to nature conservation targets

9.6 There should be strong links between the collection of data on biodiversity and the objectives of nature conservation policies. Other chapters in this action plan outline key objectives and specific targets for nature conservation, and a summary of these targets is given in Table 2. The data needs for each area of work is shown, demonstrating the close linkage to requirements 'as far as possible and as appropriate' under Article 7 of the Convention.

9.7 Information collected throughout the UK should be used actively to inform decisions on nature conservation and land use, and to provide a scientific basis for actions. Table 3 illustrates the linkages required from data collection through to actual conservation practice. Table 4 provides an outstanding example of data collection by a large number of volunteer fieldworkers used to ensure effective conservation action for wetland birds. Other less advanced systems should be developed to ensure similar effective translation of data collection to conservation action.

9.8 While in some cases data flows through to action in many others considerable interpretation, analysis and even further research is required. The actions of the native conservation agencies need to be underpinned by scientific evidence which involves further interpretation of data. This analysis may be carried out to determine population processes, controlling factors or habitat characteristics. In many cases the organisations responsible for data collection may be best placed to undertake fundamental research based on those data in collaboration with the nature conservation agencies.

CURRENT DATA COLLECTION

Species and habitats

9.9 The Convention requires the key components of biodiversity to be identified. Ideally the distribution, abundance, reproductive status and conservation status should be determined for key species and habitat types. 'Key' in this sense may be either components that are important determinants of biodiversity or those that are good indicators of overall biodiversity. Government and statutory bodies have undertaken considerable work in recent years to examine priorities for conservation action within this framework. Table 5 outlines work currently underway to provide information on the potential biodiversity resource in the UK.

9.10 While there is a long history of data gathering on the distribution and status of species and habitats, this has tended to be carried out between organisations in an unplanned and sporadic way for some groups – though work on birds is an obvious exception. Survey activity usually relates to the availability and enthusiasm of particular groups of volunteers. For this reason UK data collections of species groups such as birds, some invertebrate groups such as butterflies and for vascular plants tend to be more comprehensive than for other species groups. The recent survey by the Co-ordinating Commission for Biological Recording (CCBR) demonstrates this imbalance clearly. CCBR estimate that at least 85 million biological records are held today in the UK, over 60% of which refer to birds.

9.11 The CCBR has recently concluded the most comprehensive survey of biological recording ever made in the UK. The results of this survey will be available in 1994. The survey makes it clear that data should be collected on less frequently covered groups where they are important components of biodiversity. Notable groups where ecologically significant information is inadequate are those of soil flora and fauna, and fungi. However, it is important that any additional work in new areas of study should not be at the expense of efforts on those groups that are comparatively well covered, where these are still producing valuable monitoring information in the context of the Convention.

Inventories of key species, habitats and communities

9.12 Any future data collection strategy for the UK should consider whether a complete inventory of all species and habitats, including status, numbers, distribution, reproductive status and rate of change should be undertaken. While the Convention proposes developing inventories it also states that priority species and habitats should be selected for action. At present it would divert effort and funds from urgent conservation action, if an exercise to achieve a full inventory of species and habitats in the UK was to be undertaken. Obtaining relatively superficial data on all organisms would be less useful then getting meaningful data on those species that can be studied cost effectively and whose diversity is likely to correlate reasonably well with overall biodiversity. Table 6 outlines the types of data needed for a full inventory. Completion of this type of inventory is likely to be very time consuming and require considerable resources.

9.13 Inventories of species may of course take the form of physical collections in museums, zoos and botanic gardens. The UK has a long history in developing such collections and a deserved international reputation in many such areas. There remains however a need to develop further the accessibility of such collections.

9.14 Any inventory of species and habitats could initially concentrate upon threatened examples and those identified as national targets under the developing UK Biodiversity Action Plan.

Sites

9.15 In providing a scientific basis for statements on population ecology and habitat distribution leading to effective conservation practice, it is necessary to appreciate that patterns of biodiversity are not uniform across land or sea areas; some particular areas or sites have higher biodiversity than others.

9.16 Table 6 provides examples of some of the schemes currently undertaking data collection and monitoring on sites. It is notable that there is overlap and a lack of co-ordination between these projects. The box illustrates also the large number of organisations and individuals involved in collection of data at the site level. It should be noted that the majority of post-war biological records are, in fact, site specific.

A wider countryside framework

9.17 It is important to monitor biodiversity in the wider countryside as well as special sites since these areas comprise most of the country and support a great variety of wildlife. The wider countryside also includes the places where many people live and work, or visit for pleasure.

9.18 Countryside Survey 1990 has made a major contribution to our knowledge of the biodiversity resource of the wider countryside. The survey has established a permanent sampling framework of 508 one kilometre squares containing 11,500 fixed quadrats. The survey uses the ITE Land Classification to obtain an efficient and representative sample of environmental variation in Great Britain. A similar land classification and sampling framework has been established for Northern Ireland by the University of Ulster.

9.19 The land classification and sampling approach provides a tool for integrating surveys and data collection on a national scale and this is demonstrated in the Countryside Information System. Field surveys using the Countryside Survey 1990 methodology were undertaken in 1978, 1984 and 1990. There are plans to undertake another major survey in the year 2000. The repeat surveys provide a mechanism for monitoring the biodiversity of the wider countryside in the future.

Current collection of data on threats to biodiversity

9.20 Many factors impact on biodiversity throughout the UK including air pollution, water resources, destruction of habitats and intensive agriculture. Yet while many of these factors are threats to biodiversity, many are also legitimate land uses or form an integral part of our present lifestyle. A balance has to be struck between their use or permitted emissions in the case of pollution, and the maintenance and enhancement of biodiversity. Table 8 outlines current sources of these data for the UK. The type of information each organisation collects and a note of the work in progress are listed.

COUNTRYSIDE IMPACTS TABLE

Article 7 of the Convention requires contracting parties to identify processes and activities likely to have significant adverse impacts on biodiversity. The need to develop an appreciation of the environmental implications of policies and activities was also a key theme of the Environment White Paper This Common Inheritance (DOE, 1991). Although the need to appraise the consequences of policy changes is now widely accepted, the process of appraisal is itself complex and problematic; there is a wealth of information about the impacts of human activity on biodiversity, both in Britain and overseas. Providing access to such a variety of specialised information for decision-makers is a challenge.

A methodology for environmental policy appraisal was described in Policy Appraisal and the Environment (DOE 1992). The approach uses a matrix concept, in which an 'impacts table' is constructed. The axes of the matrix are "actions" which characterise a proposal and a set of "environmental" receptors which are potentially affected by the scheme. Entries in the cells of the matrix flag any environmental costs or benefits, or whether the effects are neutral or unknown.

This methodology formed the basis for a project which has recently been carried out for the Department of the Environment by Nottingham University, known as the Countryside Impacts Table. The aim was to develop a simple and readily accessible system that would enable policy makers to be better informed about the potential environmental consequences of changes in countryside or agricultural policy. This was achieved by bringing together the diverse literature on the effects of different agricultural enterprises on the various components of the countryside. The outcome has been an easily accessible database which relates agricultural practices to documented effects on the countryside. The axes of the matrix in this impacts table are the farm enterprise types and the farming activities associated with them (actions) and landscape features and their various attributes (receptors). The 'impacts' are recorded as a brief resume of what is available in the literature. This was a pilot project, and the Department is considering wider publication of the report, as well as developing the approach as a tool for bringing together and accessing information on impacts in a wider variety of policy areas. Other approaches to the evaluation of impacts include various forms of modelling.

Data standards

9.21 There is a need to apply common standards and common practices to data collection, collation and analysis. Many current data collection systems have been established by organisations working within a restricted remit. Volunteers are essential in the collection of biodiversity data. The work of the CCBR provides a major contribution to the development of common standards. Volunteers require standard recording systems and need to be able to see benefits to conservation practice as an end point of their efforts. If the UK is to continue to collect high quality biological data, then the volunteer worker has to be encouraged and given direction. Existing standard systems such as the Wetland Bird Survey (WeBS) for monitoring populations of non-breeding waterfowl act as models of the type of standard systems needed elsewhere.

New data collection

9.22 While it is desirable to develop new data series, it is crucial to maintain existing systems which contribute to the objectives of the Convention (while examining them

critically) especially if they already hold long runs of data. Increased data collection to quantify biodiversity does however need to be undertaken in the following areas:
- Marine: quantification of the biodiversity resource including, extent, distribution and sustainable use.
- Lower plants: information on the distribution of species, especially in some groups such as fungi and algae.
- Data to underline the sustainable use of many species and habitats.
- Investigation of the interrelationships between various animal and plant groups.

9.23 New data collection should be organised on a long-term basis. A national strategy and framework should be developed to co-ordinate action between organisations. The expertise already gained within the UK on data collection could assist with similar work in the Dependent Territories and other areas of the world. This clearly links the work on biodiversity data collection to the current Darwin Initiative.

Summary actions on data collection

The Government and its agencies will:

BIOLOGICAL SURVEILLANCE AND MONITORING

Nationwide (UK or Great Britain)
Total Coverage

ITE Land Cover Map	25 Land cover types
*ITE Biological Records Centre schemes	15 000 taxa
*BTO Breeding Bird Atlas	250 taxa
BTO Wintering Bird Atlas	200 taxa
British Lichen Society Atlas	750 taxa

Sample Coverage

DOE/ITE Land Use/Countryside Survey 90	508 1 km squares
Northern Ireland Countryside Survey	620 25 ha squares
*Bristol University Badger Survey	2 700 1 km squares
BSBI Monitoring Scheme	350 10 km sq/ 1000 tetrads
BTO Key Squares Survey	350 10 km sq/ 1000 tetrads

Regional

Phase 1 Habitat Survey	89 surveys
National Parks	10 parks
Environmentally Sensitive Areas	19 ESAs

Site Based

Environmental Change Network	9 sites
*Butterfly Monitoring Scheme	100 sites
Constant Effort Sites	90 sites
*Rothamstead Insect Survey (Moths)	70 sites
Rothamsted Insect Survey (Aphids)	24 sites
*JNCC Seabird Monitoring Programme	150 sites
*Common Bird Census	250 sites
*Waterways Bird Survey	100 sites
National Bat Colony Survey	350 sites
*Wintering Wildfowl & Waders	50 taxa
Nest Record Scheme	30 000 nests
*De Montford Univ, Amphibian Survey	150 sites
JNCC Invertebrate Site Register	10 000 sites
*National Otter Surveys	7 000 sites
*Red & Grey Squirrels in State Forests	1 000 10 km squares
*Rare Plants in Great Britain	300 taxa
*Rare Breeding Birds Panel	100 taxa

NB: All figures are approximate
   *Covered in UK Environment 1992

- develop a co-ordinated data collection system to quantify key areas of the biodiversity resource;
- identify priority species and habitats for data collection;
- improve data collection and collation for:
  - marine areas, lower plants and the sustainable use of species and habitats;
  - sites at risk or ecologically fragile.
- develop a set of guidelines for standard systems of data collection;
- develop the international context of the UK resource;
- develop and make widely available data and information on the physical collections of biodiversity material and resource e.g. those held at the Royal Botanical Gardens in Edinburgh and Kew, and the Natural History Museum collections.

MONITORING THE COMPONENTS OF BIODIVERSITY

Background

9.24 The Convention states that the components of biodiversity should be monitored with particular attention paid to certain classes of site, species and habitats. Monitoring means comparing change from a baseline with a desired state. If monitoring shows a failure to maintain or attain the desired state, then the change must be evaluated and responses decided upon. In planning monitoring it is important that data should be gathered in a way that the reasons for failure may be identified.

9.25 There is a need to establish a UK monitoring framework that will provide a baseline for future work and enable the monitoring of change against the targets shown in Chapter 10. This should take a holistic UK view.

Need to establish a baseline

9.26 There is an urgent need to establish an agreed baseline set of data for key aspects of biodiversity in the UK, and to monitor this over time. Table 5 outlines a range of schemes where a baseline has been established or where the data could be used as a baseline. Taking the 1990 Countryside Survey as an example, it would be logical to link other datasets on species and habitats to this framework. Any monitoring system building on this or other baseline datasets, needs to be co-ordinated at the UK, or ideally international level, and be planned for long term operation. For sites, information on SSSIs held by the statutory nature conservation bodies provides a useful baseline.

Monitoring biodiversity

9.27 Table 5 lists schemes currently monitoring the component parts of the biodiversity resource in the UK. This indicates the range of studies which could be integrated within a UK framework.

9.28 Countryside Survey reports on the structure of the wider countryside every 5–10 years while on a longer rotation the BTO Breeding Birds Atlases and the Rare Plants Survey of Great Britain are good examples of repeatable surveys which could contribute to an overall monitoring scheme, within an agreed national framework of frequency. The development of this framework is key to the overall success and value of these existing works as monitoring tools. In many cases large numbers of volunteer field workers are involved. Monitoring which demonstrably leads to nature conservation actions is likely to result in greater 'job satisfaction' for the volunteers and thus to improved coverage, and greater utilisation of their contribution.

9.29 Table 5 illustrates options to develop integration between schemes. This sub-divides current schemes into those where few sites are monitored annually and those giving regular sample surveys of landscapes.

Monitoring of threats to biodiversity

9.30 Biodiversity may be changed in many ways. A biodiversity monitoring scheme should include the ability both to monitor the environment generally and to quantify the extent of threats from environmental factors with measures of their impact. Possible threats may be classified as follows:
- Edaphic e.g. erosion and acidification.
- Climatic e.g. natural fluctuations and global change.
- Biotic e.g. introduced alien species such as the New Zealand flatworm (a predator of earthworms), the North American ruddy duck, or the Australian swamp stonecrop.
- Anthropogenic e.g. rapid intensification of agricultural systems, creation of large scale monocultures and pollution.

9.31 Where populations or habitats are very small, restricted, or fragmented, the chances of extinction from threats are increased. Threats should be monitored and measures taken to avoid further population decline, especially of an already fragmented resource. Human effects including land uses such as intensive agriculture and the impact of transport systems should be monitored. Consideration should be given to evaluation of the rate of change caused to biodiversity by particular impacts. In many cases the rate of change has increased causing problems through not allowing sufficient time for threatened species or habitats to adapt.

9.32 The development of a co-ordinated national monitoring system of trends which threaten biodiversity must be a priority. Methodological development of this monitoring should take account of the different nature of current threats. There must be a better understanding of the possible outcomes from these threats and impacts through the development of predictive systems.

Identification of thresholds for conservation action

9.33 While baseline monitoring systems and current practices will identify some change in the UK biodiversity resource they will not in themselves identify when conservation action is needed or indeed specify what types of action will be most useful. Thresholds for nature conservation actions should be developed for each monitoring scheme and linked to limits of acceptable change in biodiversity. Dramatic changes e.g. rapid declines in species population should trigger specific nature conservation actions.

Future actions and funding

9.34 Existing monitoring programmes will continue to be funded where they contribute useful data on biodiversity in the UK. There is a need to examine options to increase the co-occurrence of monitoring activity in the same sample areas or squares of the UK. This would improve comparison of results and lead to efficiencies in the use of fieldworkers.

Summary actions

The Government and its agencies will:
- examine and develop the integration of monitoring studies and seek to establish baselines for key components of biodiversity;
- develop UK monitoring schemes to take account of threats and impacts on biodiversity;
- develop thresholds for conservation action in relation to species population and habitat change.

MAINTAIN AND ORGANISE DATA AND INFORMATION

The need for meta-data

9.35 This section reviews current practices, identifies gaps and suggests new initiatives for the maintenance and organisational of data and information.

9.36 In order to develop a UK Biota Database information on existing data collection and monitoring systems must be compiled. Protocols for standards of storage for data and information should be developed covering data collection, collation as well as for monitoring and appropriate meta-data.

A UK Biota Database

9.37 Several countries are currently developing a common system for biodiversity data. Examples include the Australian Environmental Resource Information Network (ERIN) and the USA Countryside Model. The Government accepts as a high priority the need to examine the feasibility of developing a UK Biota Database along similar lines to provide a library of data and information sources as well as standard summary data on biodiversity. At the very least, readily accessible information is needed on biodiversity data held by research councils, the statutory agencies, academic bodies and NGOs. The situation on data collection and organisation in the UK is complex. It is therefore likely that any national data system would need to be highly distributed through a range of organisations with a central co-ordination system. This would provide a common format, co-ordinated system with access protocols agreed to allow widespread use of summary data and information. In this way the general public, especially volunteer fieldworkers, voluntary bodies, industry, and others would have ensured access and be guided on the interpretation and use of data.

9.38 Much relevant data is not currently owned by Government. The proposed system would of necessity be a partnership between Government, statutory nature conservation agencies and non governmental bodies.

Establishment of the system

9.39 In establishing a UK Biota Database, a clearly defined co-ordinating group would be necessary to ensure the effective running of a distributed and interactive system. In the creation of the database particular attention should be paid to the opportunities presented by geographical information systems (GIS) and remote sensing technology in providing an overview structure for future data collection and interpretation.

9.40 The needs of amateur field workers should not be forgotten and the contents of such an information system should be integral to their needs, available to them, and demonstrably useful to their work.

9.41 Given the many complexities involved, such a system should be established incrementally, initially by co-ordination of existing systems. Links to systems that may be developed in Europe should be strengthened in the establishment phase and during operation. The aim in creating such a system should be to bring relevant data more fully into both national and local decision making processes.

9.42 The importance of a UK Biota Database should not be under estimated in terms of its value to biodiversity and nature conservation. Nor unfortunately should the difficulty of establishing such an open access system be underplayed. The UK Biota Database should involve a wide range of current practitioners in its development and use a recognised information technology development methodology. Actions to establish the database are outlined below:

- Investigate current activities of relevant organisations.
- Specify user requirements i.e. what data and information is necessary for conservation action. A review of conservation actions and targets must therefore be linked to the creation of the new system.
- Specify technical options for delivering user requirements e.g. a distributed system or a centrally held system?
- Design the system.
- Build the system in appropriate levels of detail.
- Implement the system including data transfer, data amalgamation and all the other technical aspects.
- Review the delivered system at regular intervals and update and change as appropriate.
- Monitor the effect of the new system on nature conservation practice.

Interpretation of data from the UK Biota Database

9.43 Guidelines on data interpretation and analysis will need to be established in order to ensure correct interpretation analysis of data from the UK Biota Database. Issues such as intellectual copyright on data must be addressed. The EC Directive on Environmental

Information (which urges open access to data) is relevant and will need to be considered in the creation of the data system. However, safeguards to protect especially sensitive data will also need to be included in the system.

9.44 As a result of the seminar 'Action for Biodiversity' organised by JNCC and DoE in May 1993, the Chief Officer, JNCC chairs a group with participation from Government, nature conservation agencies and NGOs which is considering data issues relevant to biodiversity and mechanisms for tackling them. This group will develop ideas and advise on practical ways forward. Regular reports should be published and widely circulated. Options to develop the database model and to increase the speed of co-ordination between organisations (including networks for data collection and monitoring), need to be considered further.

Summary of actions on maintaining and organising data.

The Government and its agencies will arrange:

- a feasibility study on the development of a UK Biota Database to advise on data requirements, accessibility, standards and protocols, data management, technical options and costs.

ACCESS TO THE UK BIOTA DATABASE AND OTHER DATA RELATING TO BIODIVERSITY

Background

9.45 Although it is expensive to create, collate and maintain datasets in an accessible and usable form, data collection and storage is a fundamental requirement to fulfil the obligations of the Convention. Four factors are of importance in providing access to biodiversity data:

- Increasing demands are likely from researchers and others beyond the communities traditionally served by individual datasets or organisations.
- Despite reductions in the cost per unit of data archiving, overall costs continue to rise steadily due to the ever increasing volumes and complexity of data structure and integration.
- Consideration should be given to allowing low cost access to data for what has traditionally been termed bona fide research benefiting the conservation of biodiversity.
- The increase in visibility of data on biodiversity and the attendant increase in expectations arising from the implementation of this action plan should be considered carefully and a strategy developed to ensure effective delivery of a data-service.

ACCESS TO DATA FROM ROYAL BOTANIC GARDENS, KEW

The Royal Botanic Gardens, Kew has invested in professional staff for the development of specialised software products to serve the needs of professional botanists both in the UK and internationally. This has resulted in a number of products now available to the wider botanical community. These include *Vascular Plant Families and Genera, Authors of Plant Names* and *The Index Kewensis.*

A specialist programme has been developed to aid the management of botanical collections. A Windows based programme called 'Curator' which handles specimen information, geographical distribution mapping, holds images and bibliographic information. This is freely available and is already being used at the herbaria at Hull, Leicester and Leiden. RBG Kew is an active member of the International Working Group on Taxonomic Databases for Plant Sciences: an important group developing data standards ensuring the free exchange of information. Examples of other projects include the Brahms system for managing specimen data (Oxford Forestry Institute) and the Alice system for managing the names, uses, distribution and properties of species (Alice Software Partnership in collaboration with the Royal Botanic Gardens Kew). Both systems are becoming more widely used around the world. RBG Kew is a founder member of the ILDIS legume database, the IOPO *Species Plantarum Project,* and GENSUS, Genera of the *Compositae* Project.

9.46 Individual departments and agencies and organisations will be encouraged to formulate their own policies on access to data in collaboration with the UK Biota Database. Many have developed policies that differ fundamentally in implementation, covering permutations from zero charge to full economic cost as standard for access.

Charging for data and information

9.47 Under regulations governing the administration of public registers and the requirements of the EC Directive on Freedom of Access to Information on the Environment, public access to the biological data assembled by Government and Government bodies has been made easier. Government and statutory bodies are responding also to the initiatives on the Citizen's Charter, so facilitating public interest in the environment and creating conditions where environmental information can be freely distributed. Where data and information relate to rare or threatened species where disclosure could jeopardise their survival restrictions on release will operate. While much data will be freely available, charging is still likely in many cases. A standard system of access will enable the UK Biota Database to function in a co-ordinated manner. Further discussion is required noting that important decisions on charging will be required by Government and others to enable a UK Biota Database to function to its greatest effect.

Trading data

9.48 Once established the UK Biota dataset could be traded with others by agreement. Data from the UK Biota Database should be exchanged for research purposes where it is clear that the research will lead to a significant contribution to knowledge of biodiversity. Data might be exchanged with commercial organisations on a quid pro quo basis. Bona fide researchers would have "free" access to the UK Biota Database. Proposals to gain access to such data sets would need to make clear that the data is to be used in support of research into biodiversity.

Public access to the UK Biota Database

9.49 The public should have access to data and information on the biodiversity found in the UK. People are only very rarely interested in raw data, with the vast majority wishing to see summary or processed information, statistics and the generalised results of research and analysis. These types of data, describing the state of the resource should be freely available to all. There is a need to increase accessibility to such data and to provide a citizens guide to data on biodiversity. Awareness of data availability could be increased in the following ways:

- After its creation the UK Biota Database should actively distribute lists and catalogues outlining the sources of data and information on biodiversity.
- Summary statistics and information should be actively distributed in written and computerised form to schools, universities and public libraries.
- Guides to data should be written in plain English. Versions should be produced in various other community languages.
- Data and information should be made available to those in the population with disabilities or special needs.
- The establishment of one-stop information centres or data shops on biodiversity should be considered. Such a scheme is already operated in Dublin. Similar 'shops' should be considered for all other major cities.
- The establishment of biodiversity 'information' checkpoints will be considered. These might follow the 'Health point' model currently being used to promote health checks for the general public. These provide touch screen computers which supply summary information about available health services. A similar system could be used to promote the conservation of biodiversity and provide summary statistics on habitats and other relevant data. Such units could be located throughout the UK in public places such as museums, nature reserves, libraries or even in selected post offices.
- Publications summarising research, monitoring and activities under the UK Biota Database should be produced. For example annual work on seabird monitoring, WeBS, the Rare Breeding Birds Panel, the Common Birds Census and other work covering a range of bird species are currently reported in an annual BTO/JNCC report 'Britain's Birds'. Similar summary reports could be developed for other species and habitats groups. These reports could form a sub-set of the series 'The UK Environment'.

Summary of actions

9.50 The Government and its agencies will work to produce:

- a charging policy for data derived from the UK Biota Database if established. This should take into account handling and retrieval costs as well as the use to be made of the data.
- summary statistics and information to be made available from the content of the UK Biota Database to information centres such as museums, libraries and schools.

Table 1   The interrelationship between the requirements to collect data and information relevant to biodiversity under various EC directives and international conventions

Requirement for data and information	EC Birds Directive	EC Habitats Directive	Ramsar Convention	Bonn Convention	Bern Convention	Agricultural Directives	Water Directives	Forestry Directives	Fishing Directives
Requirement to gather information on:	Wild Birds	Habitats & species	Wetlands and conventions	Migratory species	Threatened habitats	Agricultural Practices	Pollution levels	Forestry practices	Yield and Population of fish
Maintain & organise data	Yes	Yes	Yes	Yes	Yes		Yes	Yes	Yes
Requirement to monitor	Bird population levels	Habitats & species	Wetlands and species	Migratory species	Threatened habitats		Water quality	Air pollution effects on forests	
Collect information on designated sites for conservation of biological diversity	SPAs	SACs	Wetland sites						
Data on sustainable use of biodiversity	Yes	Yes	Yes	Yes	Yes	Yes	Yes	Yes	Yes
Data to quantify threats to biodiversity	Yes	Yes	Yes	Yes	Yes	Yes	Yes	Yes	Yes

Table 2   Data needs in relation to the data in the action plan

Convention requirement	Identify Key ecosystems and habits	Biological Key ecosystems and habits	Diversity Genomes of importance	Monitor through sampling and other techniques	Identify threats and impacts	Maintain and organise relevant data
Protection and conservation habitats: protected areas networked						
• Enhanced site management and designation using SSSis as a basis for positive actions	✔	✔	✗	✔	✔	✔
• Establish local flora to enhance protection of biodiversity hotspots	✔	✔	✗	✗	✔	✔
• Improve database of Countryside Survey and include Northern Ireland	✔	✔	✗	✗	✔	✔
• Biodiversity audit at 10km or if possible 1km scale to identify hotspots	✔	✔	✗	✗	✔	✔
• Complete SPA and SAC classification for the UK by the year 2004	✔	✔	✗	✔	✔	✔
• Develop further the extent of National Parks in England	✔	✔	✗	✔	✔	✔
Protection and conservation of species						
• Publish Red Data Books for key components of biodiversity	✔	✔	✔	✔	✔	✔
• Monitor illegal persecution of threatened species	✗	✔	✗	✔	✔	✔
• Prepare Species Action Plans and implement by 2000 for globally threatened or endemic species	✔	✔	✔	✔	✔	✔
• Develop strategy for ex situ conservation of genetic resources	✔	✔	✔	✔	✔	✔
• Prepare guidelines on species translocations, reintroductions and introductions by 1996	✗	✔	✔	✔	✔	✔
Agri-environmental measures						
• Monitor and promote further greening of the CAP	✔	✔	✗	✔	✔	✔
• Identify and promote environmentally beneficial practices for agriculture	✔	✔	✗	✗	✔	✔
• Provide further incentives for environmentally sensitive agriculture, especially moorland management	✔	✗	✗	✔	✔	✔
• Continue Countryside Stewardship Scheme	✔	✗	✗	✔	✗	✔

Table 2 (cont)   Data needs in relation to the data in the action plan

Convention requirement	Identify Key ecosystems and habits	Biological Key ecosystems and habits	Diversity Genomes of importance	Monitor through sampling and other techniques	Identify threats and impacts	Maintain and organise relevant data
Forestry						
● Implement Forestry Plan	✔	✔	✔	✔	✔	✔
● Protect and manage ancient semi-natural woodland to conserve their character	✔	✔	✔	✔	✔	✔
● Woodland regeneration	✗	✗	✗	✗	✗	✗
● Encourage forest restructuring	✔	✔	✗	✔	✔	✔
● Encourage woodland expansion	✗	✗	✗	✔	✔	✔
● Encourage farm woodlands	✗	✗	✗	✔	✔	✔
● Encourage new native woodlands	✗	✗	✗	✔	✔	✔
● Encourage community woodlands	✗	✗	✗	✔	✔	✔
● Support the new National Forest	✗	✗	✗	✔	✔	✔
Freshwater						
● Develop long-term strategy for the sustainable management of water resources	✔	✔	✔	✔	✔	✔
● Encourage improvements in water quality	✗	✗	✗	✔	✔	✔
● Establish statutory water quality objectives and enforce pollution control regulations	✗	✗	✗	✔	✔	✔
● Ensure ground water reserves are protected from pollution	✔	✗	✗	✔	✔	✔
● In England and Wales produce water catchment management plans	✔	✔	✗	✔	✔	✔
Natural Areas: a geographical framework	✔	✔	✗	✔	✔	✔
● Encourage development of biogeographical examination of the UK leading to the construction of local action plans						
Marine						
● Develop knowledge of biodiversity in the marine area	✔	✔	✔	✔	✔	✔
● Monitor fisheries and fish populations to ensure sustainability	✗	✔	✗	✔	✔	✔
● Accurate and timely assessments of fish stocks and productivity	✗	✔	✗	✔	✔	✔
● Monitor impacts of towed fishing gear on seabed	✔	✔	✗	✔	✔	✔
● Designate and protect under the Habitats and Species Directive key marine areas	✔	✔	✗	✔	✔	✔
Information and monitoring						
● Develop guidelines for standard systems of data collection	✔	✔	✔	✔	✔	✔
● Continue long-running monitoring schemes on biodiversity	✗	✗		✔	✗	✔
● Develop integration of monitoring and establish baseline data for key components of biodiversity	✔	✔	✔	✔	✔	✔
● Develop national monitoring systems with appropriate thresholds for nature conservation action to take account of threats and impacts to biodiversity	✔	✔	✔	✔	✔	✔
● Develop National Biota Database including options for data requirements, standards management, technical options and costs	✔	✔	✔	✔	✔	✔
● Undertake a feasibility study for the creation of a UK Biota Database	✗	✗	✗	✔	✗	✔

Table 3   **Data, information and monitoring under the Convention on Biological Diversity**

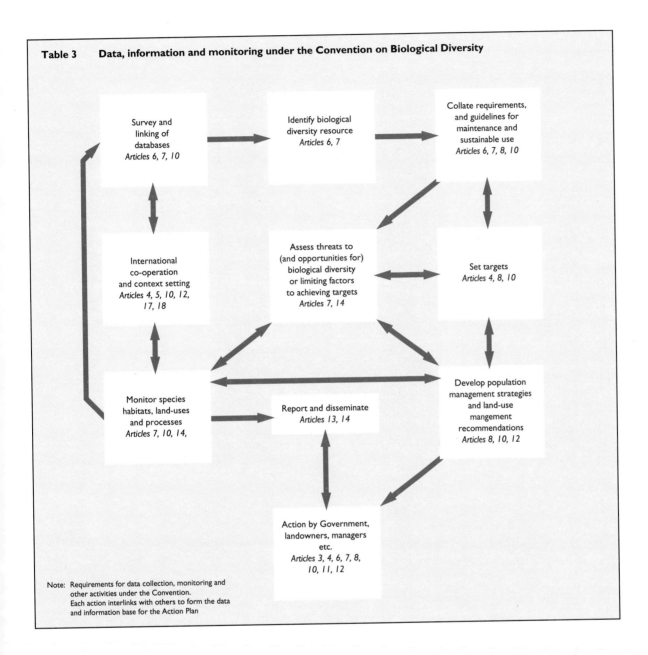

Note: Requirements for data collection, monitoring and other activities under the Convention.
Each action interlinks with others to form the data and information base for the Action Plan

Table 4   An example of Data Flow: Volunteers to Conservation Action Wetland Bird Survey (WeBS)

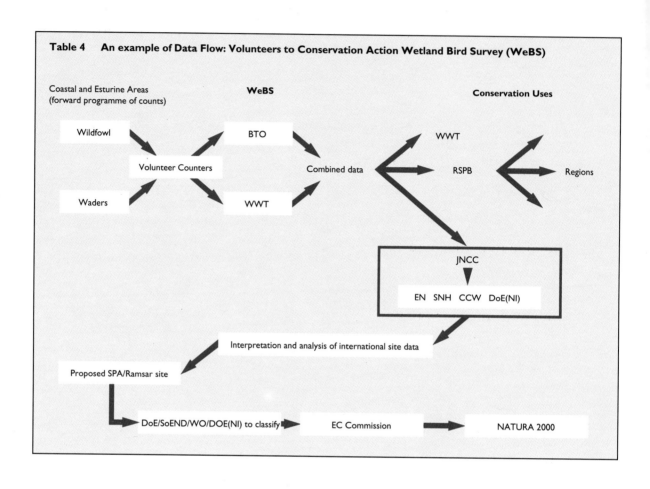

Table 5　Current biological surveillance and monitoring

	Number of sites (or other scope) N.B. all figures approximate *covered in UK Environment 1992	Frequency	Coverage: total or sample
British Lichen Society Atlas			Nationwide coverage: >750 taxa
Environmental Change Network	9	Annual	
Butterfly Monitoring Scheme *	100	Annual	
Rothamstead Insect Survey (moths) *	70	Annual	
Rothamstead Insect Survey (aphids)	24	Annual	
JNCC Seabird Monitoring Programme *	150	Annual	
JNCC Seabird Group Seabird Colony Register		5 - 10 years	Nationwide coverage
BTO Common Bird Census *	250	Annual	Sample national coverage: 240 sites
BTO New Breeding Bird Survey	1,000 sites (minimum no. of sites required: to be launched 1994)	Annual	Sample national coverage: >1,000 sites
BTO Waterways Bird Survey *	100	Annual	Sample national coverage: 130 sites
BTO Constant Effort Ringing Sites	120	Annual	Sample national coverage: 120 sites
Wetland Bird Survey (BTO/WWT/RSPB/JNCC)		Annual	Nationwide coverage
BTO Nest Records Scheme	300,000 nests	Annual	Nationwide coverage
De Montford University Amphibian Survey *	150		
JNCC Invertebrate Site Register	10,000	Baseline established (limited amount of time series data)	Nationwide coverage
National Otter Surveys *	7,000	5-10 years	Sample national coverage
FC Red and Grey Squirrel surveys in state forests *	1,000 x 10 km sqs	Annual	
FC Mammal and Bird questionnaire 1983		Baseline established	
JNCC Rare Plants database in Great Britain *	sites for 300 species	>11 years	
Rare Breeding Birds Panel *	sites for 100 species	Annual	
BTO Breeding Birds Atlases		>11 years	Nationwide coverage: 250 species
BTO Wintering Birds Atlas		Baseline established	Nationwide coverage: 200 species
BSBI Monitoring Scheme	1,125 tetrads	>11 years	Sample national coverage: 350 10km sqs/100 tetrads
BTO Key Squares Survey		Baseline established	Sample national coverage: 350 10km sqs/100 tetrads
ITE Land Cover Map	Complete cover	Baseline established	Complete nationwide coverage of GB
ITE Biological Records Centre Schemes		Baseline established (limited amount of time series data)	Nationwide coverage: 15,000 taxa
ITE Countryside Survey 1990		5-10 years	Sample national coverage: 508 x 1 km sqs
Forestry Commission Inventory of Woodlands and Trees		Continuous on 10-15 year cycle	GB mapping 100% woods>2ha plus sampling of all woods & trees in countryside
JNCC Lower Plants Biodiversity Register		Baseline established (limited amount of time series data)	Nationwide coverage
Bristol University/NCC Badger Survey		Baseline established	Sample national coverage: 2,445 x 1 km sqs
Bristol University/JNCC Brown Hare Survey		Baseline established	Sample national coverage: 970 x 1 km sqs
Bristol University/JNCC Bat Survey		Baseline established	Sample national coverage: 700 x 1 km sqs
National Bat Colony Survey	350	Annual	
NCC/SNH National Countryside Monitorng Scheme		Baseline established >11 years	Sample coverage: England & Wales
SO Land Cover of Scotland Survey		Digital baseline established	Complete coverage for Scotland
National Parks Monitoring		Baseline established	
Environmentally Sensitive Areas monitoring		Baseline established	
Phase I habitat surveys		Baseline established	Regional coverage/incomplete nation wide coverage: 89 surveys
National Parks monitoring			Regional coverage: 10 parks
Environmentally Sensitive Areas			Regional coverage: 19 ESAs
SSSI monitoring	5,700+	Variable	
NERC Survey of Grey Seals	38	Annual	Nationwide coverage
NERC Survey of Common Seals	6	Annual	Nationwide coverage
Northern Ireland Countryside Survey		Baseline established	Sample material coverage (NI): 620x25ha sqs

Table 6 COMPONENTS OF BIODIVERSITY

A. Inventory of British species/sub-species/varieties:
For each species
Distribution
Abundance
Reproductive success
Conservation status
Community membership
Significance in each community
Autecological data
Chromosome number (s)
Cell DNA content
Genotypic variation: identified genes
Sequence data

B. Inventories of British Communities
I. *Terrestrial and Freshwater*
National Vegeation Classification
Recognised variants

Recognised animal communities
Relation to plan communities
Soil decomposer communities
Other soil communities

2. *Littoral, sub-littoral and open sea (to legal limits)*
Recognised communities
Bottom living communities
Free-swimming vertebrate, invertebrate populations
Plankton and micro-organisms
Bottom-dwelling communities

3. *Aerial*
Aerial plankton
C. Genome inventories
Chromosome number
DNA content
Identified genes, especially if utilised
Chromosomal/mitochondrial sequences

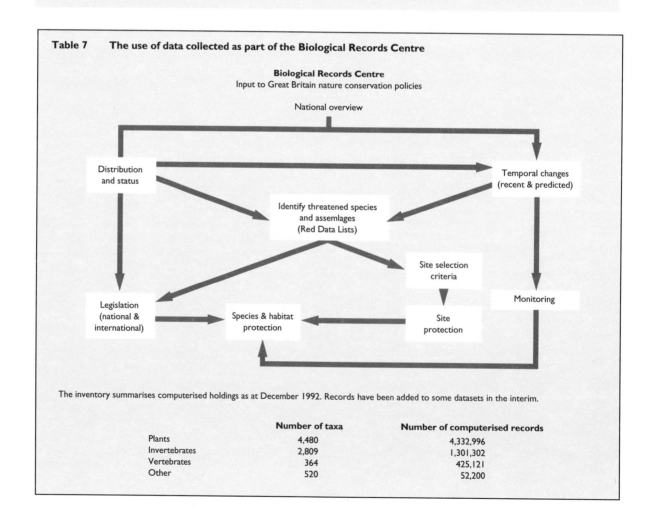

Table 7   The use of data collected as part of the Biological Records Centre

Biological Records Centre
Input to Great Britain nature conservation policies

National overview

Distribution and status

Temporal changes (recent & predicted)

Identify threatened species and assemlages (Red Data Lists)

Site selection criteria

Legislation (national & international)

Species & habitat protection

Site protection

Monitoring

The inventory summarises computerised holdings as at December 1992. Records have been added to some datasets in the interim.

	Number of taxa	Number of computerised records
Plants	4,480	4,332,996
Invertebrates	2,809	1,301,302
Vertebrates	364	425,121
Other	520	52,200

Table 8 SUMMARY OF PHYSICAL DATA IN THE UNITED KINGDOM AND WORK IN PROGRESS IN RELATION TO THESE STATISTICS

Type of information	UK data sources	Work in progress in UK
Land use/cover	Water Companies (England & Wales)	System being developed to collect summary data for the Urban Waste Water Treatment Directive
	Institute of Terrestrial Ecology (ITE)	A national land cover map for each 1 km^2 produced by ITE launched on 12 July.
	Department of the Environment (DOE)	The 1990 Countryside Survey gives national habitat and cover data. The DOE are considering a pilot project to develop a Land use Stock system for England and also updating earlier work on Rates of Urbanisation to 2011.
	Scottish Office/Macaulay Land Use Research Institute	Work is in progress to make Land Cover of Scotland Survey data compatible with other geographical information systems, including the ITE land cover map.
Energy	Department of Trade and Industry (DTI)	Continuing development of energy statistics e.g. improved methodologies for collecting information on privately generated electricity, etc.
Air emissions	Warren Spring Laboratory (WSL)	Developing methodologies to monitor particularly for VOCs. Developing estimates for ammonia emissions.
Emissions of greenhouse gases	WSL	Refining CO_2 estimates e.g. from offshore sources. Major re-estimating work on methane emissions. Development of N_2O emissons inventory.
CFCs and halones	DTI	Confidentiality restrictions regarding production statistics.
Water resources	National Rivers Authority (NRA), Scottish River Purification Boards (SRPBs)	Information on new volumes, available yields and abstractions assembled and received annually.

Table 8 (cont) SUMMARY OF PHYSICAL DATA IN THE UNITED KINGDOM AND WORK IN PROGRESS IN RELATION TO THESE STATISTICS

Type of information	UK data sources	Work in progress in UK
Waste water treatment	Scottish Office	Detailed information system covering all treatment works in Scotland has been developed.
Water quality	NRA, SRPBs	Analyses and use of Harmonised Monitoring Scheme (HMS) database are being developed. HMS contains data for up to 130 determinands at about 230 sites spread across Great Britain.
Waste generation, disposal and recycling	Local Authorities, industry, etc.	UK actively involved in the EC work on waste statistics system.
Biodiversity, nature conservation, forest condition	Countryside conservation agencies (JNCC, EN, SNH, DOE(NI) & CCW)	Exploratory work in inventories of wildlife and habitat data is being carried out by JNCC. Recent national seminar identified the need for integration of the many existing data collections into a national framework.
	Forestry Commission	In 1993 started a rolling programme of mapping types of woodland cover and of sampling woodlands and trees for compostion and condition. This project has direct links with the Land Cover of Scotland Survey and potentially with the DOE Land Use Stock System if this is developed.
Heavy metals (lead, cadmium, mercury etc)	Lead Development Association, Cadmium Association, DOE	Associations provide limited information on use and consumption of lead and cadmium in the UK. Research project started in 1993 on consumption and use patterns of mercury in the UK.
Public opinion	DOE (Earlier national surveys were carried out in 1986 & 1989)	Fieldwork for the 1993 Public Attitudes (follow up) survey started on 5 July.
Sectoral indicators: agriculture	DOE	Development work started in 1993.
Sectoral indicators: transport	DOE	Development work started in 1993.

SECTION 3

CHAPTER 10

TARGETS AND MONITORING

THE WAY FORWARD

10.1 There has been wide public debate and consultation throughout the preparation of this Plan. The many contributions received have enabled the Government to define the overall goal, underlying principles and objectives set out in Chapter 1.

10.2 These statements of the Government's overall goal and objectives are themselves a significant redefinition of policies. But the commitment to biodiversity is not new. There are many programmes and activities currently being implemented which will contribute to the goals of this Plan. Many have been developed as part of the Government's programmes for the conservation of the environment. The activity is dynamic, focused and extensive. It also includes the priorities identified by Government and the nature conservation agencies for meeting international obligations for nature conservation by conserving those habitats and species most at risk.

10.3 Our stewardship relates to what we have now and not what we had in the past. Our commitment is to pass to future generations a heritage of which we can be proud and which they in turn will wish to cherish. Government policies on biodiversity are part of a wider policy of sustainable development, and will develop and be implemented consistently with that. In many instances a realistic goal will be to hold and nurture what we have, although like all good stewards we should seek ways of increasing our wildlife and natural features or of repairing past damage. Attaining these goals presents formidable scientific and technical challenges and hard choices for Government and its agencies, local authorities, businesses, landowners and indeed for every individual. This Plan demonstrates that the Government is ready to play its part.

10.4 What follows is a summary of the intended effect of individual policies and programmes over the coming years and some examples of the habitats and species that will be targeted under each of the key elements of the Plan. The Government is committed to the need for 'sound science' to underpin policy development. It recognises that further work is needed to develop and implement the programmes outlined in this Plan. The Plan does, however, give a sound basis for programmes aimed at delivering clear conservation gains by the years 2000 and 2010. It will be necessary to review this Plan from time to time in the light of the results of that further work and the resources that can be made available for these purposes.

EXISTING PROGRAMMES

Protection and Conservation of Species

10.5 The Government is formally committed under the Wildlife and Countryside Act 1981 to review every five years the status of wild plants and animals (other than birds) and to determine what protective status is appropriate. English Nature's Species Recovery Programme assists endangered native plants and animals. Specific action plans are devised which aim to restore the species to a satisfactory conservation status. The budget in 1993 is £250k and supports projects for 20 species. Included within it is a small grants programme which supports other species work. Species that have been or are the subject of such plans include Plymouth Pear, Fen Ragwort, Fen Raft Spider, Rough Marsh Mallow, Lady Slipper Orchid, Wart Biter Cricket, Large Blue Butterfly, Dormouse, Essex Emerald Moth, Natterjack Toad, and Red Squirrel. A small breeding population of the White Tailed Sea Eagle which had been lost by persecution has been re-established in Scotland. Work on Red Kite re-establishment has also been undertaken in Scotland and England by JNCC and RSPB in partnership. Important work by Scottish Natural Heritage and the Royal Botanic Gardens in Edinburgh is going forward on strategies to aid the recovery of 22 endangered plants. In Wales species including the Red Kite, Wild Cotoneaster and Tufted Saxifrage are receiving special attention. Further plans will be drawn up based on analysis of population trends and ecological requirements. The success of these programmes will demonstrate the capability to enhance biodiversity which has declined through man's influences.

Protected Area Network

10.6 The present nationally important network of some 6,000 SSSIs covering almost 2 million hectares will continue to be used as the basis for securing the conservation and enhancement of the best sites for wildlife. Further sites will be added where significant gaps in representation are identified; for instance in relation to implementing the EC Habitats Directive or as a consequence of ongoing review by the nature conservation agencies.

10.7 Government and the nature conservation agencies have a range of programmes and policies which are designed to support the effective conservation of these sites. There is strong co-operation between Government departments such as the Forestry Commission and the Ministry of Defence and the conservation agencies to ensure stewardship of SSSIs within their ownership. Government policies support the conservation of sites through the requirements under the planning system and statutory consultation processes. English

Nature's Wildlife Enhancement Scheme is a pilot scheme which already covers nearly 5,000 hectares of SSSIs. The voluntary conservation organisations such as the County Wildlife Trusts (in Scotland the Scottish Wildlife Trust) and RSPB play a major role in the conservation of SSSIs through their ownership and management of sites. Help is provided by the conservation agencies through schemes such as English Nature's Reserves Enhancement Scheme and Scottish Natural Heritage's Voluntary Peatland Management Scheme which is currently dedicated to enhancing the management of the Flow country of Caithness and Sutherland.

10.8 Within this network, additional measures are taken to conserve Special Protection Areas for birds, Ramsar sites and National Nature Reserves. Soon Special Areas of Conservation (SAC) under the Habitats Directive will be added. On the advice of the nature conservation agencies the Government designates internationally important sites with a programme aimed at completing the SPA programme and complying with the timetable set down in the Habitats Directive for the designation of SACs by 2004.

10.9 An important objective of the 11 National Parks in England and Wales covering 1,450,451 hectares is the conservation of nature. The Government has stated its intention to give greater statutory protection to the New Forest, an area of forest, heath and lowland mires covering 57,300 hectares of land. The new Natural Heritage Area designation in Scotland provided in the Natural Heritage (Scotland) Act 1991 will give further opportunities to protect areas of outstanding natural heritage value. Work consequential to the deliberations of two working parties examining the management problems in the Cairngorms and at Loch Lomond and the Trossachs should enhance the conservation of these areas.

Agri-Environment Measures

10.10 Developments within the CAP have expanded the opportunities for encouraging the management of agricultural land in ways that are more sensitive to maintaining wildlife and their habitats. The most developed programme is that for Environmentally Sensitive Areas, under which Agricultural Departments plan to designate 2.7 million hectares, or some 15% of UK agricultural land by 1994. Farms participating in ESA agreements undertake to farm in ways which protect and enhance the environment on their farms in return for annual management payments. These agreements, which continue for 10 years, offer higher levels of payment for higher environmental achievements. The habitat types targeted in England include heathland, moorland, wet grassland, downland and semi-natural rough grazing. In Scotland the Uist Machairs

and the extensive heather conservation scheme in the Southern Uplands are particularly significant. In Wales targetted habitats include wetlands, hay meadows, semi-rough grazing and maritime heaths. Designed to maintain and improve the range and biodiversity of habitats and to maintain valued landscapes within the ESAs the measures are expected to maintain and improve the vulnerable species such as the Red Kite, Merlin, Stone Curlew and the Marsh Fritillary butterfly. They will contribute to reducing overgrazing in the uplands, leading to heather recovery, together with enhanced populations of moorland bird species. In a number of ESAs the objective is to enhance the proportion of breeding waders and over-wintering birds. The management regimes such as prevention of ploughing of hedge removal and measures to conserve the specifically targeted habitat will contribute to combatting the fragmentation of habitats and their associated ecosystems. The raising of water levels has already made a significant contribution to the recovery of plants and invertebrates, for example in the Somerset Levels.

10.11 New agri-environment schemes which Agricultural Departments plan to launch in 1994 will also contribute to the enhancement of biodiversity. The Moorland scheme will target heather moorland not already covered by the ESA programme, and the Habitat scheme will target specific wildlife habitats such as saltmarsh and water fringes to the benefit of the plant, invertebrate and bird species associated with them. The organic conversion scheme will help farmers to convert to this particular form of balanced agriculture which should be to the advantage of birdlife in particular.

10.12 The schemes provide incentives to farmers and landowners to manage these key habitats and maintain their conservation value. The development of Codes of Good Practice for farming, the provision of advice, by farm advisers, and the availability of grant will all contribute to the continuing conservation effort.

10.13 Countryside Stewardship is an associated scheme, which is intended to form a component of the overall Agri-Environment programme under the CAP. It is operated on an experimental basis by the Countryside Commission in partnership with English Nature and English Heritage. The scheme offers farmers and landowners a 10 year contract to enhance and conserve important landscapes and wildlife habitats. The agreements can apply to: chalk and limestone grasslands, lowland heath, waterside landscapes, coastal land uplands, historic landscapes and old orchards, the old meadows of the Culm in Devon and of Hereford and Worcester. By end 1993 some 85,100 hectares were subject to agreements under the scheme and the target is a further 3000 hectares by 1995. The equivalent scheme in Wales is

Tir Cymen. It offers annual payments for positive management to benefit wildlife, landscape and access provision and covers a range of habitats. It adopts a whole farm approach, and is available on a pilot basis in three Local Authority districts.

10.14 Similar schemes in Scotland include the Islay Goose Management scheme; Corncrake protection (run in co-operation with the RSPB); and a grant scheme to assist the development of whole farm/estate natural heritage conservation plans.

Forestry

10.15 Policies and programmes have as their objective to maintain the present area of ancient and semi-natural woodlands; to expand the area of native woodland of a natural character; to improve all forests as habitat for wildlife, and to design and locate new forests in harmony with the environment. The Forestry Commission and, in Northern Ireland, the Department of Agriculture, employ a range of instruments to pursue these targets, including felling controls (GB only), environmental assessment, woodland grant schemes, conservation plans, and nature conservation guidelines. An important initiative recently announced by the Forestry Commission aims to identify methods for improving biodiversity in managed forests and develop standards of biodiversity. The Countryside Commission's National Forest Initiative aims to create landscape improvement and environmental benefits within a 200 square mile area in the heart of England. Community Forests are being developed jointly by the Countryside Commission, Forestry Commission and local authorities to make degraded areas on the edge of cities more attractive places for wildlife and city dwellers. The Farm Woodland Premium Scheme, operated by the territorial agricultural departments, will help improve biodiversity in the farmed environment.

10.16 In Scotland the Indicative Forestry Strategies prepared by most Regional Councils are an important mechanism for steering afforestation to the right place and for securing benefits to biodiversity from the creation of new forests. In England and Wales, local authorities have received Departmental guidance on the preparation of similar strategies. In Northern Ireland, the Department of Agriculture has published environmental guidance on the location of new forests.

Freshwater

10.17 A long term strategy for the sustainable management of water resources is being prepared for England and Wales by the National Rivers Authority, which will focus on demand management and measures to conserve water resources and their biodiversity. The Government is encouraging improvements in water quality by establishing statutory water quality objectives as appropriate; by enforcing pollution control regulations, and by ensuring that ground water reserves are protected from pollution and depletion, and that abstraction from surface and ground water surface allows adequate flows to be maintained. Where flood defence and water supply reservoir schemes are necessary they should be environmentally acceptable and where possible will be designed and managed to enhance the environment.

10.18 In Scotland river quality surveys continue to show steady improvement with 99% of inland waters in the highest quality classes in 1990. The Government is promoting further research through the Scotland and Northern Ireland Forum for Environmental Research into water biodiversity issues and has recently published a Code of Practice on Conservation, Access and Recreation to encourage the water industry and regulators to use environmentally friendly working practices.

10.19 The most important wetlands for nature conservation have been designated as Sites of Special Scientific Interest and 68 wetland areas of international quality had been designated under the Ramsar Convention by November 1993. English Nature has embarked on a programme of notifying a representative series of rivers as SSSIs; some of these are being targeted as Environmentally Sensitive Areas or as pilot water fringe areas under the Habitat Scheme (part of the EC Agri-Environment programme).

10.20 Water Level Management Plans are being prepared for wetlands within drainage systems with priority given to those of high nature conservation interest. English Nature, Internal Drainage Boards, the National Rivers Authority and individual landowners are involved in the process, and MAFF is actively involved in encouraging their production. The objective is to provide an agreed procedure for the management of water levels in order to ensure that the conditions are favourable to wintering and breeding birds, particularly waders and wildfowl, and for characteristic ditch and meadow plants and invertebrate animals.

10.21 A demonstration project for river restoration is being developed with the help of an EC LIFE grant. The production of river Catchment Management Plans and water resource plans has been started by the National Rivers Authority for 180 catchments in England and Wales.

Conserving Local Character

10.22 English Nature have drawn up a draft Natural Areas map for England (see Chapter 4). The aim is to agree five key objectives for each area. These objectives will provide the focus for planning management and other co-ordinated actions designed to conserve and enrich the distinctive character of these areas. English Nature are piloting this approach in six Natural Areas. In Wales CCW is assessing the usefulness of identifying a natural zonation based upon structural and biogeographical features.

10.23 Scottish Natural Heritage is exploring the identification of biogeographical zones in Scotland which it can use as a framework for determining natural heritage targets and monitoring progress. To date, work has concentrated upon the uplands which constitute over 70% of Scotland's land area. It is intended that this should be extended into the whole of Scotland and into coastal and marine zones, and refined to account for the cultural aspects which impact upon and contribute to the natural heritage. When this work is complete these zones will form the basis of SNH's strategic approach to conserving biodiversity, and indeed other components of the natural heritage.

Marine

10.24 While much is known about our terrestrial wildlife and its distribution, far less is known about the marine environment. It represents a huge area for enormous diversity. Government and the nature conservation agencies are working on further measures to conserve the biodiversity of the marine environment. Inevitably, the subject and the actions are much less developed.

10.25 The Government and the nature conservation agencies are committed to the implementation of the EC Habitats Directive; conserving endangered species and contributing to the Community wide network of internationally important sites, known as Natura 2000. This network will extend to marine habitats and species and will be a significant step forward in conservation. Fulfilling the obligations accepted under the Directive will represent a major commitment over the coming years.

10.26 There is legislative provision for setting up Marine Nature Reserves, but the mechanisms have sometimes proved cumbersome. Consequently there are only two Marine Nature Reserves in the UK with a further two under consideration. However, SSSIs make a significant contribution to the coastal environment and considerable progress has been made through the 16 voluntary marine nature reserves now in existence. Scotland has 29 marine

consultation areas. These have no statutory locus, but are areas of nature conservation importance.

10.27 The Government is promoting, where appropriate, integrated management plans to foster the sustainable use of vulnerable marine areas. Such plans will normally be local authority led and form the basis for a broader strategy for evaluating priorities in these areas. English Nature has launched a new initiative for the conservation of estuaries. Working with local interests, the programme produces management plans which are centred on the principle of the sustainable utilisation of the estuarine resource. The Firth initiative by Scottish Natural Heritage is aimed at securing integrated environmental management plans for the Moray Firth, Solway Firth, the Firth of Forth and, in due course, the other significant estuaries in Scotland. Similarly the collaborative venture in the Minch involving Western Isles Islands Council, Highland Regional Council and SNH will provide a comprehensive review of existing resources and, through consultation, identify alternative management regimes. At Strangford Lough, the Department of Environment for Northern Ireland is working alongside other interests towards an integrated plan which will complement the proposed Marine Nature Reserve. The Countryside Council for Wales too has specific programmes directed at the marine environment. All the country agencies through the Joint Nature Conservation Committee are working towards the completion of the Marine Nature Conservation Review, a major long term programme to describe features of special interest in the marine environment.

10.28 The aims of UK and EC Fisheries policies is to ensure the sustainable use of target species and the general protection of marine biodiversity. However much more needs to be known about the inter-relationship of all the factors, natural and man induced, on population levels before we can know whether present policies need to be changed. The best information available indicates that fisheries management policies are unlikely to result in any significant change in marine biodiversity over the next 10–20 years. There are significant initiatives under way planned to reduce the danger of polluting the marine environment. These are dealt with in more detail in the Sustainable Development Strategy.

10.29 Particular attention is given to marine mammals, already highly protected under the Conservation of Seals Act 1970 as well as the Wildlife and Countryside Acts. Government funds a major research programme, much of which is carried out by the Sea Mammals Research Unit in Cambridge. The UK is also taking a vigorous approach to implement the new Agreement on the Conservation of Small Cetaceans of the Baltic and North Seas (ASCOBANS).

Current initiatives include a joint survey of small whale populations in the North Sea led by SMRU and a dolphin awareness scheme organised by SNH in the Moray/Cromarty Firths to protect harbour porpoises and bottle nosed dolphins from being harmed by recreational boating.

Information and Monitoring

10.30 Britain's long established tradition in natural history means that we have a wide range of well developed systems to measure the distribution of many species. Programmes of monitoring birds directed by the British Trust for Ornithology, and the Wildfowl and Wetlands Trust have been in progress for more than 30 years and a new Atlas of British Birds will be published in 1993.

10.31 The Biological Records Centre, part of the Institute of Terrestrial Ecology, also has a long history extending back over 30 years. Much work has been done in the last five years to improve its quality and the extent of the analysis. Many other societies also run schemes, and the nature conservation agencies have commissioned some specific schemes, such as butterfly monitoring or rare plant monitoring, and contribute to other programmes such as those on waders and wildfowl with the BTO, RSPB and the WWT.

10.32 The Co-ordinating Commission for Biological Recording brought together all the key recording groups some four years ago. It now works closely with the programme being encouraged by the nature conservation agencies through the Joint Nature Conservation Committee to develop further the co-ordination of this work. This Plan provides an opportunity to increase the momentum of this work and to ensure that its priorities are directed towards the species, habitats and ecosystems identified as specific performance measures under the Plan.

10.33 Overall, to varying degrees of precision, there is monitoring of about 300 species of birds and about 50 butterflies on at least an annual basis. JNCC are actively investigating how to widen this net in a cost-effective way and developing common standards for monitoring and survey projects. They will also be undertaking a review of the appropriateness of the current selection of monitored species as indicators of environmental change.

10.34 SNH is developing state of the natural heritage reporting based upon a disciplined monitoring and survey strategy. This, in turn, will improve its ability to monitor the conservation of biodiversity in Scotland. CCW has a programme of habitat surveys and of monitoring rare species and habitats.

10.35 The National Rivers Authority has a number of important monitoring programmes in the freshwater environment particularly on fish and invertebrate communities. This work is paralleled in Scotland by the River Purification Boards in particular with a biological monitoring and classification system for river quality (RIVPACS) developed by the Institute of Freshwater Ecology. Government has brought together an important consortium to develop the Countryside Survey originally initiated by ITE. This 1km square basis for recording will provide the standard for all such work. The Scottish Office's Land Cover Survey of Scotland based on aerial photographs of the entirety of Scotland taken in 1988 and 1989 has produced a digital database of land use across rural Scotland. The RSNC and WWF in particular have stimulated important programmes involving biological recording. These offer major scope for the future in increasing the involvement of volunteers in data collection.

Future Work

10.36 Existing policies will be continued through a range of programmes and tasks which are set out below. These form the broad targets of the Government and its nature conservation agencies in partnership with others over the next 20 years which will contribute to the achievement of the objectives of this Plan. They will be refined, prioritised and spelt out in more detail over the next two years (see para 10.40).

PROGRESS TOWARDS OBJECTIVES

To conserve and where practicable enhance wild species and wildlife habitats the Government and its agencies will aim to:

Habitats

1 Ensure that summary management plans are prepared and, where possible, implemented for each biological SSSI by the year 2004.
2 Continue to designate additional protected areas to deal with acknowledged gaps in the existing coverage, eg in relation to freshwater habitats, peatlands and intertidal wildlife habitats and species.
3 Complete the designation of all identified Special Protection Areas and Ramsar sites. Comply with the timetable for the designation of Special Areas of Conservation set down in the Habitats Directive by the year 2004.
4 Create mechanisms for effective protection and management of key wildlife areas in the marine environment in the UK.
5 Ensure that development control conforms to Government policies for the conservation of biodiversity.

6 Improve the databases of the Countryside Survey and Northern Ireland, while further developing the Scottish Office Land Cover of Scotland survey.

7 Utilise existing knowledge to identify prime biodiversity areas in the UK based on best available levels of data recorded and agree a strategy to protect and enhance them involving all interested parties.

8 Revise the Natural Area map for England in 1994, completing a strategy for 6 natural area schemes with key objectives by 1995. In Scotland publish maps of biogeographical zones by 1995.

9 Complete the Marine Nature Conservation Review under the aegis of the Joint Nature Conservation Committee.

10 Continue to implement new approaches to coastal flood defence and coast protection which manipulate, and work with, natural processes.

11 Designate sufficient marine SACs and SPAs and ensure that mechanisms are in place for their effective conservation under the Habitats and Birds Directives.

12 Produce estuaries management plans for 27 key estuaries in England by 1997, and in Scotland work towards the preparation of integrated management plans and co-operative frameworks for their implementation for the Moray Firth, Solway Firth and the Firth of Forth by 1998; to be followed by other significant Scottish estuaries in due course. In Northern Ireland complete plans for Strangford Lough and Belfast Lough.

13 Promote the preparation of coastal zone management plans where required, following consultation on coastal policy discussion papers for England and Wales, stressing among other things, the importance of conserving and enhancing biodiversity. Issue a separate Scottish consultation paper covering coastal issues in due course.

14 Undertake further research to assess the scope for habitat creation through managed retreat of the coast linking research projects around a full scale trial.

15 Utilise voluntary and statutory marine reserves and other relevant initiatives as mechanisms to involve individuals and communities in practical marine conservation work.

16 Encourage local planning authorities to make reasonable provision for Local Nature Reserves and natural green space in local plans and environmental charters.

17 Continue to support voluntary sector initiatives aimed at enhancing the conservation value of urban and urban fringe land, for example continued support to the Groundwork Trust movement, enabling more urban trusts to be established, and to the Royal Society for Nature Conservation to enable it to extend its 'Environment City' scheme in co-operation with local authorities. In Scotland, continue Scottish National Heritage's Countryside Around Towns programme to enhance the value of degraded land, and continue to underpin UK2000 Scotland's role in forging partnership between private, voluntary and public sectors for environmental purposes.

18 Continue to promote further 'greening' of the CAP while recognising the need to work within the framework of the reformed CAP, press for closer linkage between agricultural and environmental policies and objectives.

19 Continue to monitor existing financial incentives to encourage environmentally sensitive forms of agriculture to ensure they are having positive effects on the habitats and landscapes targeted and are thus contributing to biodiversity objectives. Tailor new incentive schemes planned under the agri-environment programme to complement existing schemes and keep under review.

20 Enforce strictly regulations controlling the use and storage of environmentally damaging pesticides and fertilisers, if necessary introducing new measures.

21 Support organic farming and encourage more extensive livestock farming in selected areas.

22 Expand Government research on environmental management and continue support and advice to farmers to help them to identify and adopt environmentally beneficial management practices, which will conserve, and where practicable, enhance wildlife habitats on their land.

23 Continue to support measures for hedgerow management and restoration in England and Wales.

24 Implement the biodiversity aspects of the UK Sustainable Forestry Programme.

25 Continue to protect ancient semi-natural woodlands and encourage forms of management which conserve their special characteristics.

26 Continue to encourage the regeneration of woodland.

27 Encourage the restructuring of even-aged plantations to create more varied forests with a mixture of types and ages of trees, including the implementation of forest design plans in State forests.

28 Continue to encourage a steady expansion of woodland and forest cover.

29 Encourage the extension and creation of native woodlands, including extending the area of Forestry Commission Caledonian Forest (native pine and broadleaves).

30 Support the creation of community woodlands near population centres.

31 Support the creation of a new National Forest in the English Midlands, and the creation of multi-purpose woodlands in Scotland's central belt through the Central Scotland Woodlands Initiative.

32 Continue to encourage urban tree planting and care through research, support to voluntary organisations, and urban regeneration initiatives.

Species

33 Prepare action plans for threatened species in priority order: globally threatened; threatened endemics; other threatened species listed in the relevant schedules and annexes to UK and EC legislation and international agreements to which the UK is a party; endangered and vulnerable species listed in Red Data Books, aiming to complete and put into implementation plans for at least 90% of the presently known globally threatened and threatened endemic species within the next ten years.

34 Continue English Nature's Species Recovery Programme by adding at least five new species each year.

35 Establish priorities for Red Data Books for the main taxonomic groups without them.

36 Update and publicise guidelines on trans-locations, re-establishments, introductions and re-stocking.

37 Review microbial (and possibly botanical and animal) genetic resources, and then consider whether to develop a formalised strategy for future ex-situ conservation across all genetic resources taking account of international obligations and developments in this field.

38 Continue to have regard to the need to conserve marine fauna and flora in carrying out the Government's duty to regulate fisheries.

39 Seek to control levels of fishing effort in the UK fleet by a package of measures to reduce capacity (eg decommissioning) and fishing activity (eg restrictions on days spent at sea).

40 Ensure that fisheries research continues to provide:
– effective understanding of the natural processes that control the production and survival of fish and shellfish larvae;
– the means of making accurate and timely assessments of fish stock numbers;
– assessment of topical issues such as the inter-action between towed gear and the seabed and by catches.

41 Draw up priority action statements to guide UK implementation of the new agreements on European bats and small cetaceans of the Baltic and North Seas.

42 Continue to give legal protection to threatened species and prohibit both the persecution of protected species and the use of illegal means of killing/taking.

To develop public awareness and understanding the Government and its agencies will:

43 Encourage voluntary bodies involved in tourism and heritage activities to raise funds locally for initiatives on the conservation of biological resources.

44 Encourage the tourism industry to include more information about the need for environmental conservation in its promotional literature, and to develop the necessary skills to provide high quality information and interpretation, including information about local biodiversity.

45 Consider a publicity strategy to explain the meaning and importance of biodiversity and to explain what needs to be done to conserve and enhance it. The campaign could:
– support initiatives that enhance people's understanding of what is special about their local environment;
– encourage the creation of a network of community wardens;
– support initiatives that promote local action to conserve and improve local biodiversity.

46 Incorporate environmental principles, including biodiversity, in their policies and programmes.

47 Encourage where possible the adoption of agreed measures arising out of the Scottish Working Group report *Learning for Life*, and the adoption of measures proposed in the Toyne Report.

48 Establish a Citizens' Environment Network to carry the message to individuals throughout local communities.

49 Promote a co-ordinated programme of research through the Government's environment agencies to include understanding of the impact of recreation on biodiversity and to develop visitor management techniques to reduce negative effects eg the Sustainable Tourism Project in Northern Ireland.

50 Improve the accessibility and coordination of existing biological datasets; provide common standards for future recording.

To contribute on the conservation of biodiversity on a European and Global scale the Government and its Agencies will:

51 Participate actively at all levels of the Biodiversity Convention.

52 Plan an active part in developing effectively existing international conventions for nature conservation, particularly CITES, the Bern, Ramsar and Bonn conventions and the specific agreements under the last of these.

53 Play a full part in ensuring a sound scientific basis for conservation in Europe.

54 Participate in the identification of sensitive areas at high risk from shipping.

55 Participate fully in the Agreement on the Conservation of Small Cetaceans in the North and Baltic Seas (ASCOBANS) which will improve on an international scale, measures for conservation, management and research.

56 Take full account of the EC 5th Environment Action Programme in respect of its implications for biodiversity.

57 Assist the conservation and sustainable use of biological resources in countries otherwise unable to afford it and rich in biodiversity through the Darwin Initiative.

58 Through the aid programme support national development programmes in developing countries that aim at or involve the conservation and sustainable use of biodiversity; and assist developing countries to take action to conserve biodiversity in the global interest through the Global Environmental Assistance Programme.

59 Encourage individual Dependent Territories to develop strategies for biodiversity conservation, including updating existing legislation and developing new legislation to protect species and habitats as appropriate.

SOME EXAMPLES OF SPECIES AND HABITATS IMPORTANT TO THE MAINTENANCE OF BIODIVERSITY IN THE UK FOR WHICH TARGETS COULD BE ELABORATED

10.37 Consideration of the measures that could be taken to promote the underlying principles of the Action Plan, and to advance towards the stated objectives has led to the identification of key elements which the programmes, policies and actions of Government departments, the nature conservation agencies, NGOs and public participation should seek to secure. These key elements are:

- Maintenance of the natural range of native species.
- Identified species (which may be recognised as key species in their own right or indicative of more general states of biodiversity) to be increased by a measurable amount with the milestone dates being 10 and 20 years from now.
- Identified key habitats or assemblages of plants and animals to be measurably enhanced over the period of the plan.
- The fragmentation or isolation of key habitats to be avoided and, wherever practicable past fragmentation to be reversed.
- The involvement of local communities and the voluntary effort to be fostered.
- Specific programmes to be developed – or existing ones enhanced – to improve information and access and to monitor trends in populations and habitats.

10.38 Further consideration of these key elements will lead to the elaboration of targets against which progress towards the objectives will be measured. The following selection of habitats and species are included as examples for which specific targets could be defined, and the impact of the effect of achieving such targets on the biodiversity of the UK assessed. The performance indicators shown

---

EXAMPLE OF SPECIFIC TARGETS FOR KEY HABITATS AND SPECIES

HABITATS
Caledonian Pinewoods
Caledonian pinewoods consist of a mixture of mature Scots pine and birch woodland with a rich understorey of shrubs, the presence of dead and rotting wood and some open areas. The level of natural regeneration of canopy and shrub species must be sufficient to ensure the maintenance of the habitat. The presence and numbers of various birds, insects and flowering plants, ferns, bryophytes and lichens are important indicators of habitat quality.

Performance Indicator
Maintain and manage where necessary, all existing Caledonian pinewoods (12,500 ha) and produce the correct conditions during the next 4 years to begin the process of regeneration of a further 5,000 ha.

Lowland Heathland
Lowland heathland is a range of habitats characterised by plants such as heather and cross-leaved heath found below about 250m. It supports a number of rare plant and animal species such as the marsh gentian, Dartford warbler and sand lizard. Only one sixth of the area of lowland heath present in 1800 now remains, representing less than 0.3% of England's land surface. This nevertheless represents an important proportion of the international total. It is now highly fragmented and often threatened by a lack of management and development.

Performance Indicator
Maintain, and improve by management, all existing lowland heathland (58,000 ha) and produce conditions during the next ten years to begin the process of heathland re-establishment of a further 6,000 ha in Dorset, Hampshire, Surrey, Devon, Suffolk and Norfolk.

The aims of re-establishment should be: to increase the total heathland area; to increase the heathland patch size; to link heathland patches.

SPECIES
GLOBALLY THREATENED
Kite
A globally threatened species found in parts of Wales and recently successfully re-introduced into England and Scotland.

Performance Indicator
To maintain the annual red kite population increase in Wales at more than 5% per annum, which should result in 120 breeding pairs by 1997.

In the longer term see the species re-established throughout its former range.

ENDEMIC
Scots Primrose
A scarce endemic confined to parts of northern Scotland.

Performance Indicator
Every effort should be made to maintain the present distribution of the species 15 sites in Orkney and 26 in Caithness and Sutherland.

INTERNATIONALLY IMPORTANT
Gannet
A widespread but localised breeding bird found in internationally important numbers in Britain.

Performance Indicator
Maintain UK population at 160,000 pairs. Maintain population at current levels in the 14 well established colonies in Britain.

RED DATA BOOK SPECIES (DECLINING)
Bittern
A rare and declining resident, confined almost entirely to lowland marshes dominated by Phragmites needs. In winter the population is supplemented by birds from elsewhere in Europe.

Performance Indicator
Arrest the decline and maintain at least 20 booming males within the present area of distribution. Seek to increase numbers by creating suitable large reed beds in England and aim for a population of 50 pairs by 2005 and 100 by 2020.

Stone Curlew
A rare breeding summer visitor to some natural grasslands in south east England with a declining population of less than 160 pairs. Its survival depends on the correct management of grazing in its breeding grounds and the protection of nests from farming operations.

Performance Indicators

Increase the breeding population to 200 pairs by the year 2000 within their present range. Encourage recolonisation of the past breeding range of Stone Curlews within England.

To increase the proportion of the Stone Curlew population breeding on semi-natural grassland habitats.

THREATENED SPECIES
Dormouse

The dormouse is currently the subject of a Species Recovery Programme, which will begin the process of restoring populations to areas from which they have disappeared and reinstating appropriate woodland management.

Performance Indicator

Within the next 10 years to reintroduce dormice to 10 woodland sites in 5 counties where the dormouse is rare or absent. In addition, at least 20 further sites will be the subject of long-term monitoring to ensure the survival of existing populations.

Greater Horseshoe Bat

Twelve discrete populations of this endangered European species are known in Britain, ten of which are in England.

Performance Indicator

By the year 2000 ten main maternity roosts will be protected by notifying them as SSSIs or SACs and implementing management agreements where necessary. At least 10 major hibernation sites will be protected. The protection of critical feeding areas around the maternity sites will also be started.

Smooth Snake

Considered 'endangered' and vulnerable in a European context. It is found on dry sandy heaths with native strands of heather and gorse. It suffers from encroaching scrub and woodland and requires a diverse heathland structure and avoidance of fire.

Performance Indicator

Prevent further loss or contraction of the range. Re-introduce the smooth snake to sites within its known or presumed range from sites at carrying capacity. The management of those sites to allow for maximum populations without avoidable adverse effects on other valued ecosystem components.

Natterjack Toad

'Vulnerable' and declining species despite reintroductions. Often found in dune slacks, lowland heath and coastal marshes with pools which hold water at least until mid-summer. It suffers from scrub encroachment, changes in water levels leading to pools being too deep or drying out too early.

Performance Indicator

Recovery goal achieved when general historical distribution has been restored by the maintenance of existing populations and the re-establishment and subsequent monitoring of at least 4 populations on heathland sites in Hampshire and Surrey, at least 3 in East Anglian heathland sites and north Wales, and four other sites where they have recently become extinct. One in Lancashire, two in Cumbria and one in Merseyside.

Marsh Fritillary

A formally widespread but now nationally scarce butterfly (less than 100 10 km squares in Britain) mainly in south west Wales and north west Scotland. Dependent on its foodplant Devil's Bit Scabius, growing in a structurally diverse grass sward, either in wet pasture or downland turf and dependent on a tussock structure usually achieved by cattle grazing, rather than sheep grazing. A mobile species, it seems that isolated populations are unlikely to survive without the possibility of interchange with satellite populations.

Performance Indicator

To halt the decline in range and reinforce existing core populations by increasing the area of appropriate grazed swards with Succisa in the immediate vicinity of extant populations.

White Faced Darter Dragonfly

Nationally scarce (less than 100 10 km squares in Britain). Scattered distribution but only in wet heathland in Surrey and a small number of peat mosses in Shropshire, Cheshire and Cumberland in England and in Sphagnum bogs in the Scottish Highlands. It breeds in highly acidic Sphagnum choked pools of clean water and is highly vulnerable to the effects of afforestation of bogs and heaths, peat cutting, moss collection, the drainage of adjacent land and neglect of habitat leading to the dominance of scrub.

Performance Indicator

Targets should prevent drying out or scrub invasion on existing sites and possibly the removal of conifer forest or old peatbogs near to existing colonies and where there is a realistic chance of re-establishing bog vegetation with pools.

Burnt-tip Orchid

A plant of short well grazed limestone and chalk downland turf. Its distribution has contracted to about 25% of its historical range; mainly in the last 50 years. The chief reasons for this decline have been through adverse agricultural practices such as ploughing, failure to maintain traditional grazing regimes and the use of artificial fertilizers and herbicides.

Performance Indicator

Maintain in the remaining 53 10 km squares of its range.

are by way of illustration and have not been agreed by Government.

BIODIVERSITY ACTION PLAN STEERING GROUP

10.39 The Government has been impressed by the extent and constructive nature of the response from non-governmental organisations and institutions during the preparation of this Action Plan. This has included the written responses to the framework document issued in February 1993, participation in the seminar held at the Royal Geographical Society in May 1993 and the contribution of a number of the chapter editors and others who have been invited to comment on or contribute to sections of the plan which they have seen in draft. Within Government the work has been co-ordinated by a Steering Group consisting of all relevant departments and agencies and chaired by the Department of the Environment.

10.40 In order to strengthen this collaboration and to focus efforts within and outside the Government to maintain and enhance the biodiversity of the United Kingdom, the Government proposes to establish a Biodiversity Action Plan Steering Group. This Group would take as its basis the existing official group but would be widened to include senior people drawn from the world of non-governmental organisations (NGOs), academic institutions and local government. The Group would be advisory in nature and would not affect the responsibilities of the Government, government agencies or any of the bodies from which members of the Group were drawn. It would be for the Government ultimately to adopt conclusions arising from the work of the Group and for the nature conservation agencies to discharge their responsibilities within the statutory and financial frameworks provided for them. The

Government hopes nevertheless that such a Steering Group could help to overcome some of the fragmentation of effort currently evident in the field of nature conservation and biodiversity and make all those concerned feel that they can make a positive contribution in the context of a set of broadly agreed objectives for the biodiversity of the United Kingdom. The Group would have as its immediate remit overseeing:

- the development of a range of specific costed targets for key species and habitats for the years 2000 and 2010 to be published in European Nature Conservation Year 1995;
- a working group already established following the May Seminar designed to improve the accessibility and co-ordination of existing biological datasets, to provide common standards for future recording and to examine the feasibility in due course of a single UK Biota Database;
- the preparation and implementation of a campaign to increase public awareness of, and involvement in, conserving UK biodiversity;
- the establishment of a review process for the delivery of the commitments contained in the plan and set out in the preceding part of this chapter.

10.41 Possible membership of such a Steering Group is set out in the box below. Ministers might wish to chair it from time to time, but it would normally be chaired by an official from the Department of the Environment, who would also provide the secretariat. It is envisaged that the Group would initially be set up for a two-year period with the target of reporting on the specific elements of its remit and particularly on targets for key species and habitats for publication during European Nature Conservation Year 1995. The remit, membership and need for the Group in its initial form would be reviewed at that point in the light of experience of its work and the monitoring process established. It is suggested that non-governmental members of the Group should be selected on the basis of their personal contribution rather than as representatives of particular organisations but the Government wishes to achieve a good balance of interests and territorial representation.

10.42 In the Sustainable Development Strategy the Government is announcing that it will establish a Panel on Sustainable Development comprised of a small number of very senior people to advise and review the Government's implementation of the four post-Rio documents being published at this time, including the Biodiversity Action Plan. This will strengthen the process of review at a strategic level while the Steering Group will concentrate on carrying forward or supporting the tasks and targets set out earlier. The Government will also look forward to receiving comments on the Action Plan from Governments and conservation organisations in other parts of the world. It hopes that this document will provide a useful contribution and stimulus to the process established under the Convention on Biological Diversity.

PROPOSED COMPOSITION OF BIODIVERSITY ACTION PLAN STEERING GROUP

Departments

Department of the Environment
Scottish Office
Welsh Office
Department of the Environment, Northern Ireland
Ministry of Agriculture, Fisheries and Food
Foreign and Commonwealth Office
Forestry Commission

Agencies

English Nature
Scottish Natural Heritage

Countryside Council for Wales
Joint Nature Conservation Committee
Countryside Commission
Natural Environment Research Council
National Rivers Authority

Collections
Natural History Museum
Royal Botanic Garden, Kew or Edinburgh

Local Government
3 persons

NGOs
4 persons

Academic Bodies
3 persons

ANNEXES

GLOSSARY

Acidification
The result of changes in chemistry in any area which results in a more acid environment (ie with more H+ ions). Very often the input of so-called 'acid rain' results in the unnatural acidification of habitats that have limited capacity to neutralise such changes in chemistry (habitats with limited buffering capacity).

Alien species
A species which does not naturally occur within any area (most usually a country) and which has either arrived naturally, or more usually as a result of man's intervention (whether deliberate or accidental). Alien species often have adverse effects on native species as a result of competition.

Alluvial plains
Flood plains of rivers commonly composed of sand and gravels.

Ancient woodland
Woodland that is known to have existed before 1600.

Anthropogenic
Literally 'man-made'. Any factor or influence resulting from human intervention or activity, for example farmland is an anthropogenic landscape.

Area of Outstanding Natural Beauty
A region of England and Wales which is not a National Park but which is considered sufficiently attractive to be preserved from over-development.

Atoll
A coral reef or ring of islands surrounding a lagoon.

Avifauna
The birds which live naturally in a certain area.

Biodiversity
Biological diversity. The definition given by article 2 of the Biodiversity Convention is – 'The variability among living organisms from all sources including inter alia, terrestrial, marine and other aquatic ecosystems and the ecological complexes of which they are part; this includes diversity within species, between species and of ecosystems'. A simpler definition is the total range of the variety of life on earth or any given part of it.

Biodiversity Convention
The Convention on Biological Diversity. This Convention was signed by the Prime Minister and 150 other Heads of State or Governments at the Earth Summit (the United National Conference on Environment and Development) in Rio de Janeiro in June 1992. Under article 6A of the Convention signatories must develop national strategies, plans or programmes for the conservation and sustainable use of biological diversity or adapt existing strategies, plans or programmes for this purpose.

Biogenetic Reserve
A site nominated by the UK Government under various Council of Europe resolutions and recommendations for the conservation of biotopes.

Biogeographical realms
Major parts of the land surface characterised by distinctive assemblages of plants and animals.

Biogeography
Study of the geographical distribution of species.

Biological trait
Any feature or property of an organism.

Biomass
The total weight of living organisms in any given area.

Biosphere Reserve
A site designated by the UK Government under the UNESCO Man and the Biosphere programme.

Biosphere
The part of the earth which includes living organisms.

Biota
Pertaining to living things. Thus a UK Biota database would hold all types of information about the range of species occurring in the UK.

Biotic factor
Any influence of animals or plants affecting another organism.

Boreal Period
From c.9,000 to 7,500 years before present; characterised by warm and dry conditions.

Broadleaved forest
Forest made up of trees that are not conifers.

Bryophytes
A major group of plants that includes mosses and liverworts.

Cetaceans
Large mammals such as dolphins, porpoises and whales which live in the sea.

Climax vegetation
The plant communities which would develop and be present in the absence of human intervention.

Coastal squeeze
The loss of intertidal habitat arising from: (i) the presence of sea walls that do not allow habitat to move inland and recreate itself in response to rising sea levels; or (ii) loss under further reclamation.

Coed Cymru
An initiative supported by all of the statutory and voluntary bodies in Wales who have an interest in native, broad-leaved woodlands and the industries they support. Funding is provided by the Countryside Council for Wales, Welsh Local Authorities and National Parks, the Forestry Authority and the World Wide Fund for Nature.

Common Agricultural Policy
An agreement between members of the EEC to protect farmers by paying subsidies to fix prices of farm goods.

Community Action for Wildlife
An English Nature grant scheme aimed at involving new and established community groups and others in practical projects with clear benefits for wildlife and for the local community in towns and cities in England.

Convention on Climate Change
Signed by the Prime Minister and other Heads of State and Governments at the Earth Summit in Rio de Janeiro in June 1992. This Convention commits countries to prepare national programmes to contain greenhouse gas emissions and to return emissions of carbon dioxide and other greenhouse gases to 1990 levels by the year 2000.

Convention
An international agreement through which nations agree to work together cooperatively to implement certain defined policies or take other action. International conventions are voluntarily entered into by countries, although once a country has signed a convention it agrees to implement or be bound by the conditions specified, eg through its signature of the Ramsar Convention on

wetlands the UK has agreed to promote the conservation and wise use of all wetlands in the UK.

Countryside Survey 1990
A survey initiated by the Institute of Terrestrial Ecology and developed by a consortium of other bodies co-ordinated by DoE. Consists of a series of maps covering a sample of 508 1 km squares recording details of land cover, field boundaries of habitats and soils. The satellite images, analyses and detailed ecological surveys provide an overview of the condition of the British countryside.

Countryside Stewardship
A voluntary scheme which offers management agreements to land managers to enhance and conserve important landscapes and wildlife habitats. The scheme is administered by the Countryside Commission in partnership with English Nature and English Heritage.

Crown Dependencies
The Channel Islands and the Isle of Man. They are not part of the United Kingdom but are self-governing dependencies of the Crown with their own legislation assemblies and systems of law and administration.

Cryo-preservation
A method of preserving or freeze-drying living tissues such as bacteria and fungi.

Cultivar
A plant variety that is found only under cultivation.

Cultural landscape
Countryside modified by human activities, where signs of traditional management practices are reflected in the features present.

Detritus
Dead organic matter.

Dolomite
Rocks with more than 15% magnesium carbonate.

EC Common Fisheries Policy
A 20 year programme agreed in 1983 by EC Member States for the management and conservation of fish stocks; the maintenance and improvement of the market structure associated with the fishing industry and international fisheries agreements.

EC Directive
A legal instruction from the European Community which

is binding on all member states but which leaves the method of implementation to national governments.

EC Regulation
European Community legislation that has legal force in all member states.

Ecological pyramid
A depiction of the feeding structure of a community, with more abundant producers at the base of the pyramid and successive levels representing fewer consumers at higher levels.

Ecosystem
A community of interdependent organisms and the environment they inhabit.

Edaphic
Environmental conditions that are determined by the physical, chemical and biological characteristics of the soil.

Embayment
A coastal inlet or bay.

Endemic species
A species of animal or plant confined to a particular region or island and having, so far as is known, originated there.

Endemic Bird Area
An area with concentration of bird species not found outside that area.

Environment City Scheme
A scheme operated by the Royal Society for Nature Conservation in cooperation with local authorities.

Environmental Statement
The written output of an environmental impact assessment with the primary purpose of informing decision makers of the likely significant environmental impacts of a project. The environment statement must contain a non-technical summary to enable non-experts to understand the findings.

Environmentally Sensitive Area
A scheme run by the Ministry of Agriculture, Fisheries and Food which rewards farmers for farming in an environmentally sensitive manner according to a set of management prescriptions for each payment level.

European Nature Conservation Year 1995
A Council of Europe initiative planned for 1995 promoting nature conservation outside protected areas.

Evolutionary potential
The future possibilities for changes in the characteristics of a species, including the development of one or more new species amongst the descendants of the species.

Evolutionary relationships
Occur between organisms linked by common ancestors, or between organisms and their descendants.

Farm and Conservation Grant Scheme
A scheme run by the Ministry of Agriculture, Fisheries and Food to help farmers maintain efficient farming systems and meet the cost of combatting pollution and conserving the countryside and its wildlife.

Farm Woodland Premium Scheme
A scheme administered by the Ministry of Agriculture, Fisheries and Food. It provides annual payments to farmers who convert agricultural land to woodland.

Fen
A wetland of high nutrient status resulting from inputs via flowing water.

Flush
A patch of wet ground, usually on a hillside, where the water flows diffusely and not in a fixed channel, leading to the deposition of nutrients in the upper layers of soil.

Food chain
A term devised by ecologists to show how all organisms are dependent on others within a community. Each member of a hypothetical food chain feeds on the one below and may be eaten by the one above. There are usually not more than six links in a chain.

Food web
The interlocking patterns formed by a series of interconnected food chains.

Forest Nature Reserve
A non-statutory designation, made by Forest Enterprise on appropriate areas of land on their estate. They contain species or habitats which are of national importance and are identified, designated and managed by FE's forest managers.

Gamete
A male or female reproductive cell.

GEF
Global Environment Facility; a fund set up in 1992 and managed by the United Nations to help developing countries.

Gene
The basic physical unit of inheritance of animals and plants.

Gene pool
The total genetic information possessed by the reproductive members of a population of sexually reproducing organisms.

Genetic constitution
The genes present in an individual (or species).

Genome
Strictly, the set of chromosomes found in each nucleus of a given species. More loosely used to describe general genetic variation between species.

Genotype
The genetic composition of an organism.

Geomorphology
The study of the evolution of land forms, or the arrangement and forms of the earth's crust.

Germplasm
Hereditary material transmitted to offspring via the gametes.

Government view procedure
Areas outside planning control development such as oil wells, the marine dredging of sand and gravel and other minerals are subject to Government review procedure. The Department of the Environment (for England and Wales) consult other Government departments, relevant planning authorities and statutory conservation bodies and on the basis of these discussions the Secretary of State determines the Government view on whether the development is acceptable.

Habitat
A place in which a particular plant or animal lives. Often used in a wider sense, referring to major assemblages of plants and animals found together.

Habitat Scheme
A scheme proposed by the Ministry of Agriculture, Fisheries and Food to create a range of wildlife habitats by taking land out of production for 20 years and managing it in an environmentally beneficial way.

Heritage Coast
Undeveloped coasts for informal recreation. No specific statutory legislation applies.

Hill Livestock Compensatory Allowance
Social payments made to farmers in less favoured areas per breeding ewe or breeding cow, under the European Commission Less Favoured Areas Directive (75/268) to maintain rural populations by compensating for natural hardships.

Indicative Forestry Strategy
The Department of Environment Circular 29/92 encourages local planning authorities in England and Wales to prepare indicative forestry strategies to guide the development of forestry in their area. The production of such strategies is voluntary and their status advisory.

INSET programme
In service training for teachers.

Invertebrates
Animals without a backbone.

Isolate
A pure culture of a micro-organism.

Isolating mechanism
Any physical or other barrier preventing dispersal of a species, leading to separation from other populations of the same species.

Isthmus
A narrow piece of land linking two areas of land.

ITE land classes
Thirty-two categories of land classified by physical and other attributes.

Jurassic limestone
Sedimentary rock consisting essentially of carbonates laid down in the Jurassic period (195 million years ago – 135 million years ago).

Leguminous species
Members of the pea species, eg peas, beans and clovers.

Local Agenda 21 initiative
An initiative set out in the publication Agenda 21: a guide for local authorities in the UK.

Local Nature Reserve

An area of land that is of special nature conservation interest locally. LNRs are declared and managed by local authorities under the National Parks and Access to the Countryside Act 1949.

Managed retreat

This progressively shifts the boundary of natural coastal and maritime habitat landward, by moving man-made sea defences back or removing or re-modelling them, creating new intertidal areas in the process.

Marine Nature Conservation Review

Initiated in 1987, a major research programme being undertaken within the support unit of the Joint Nature Conservation Committee and the nature conservation agencies, to consolidate and complete the information already collected on British marine ecosystems.

Marine Nature Reserve

Declared by Nature Conservancy Council and its successors under the Wildlife and Countryside Act 1981 for the purpose of conserving marine flora or fauna or geographical or physiological features of special interest in the area and providing opportunities for study and research.

Matrix

A means of displaying information with many attributes. A simple table with columns and rows is a two dimension matrix. More complex matrices can be developed using computers.

Meadow

An area of permanent grass cut for hay.

Meiofauna

Small animals that live between sediment particles.

Meristem

A region of active cell division in a plant.

Metadata

Data about data. A second level of information about other data sources. Thus a dictionary of all those who hold information on different groups of species could be described as species metadata.

Montane

Above the potential tree line (at about 700 m).

Moorland Scheme

A scheme due to be introduced by the Ministry of Agriculture, Fisheries and Food under the Agri-Environment proposals in the summer of 1994. Its aim will be to reward farmers for reducing sheep numbers on moorland in given circumstances.

Morphology

The physical form of an organism.

National and Scottish Vocational Qualifications

Drawn up by industrial lead bodies to provide clear attestation that the holder of such a qualification possesses specific competences needed to function at a given level in a given occupation.

National Nature Reserve

An area of high nature conservation value, managed to provide opportunities for research or to preserve animals and plants and geological or physiographical features of special interest. NNRs are declared by the country conservation agencies or their predecessors under the National Parks and Access to the Countryside Act 1949 or the Wildlife and Countryside Act 1981.

National Park

Designated in England and Wales under the National Parks and Access to the Countryside Act 1949 for the purpose of preserving and enhancing the natural beauty of areas specified by reason of their natural beauty and the opportunity they afford for open-air recreation.

National Scenic Areas

Have their statutory base in the Town and Country Planning Act 1972 (as provided for under the Housing and Planning Act 1986) and as amended by the Natural Heritage (Scotland) Act. Certain categories of development in National Scenic Areas are notified to Scottish Natural Heritage under Town and Country Planning (Notification of Application) (National Scenic Areas) (Scotland) Direction 1987.

Native species

Species that occur naturally in an area, and therefore one that has not been introduced by humans either accidentally or intentionally.

Natural Areas

These reflect the geological foundation, the natural systems and processes and the wildlife in different parts of England and provide a framework for setting objectives for nature conservation.

Natural range
The area in which a species can colonise and maintain its population naturally. The limits of the geographical distribution of a species.

Neolithic
The New Stone Age (c.4,000 to 2,500 years before present).

Niche
A small place or specialised habitat which is occupied by species which are adapted to its particular environmental conditions.

Pasture
An area used for grazing cattle, sheep or horses.

Pedunculate oak
An oak tree with stalked acorns.

Phylogenetic
Concerning evolutionary relationships within and between groups of organisms.

Phytoplankton
Small plants that float in fresh or salt water.

Plagioclimax habitats
Where the composition and structure of communities has been altered or deflected by human activities.

Plankton
Small animals and plants which float in the sea drifted by tides and currents.

Plant community/society
Interacting collection of species found in a common environment or habitat.

Pollard
A tree which has been cut about two metres from the ground so as to produce a crop of branches suitable for fencing or firewood,

Precautionary principle
Defined in the 1990 White Paper in the following terms 'Where there are significant risks of damage to the environment, the Government will be prepared to take precautionary action to limit the use of potentially dangerous materials or the spread of potentially dangerous pollutants, even where scientific knowledge is not conclusive, if the balance of likely costs and benefits justifies it'.

Protocols
Formal agreements that define means of working together, usually by different organisations. A protocol defines the components of such interaction and how it is to happen in practice so that all parties are clear as to the scope of collaboration.

Quadrat
A square area of vegetation marked off for study.

Races
A group of organisms with distinctive features below the level of a species (often qualified by geographical, ecological or physiological properties).

Ramsar site
A site designated as a wetland of international importance under the Ramsar Convention of Wetlands of International Importance especially as a waterfowl habitat.

Raptors
A term used to cover birds of prey such as falcons, hawks and osprey.

Red Data Book species
Catalogues published by the International Union for the Conservation of Nature (IUCN) or by National Authorities listing species which are rare or in danger of becoming extinct globally or nationally. Sometimes species are included for which the national authority hosts a large part of the world's population and has an international responsibility to conserve them.

Ride
An open unmade track through a wood.

Riparian zone
The land immediately adjacent to a river which may extend to the edge of the flood plain (where one exists) stretch partially across it or merely form narrow "riparian strips" banding the top of the banks.

Rural Action
A scheme co-funded by English Nature, the Rural Development Commission and the Countryside Commission to help people living in the English countryside to care for their own environment by promoting a wide variety of local projects.

Sandford principle
A principle that stems from the 1974 Review of National Park Policies by Lord Sandford. Where there is conflict

between the two National Park purposes, conservation of natural beauty and public enjoyment, the first must prevail.

Saproxylic
Feeding on dead wood.

Semi-natural habitats/communities
Habitats or communities that have been modified to a limited extent by man.

Sessile oak
An oak tree with unstalked acorns.

Set-aside
Using a piece of formerly arable land for something else, such as allowing it to lie fallow, using it for woodland or for recreation.

Slack
A damp hollow between the ridges of sand dunes, with its own specialised plants.

Special Area of Conservation
A site designated by the UK Government under EC Directive 92/43 on the conservation of natural habitats and of wild fauna and flora.

Special Protection Area
A site designated under Article 4 of EC Directive 79/409 on the conservation of wild birds.

Species Action Plan
A conservation plan for a species based upon knowledge of its ecological and other requirements, which identifies the actions needed to stabilise and improve its status.

Species evenness
The extent to which assemblages are dominated by relatively few species.

Species richness
The number of species in an ecosystem

Spring
An upwelling of water from the land surface, which may flow into a watercourse.

SSSI – Site of Special Scientific Interest
An area of land notified under the Wildlife and Countryside Act 1981 as being of special nature conservation interest. The SSSI designation applies

throughout GB. Sites are notified by the appropriate country conservation agency.

Sub-Atlantic Period
From c.2,500 years before present until now; characterised by mild and wet conditions.

Subspecies
A group of interbreeding populations with different characteristics (physical and genetic) from other populations of the same species, frequently isolated geographically from other populations of the same species.

Substrate
The material or surface to which an organism is attached or which it grows upon.

Succession
The distribution of living things through time in an area; commonly the sequence of organisms colonising and successively present in an area where plants and animals have been removed or changed by external factors.

Sustainable development
Development that meets the needs of the present without compromising the ability of future generations to meet their own needs.

Sward
An area of grasses and herbs.

Systematics
The study and arrangement of living things into groups as closely as possible according to their evolutionary relationships.

Taxa
General term for taxonomic groups at any level (eg species, genera etc). Taxon in the singular.

Taxonomy
The science of describing, naming and classifying living things.

The Hedgerow Incentive Scheme
A scheme run by the Ministry of Agriculture, Fisheries and Food designed to address the problem of deterioration of hedges due to under or inappropriate management.

The Fifth Environmental Action Programme
Produced by the European Commission to set the strategic framework for the Community's environmental policy until the year 2000.

The Earth Summit
The United Nations Conference on Environment and Development.

The Convention of Scottish Local Authorities
A formal convening of all regional and district councils in Scotland.

Tir Cymen
A voluntary whole farm scheme for countryside conservation in Wales, designed and operated by the Countryside Council for Wales. Farmers may be offered annual payments in return for the positive management for the benefit of wildlife, landscape archaeology and geology and for providing new opportunities for quiet enjoyment of the countryside.

Topography
The physical features of a geographical area.

Trophic relationship
A feeding relationship, such as [between] animals grazing on plants.

Tundra
Treeless regions that may be bare of vegetation or may support mosses, lichens, herbaceous plants and dwarf shrubs.

Type specimen
The actual specimen from which a given species was first described.

Vascular plants
Plants that have a vascular system, ie contain vessels for conducting liquids.

Vertebrates
Animals with a backbone; mammals, birds, reptiles, amphibians and fish.

Wildlife corridor
A linear habitat (or habitats) linking two or more areas of wildlife significance, which may facilitate the dispersal of species.

Wildlife Enhancement Scheme
A scheme set up by English Nature designed to develop an effective partnership with managers of land in Sites of Special Scientific Interest. Under the scheme a straightforward management agreement and management plan is agreed with English Nature in return for a fixed annual payment which reflects the cost of managing the SSSI for wildlife.

Wildwood
The original woodland cover, relatively unaffected by human activity.

World Heritage Site
A site designated by the World Heritage Committee after nomination by the UK Government under the 1972 Convention on the Protection of the World Cultural and Natural Heritage.

ANNEX B

INTRODUCTION

1 The preparation of the Action Plan has benefited from contributions from all sectors of society including central and local government, learned societies, universities, research institutes, collections, voluntary organisations and individuals.

2 This annex explains how this process was organised and managed. We would like to place on record our thanks and gratitude to the many people who have contributed to the Plan, often as a substantial additional task to their day to day duties.

Inter-Departmental/Agency Steering Group

3 The work was managed by an Inter-Departmental/Agency Steering Group chaired by Robin Sharp CB, Director of Rural Affairs, Department of the Environment. Other members were:

Derek Beames	–	Welsh Office
Roger Bendall	–	Department of the Environment
Colin Bodrell	–	Ministry of Agriculture, Fisheries and Food
Roy Bunce	–	Department of the Environment
Dr Eileen Buttle	–	Natural Environment Research Council
Roger Clarke	–	Countryside Commission
John Compton	–	HM Treasury
Roger Crofts	–	Scottish Natural Heritage
Hamish Daniel	–	Foreign and Commonwealth Office
Dr Patrick Denny	–	English Nature
Dr John Faulkner	–	Department of the Environment, Northern Ireland
Dr Ian Gauld	–	Natural History Museum
Graham Gill	–	Forestry Commission
David Grundy	–	Forestry Commission
Stephen Hampson	–	Scottish Office
Rob Hepworth	–	Department of the Environment
Hamish Laing	–	Scottish Office
Dr Derek Langslow	–	English Nature
Stephen Marston	–	Cabinet Office
Kate Mayes	–	Department of the Environment
Ian Mercer	–	Countryside Council for Wales
Mike Pienkowski	–	Joint Nature Conservation Committee
Jill Rutter	–	No 10 Policy Unit
Roy Walker	–	Joint Nature Conservation Committee

Minutes and papers were circulated widely to colleagues in government departments, agencies and collections.

Editorial Team

4 The editorial and production team were:

Roger Bendall	–	Department of the Environment
Dr Patrick Denny	–	On loan from English Nature
Susan White	–	On loan from English Nature
Jean Marsh	–	Department of the Environment

Sub-Committee

5 The Steering Group was supported by a small Sub-Committee chaired by Roger Bendall, who provided scientific and technical assurance. Other members were:

Dr Leo Batten	–	English Nature
Dr Patrick Denny	–	English Nature
Dr Colin Galbraith	–	Joint Nature Conservation Committee

John Gilmour	–	Scottish Office
Rowena Harris	–	Natural Environment Research Council
Sandy Kerr	–	Scottish Natural Heritage
Dr Malcolm Smith	–	Countryside Council for Wales

Chapter Editors

6 Government takes responsibility for the production and content of the Plan, but is grateful for the assistance of chapter editors who had the lead responsibility for drafting individual chapters, drawing on the many contributions received from organisations and individuals. The chapter editors were as follows:

Chapter 1	Introduction	Roger Bendall	Department of the Environment
Chapter 2	UK Science Base	Professor John Sheail Professor Robert May	Institute of Terrestrial Ecology University of Oxford
Chapter 3	UK Biodiversity	Dr Ian McLean	English Nature
Chapter 4	Conservation Within Habitats	Dr Leo Batten Sandy Kerr Dr Malcolm Smith	English Nature Scottish Natural Heritage Countryside Council for Wales
Chapter 5	Conservation Outside Habitats	Dr Nigel Stork	The Natural History Museum
Chapter 6	Sustainable Use	Richard Lloyd Andy Neale	Countryside Commission Countryside Commission
Chapter 7	Partnership and Education	Professor John Smyth OBE	
Chapter 8	UK Support to Biodiversity Overseas	Sara Oldfield Kate Mayes David Turner Jim Maund	NGO Conservation Forum Department of the Environment Overseas Development Administration
Chapter 9	Information and Data	Dr Colin Galbraith	Joint Nature Conservation Committee
Chapter 10	Targets and Monitoring	Robin Sharp	Department of the Environment

7 A consultation letter was issued to over 300 organisations throughout the United Kingdom in February 1993. Over 1,000 pages of text were received by way of response. This was followed by a two-day seminar held in May at the Royal Geographical Society in London, chaired by the Earl of Selborne, Chairman of the Joint Nature Conservation Committee, which was attended by over 100 delegates, including leading experts in the nature conservation field. A series of workshops were held, which together with follow up Working Groups on objectives and principles, chaired by Dr Derek Langslow, English Nature, and information and data, chaired by Roy Walker, JNCC, helped to inform those responsible for drafting the Action Plan. The first of these Groups received valuable input from a consortium of NGOs; organised by Graham Wynne, RSPB.

8 It is not possible in the space provided to refer to all those who have contributed, but perhaps special recognition should be given to the following non-governmental sources:
National Academies Policy and Advisory Group (NAPAG)
RSPB
British Trust for Ornithology (BTO)
WWF(UK)
The British Ecological Society
The Linnean Society
Institute of Oceanographic Sciences Deacon Laboratory
Institute of Terrestrial Ecology
RSNC
Royal Botanic Gardens Kew and Edinburgh

ANNEX C

FURTHER READING

Chapter One

This Common Inheritance. Britain's Environmental Strategy. Cm 1200. HMSO, 1990.

This Common Inheritance. The First Year Report. Cm 1655. HMSO, 1991.

This Common Inheritance. The Second Year Report. Cm 2068. HMSO, 1992.

Our Common Future (The Brundtland Report) – Report of the 1987 World Commission on Environment and Development. Oxford University Press 1987.

Rio Declaration on Environment and Development, 1992.

Agenda 21 Document – Action Plan for the Next Century, endorsed at UNCED. Full text of Agenda 21 available from: Regional Office for North America, UNDC Two Building, Room 0803, 2 United Nations Plaza, New York, NY10017, USA.

Sustainable Development – The UK Strategy. Cm 2426. HMSO, 1994.

Climate Change: The UK Programme. Cm 2427. HMSO, 1994.

Sustainable Forestry: The UK Programme. Cm 2429. HMSO, 1994.

The Diversity of Life, E O Wilson, London, Allen Lane, 1992.

Chapter Two

Realising our Potential: A Strategy for Science, Engineering and Technology, Cm 2250. HMSO, 1993.

Evolution and Biodiversity: The New Taxonomy, NERC 1992.

The Ecology of Animals, Elton, London 1933.

Biodiversity, Ocean Challenge, M Angel 1991.

The Modern Biologist's View of Nature, R May in the Concept of Nature (Ed J Torrance), Oxford Clarendon Press 1992.

Population Extinction and Saving Biodiversity, Ehrlich and Daily, Ambio 22, 1993.

Range Population Abundance and Conservation, Trends in Ecology and Evolution, J Lawton 1994.

Biodiversity and the Precautionary Principle, N Myers, Ambio 22, 1993.

Gilbert White's Journals, W Johnson, Cambridge, Mass., MIT Press, 1970.

The Naturalist in Britain: A Social History, D Allen, Harmondsworth, Allen Lane, 1976.

The Flora of River-Shingles, Scottish Naturalist, F B White, 1890.

Seventy Five Years in Ecology: The British Ecological Society. J Sheail, Oxford, Blackwell Scientific, 1987.

Nature Reserves, Nature, 93, E Ray Lankester, 1914.

Two Nature Reserves, Country Life, 33, W B Crump, 1913.

Biological Collections UK, Museums Association Working Party, London, Museums Association, 1987.

Natural Environment Research Council: A History, J Sheail, Natural Environment Research Council, 1992.

Taxonomy of Taxonomists, Nature, 356, K J Gaston and R M May 1992.

Beyond Opportunism: Key Principles for Systematic Reserve Selection, Trends in Ecology and Evolution, 1993 R L Pressey, C J Humphreys, C R Margules, R I Vane-Wright and P H Williams.

Chapter Three

Countryside Survey 1990 Main Report. Countryside Series 1990 Volume 2. Department of the Environment, 1993.

Land Use Change in England. Department of the Environment, Annual.

The History of the Countryside, Rackham 1986.

National Survey of Breeding Birds: British Trust for Ornithology.

National Survey of Wintering Birds: British Trust for Ornithology.

Atlas of the British Flora, F H Perring and S M Walters, London, Nelson, 1962.

Atlas of Mammals in Britain, H R Arnold, London, NERC, ITE Research Publication, 1993.

Atlas of Butterflies in Britain and Ireland, J Heath, E Pollard and J Thomas, London, Viking, 1984.

British Red Data Books, 1 – *Vascular Plants*, F H Perring and L Farrell, Lincoln, RSNC, 1977. 2 – *Insects*, D B Shirt, Peterborough, NCC, 1987. 3 – *Invertebrates Other Than Insects*, J H Bratton, Peterborough, JNCC, 1991. 4 – *Red Data Birds in Britain*, L A Batten, C J Bibby, P Clement, G D Elliott and R F Porter, London, Poyser, 1990.

How Many Species Inhabit the Earth? Scientific American, R M May, 1992.

A Nature Conservation Review, D A Ratcliffe, Cambridge, University Press, 1977.

Important Bird Areas in the UK, D E Pritchard, S D Housden, G P Mudge, C A Galbraith and M W Pienkowski, RSPB 1992.

Chapter Four

Conserving Peatlands in Northern Ireland: A Statement of Policy, DOE Northern Ireland, Environment Service, 1993.

Environmental Protection Act 1990, HMSO 1990.

Trees in Towns, DOE. HMSO, 1993.

Planning Policy Guidance Note 20, Coastal Planning. DOE, HMSO, 1992.

Planning Policy Guidance Note 13, Transport, (Consultation Draft), DOE, April 1993.

Annual Review of R and D, 1993. Office of Science and Technology. HMSO 1993.

Recovery: A Proposed Programme for Britain's Protected Species, NCC 1990.

Wildlife Introductions to Great Britain, NCC 1979.

Towards an Introduction Policy, Wildlife Link 1988.

Guidelines for Selection of Biological SSSIs, NCC 1989.

Chapter Five

Conservation in Progress, F B Goldsmith and A Warren, Chichester, John Wiley, 1993.

UK Directing of Culture Collections of Micro Organisms, Wallingford Oxon, UK: CAB International, 1978.

Museums Association Working Party of Natural Science Collections: Report of Biological Collections Survey, National Museum of Wales 1986.

Review of UK Policy on the Ex-Situ Conservation of Plant Genetic Resources, MAFF/SOAFD 1992.

European Culture Collections: Microbial Diversity in Safe Hands, Information on Holdings and Services, Braunschweig, Germany: Information Centre for European Culture Collections, 1992. Systematic Biology Research: Government Response to the First Report of the House of Lords Select Committee on Science and Technology, 199192 Session, London: HMSO 1993.

Chapter Six

Using Water Wisely. Consultation Paper. Department of the Environment, 1992.

Code of Good Agricultural Practice for the Protection of Soil. Ministry of Agriculture, Fisheries and Food. MAFF Publications, 1993.

Code of Good Agricultural Practice for the Protection of Water. Ministry of Agriculture, Fisheries and Food. MAFF Publications, 1991.

Development Below Low-Water Mark: A Review of Regulation in England and Wales. Department of the Environment/Welsh Office. 1993.

Managing the Coast: A Review of Coastal Management Plans in England and Wales and the Powers Supporting Them. Department of the Environment/Welsh Office, 1993.

The Second European Ministerial Conference on the Protection of Forests in Europe – Helsinki, June 1993.

Tourism and the Environment: Maintaining the Balance, Report of the Task Force, Department of Employment, May 1991.

Tourism in National Parks – Guide to Good Practice, English Tourist Board, 1991.

Tourism in Northern Ireland – A Sustainable Approach, Northern Ireland Tourist Board, December 1993.

Tourism 2000, Welsh Tourist Board, 1994.

Tourism and the Scottish Environment, Scottish Tourist Board, 1992.

Policy Appraisal and the Environment: A Guide for Government Departments, DOE. HMSO, 1990.

Environmental Appraisal in Government Departments. DOE, 1994.

Fit for the Future, Countryside Commission 1991.

Action for Biodiversity in the UK, JNCC 1993.

Chapter Seven

Local Agenda 21 – Agenda 21: A Guide for Local Authorities in the UK, LGMB.

Environmental Responsibility: An Agenda for Further and Higher Education, HMSO, 1993.

Learning for Life: A National Strategy for Environmental Education in Scotland, Scottish Office, 1993.

Systematic Biology Research Select Committee on Science and Technology, First Report, Parliamentary Papers, Lords 1991/2.

Chapter Eight

Biological Diversity and Developing Countries: Issues and Options, ODA 1991.

Global Diversity: Status of the Earth's Living Resources, B Groombridge, Chapman and Hall, London, 1992.

Putting Biodiversity on the Map: Priority Areas for Global Conservation, C J Bibby, ICBP, Cambridge 1992.

British Virgin Islands National Report Prepared for the United Nations Conference on Environment and Development, G Cambers, 1992.

Birds To Watch: The ICBP World Checklist of Threatened Birds, N J Collar and P Andrew, ICBP Technical Publications No 8 ICBP, Cambridge, 1988.

Management Plan for the Gough Island Wildlife Reserve, Cooper and Ryan, 1993.

National Report on Environmental Issues in Montserrat, S Cross, UNCED 1992.

UK Dependent Territories Ramsar Study: Stage One, I Hepburn, S Oldfield and K Thompson, 1992.

Fragments of Paradise: A Guide for Conservation Action in the UK Dependent Territories, S Oldfield, Pisces Publications, 1987.

The Ramsar Convention in the Caribbean With Special Emphasis on Anguilla, D Pritchard, RSPB Sabbatical Report, 1990.

Important Bird Areas in the United Kingdom Including the Channel Islands and the Isle of Man, D Pritchard, RSPB 1992.

Printed in the United Kingdom for HMSO
Dd 5061682 1/94 C75 51-4163 32956 ORD 271887

Picture of the Earth shown as section dividers supplied by Still Pictures/Space Sector, DRA 1992.